The Tso chuan

TRANSLATIONS FROM THE ORIENTAL CLASSICS

TRANSLATED BY

BURTON WATSON

COLUMBIA UNIVERSITY PRESS

NEW YORK

The Tso chuan

SELECTIONS FROM

China's Oldest Narrative History

COLUMBIA UNIVERSITY PRESS
New York Guildford, Surrey

LIBRARY OF CONGRESS CATALOGING-IN-PUBLICATION DATA

Tso-ch'iu, Ming.
[Tso chuan. English. Selections]
The Tso chuan :
Selections from China's oldest narrative history /
translated by Burton Watson.
p. cm. — (Translations from the Oriental classics)
Selected translation of: Tso chuan.
Includes bibliographical references and index.
ISBN 0-231-06714-3
1. Confucius. Ch'un ch'iu. I. Watson, Burton, 1925–
II. Title. III. Series.
PL2470.KB 1989
931'.03—dc19 88-23708
CIP

Printed in the United States of America

Casebound editions of Columbia University Press books are Smyth-sewn and are printed on permanent and durable acid-free paper

When the Tso chuan *narrates events, if it is describing an army on the move, then rosters and written documents seem to crowd our vision and confused clamor and hubbub well up all around us. . . . When it records a glorious victory, the captives and spoils are listed in detail; when it speaks of a disastrous rout, the fleeing remnants stream across the scene. When it portrays oaths and alliances, its words overflow with noble spirit; when it touches on treachery and bad faith, we can see where the falsity and deception lies. When it recounts acts of gratitude and bounty, it is as warm as the spring sun; when it chronicles sternness or severity, there's a chill like autumn frost. Speaking of states that flourish, its words take on a boundless flavor of fulfillment; listing the nations that have perished, its tone is melancholy with regret. . . . Few are the writings that can match its reputation. Past and present, it stands in a class apart.*

From Shih t'ung *or* Understanding History *(Outer Chapters, Miscellaneous Remarks I) by Liu Chih-chi (661–721)*

C O N T E N T S

INTRODUCTION

The *Tso chuan,* a lengthy text running to thirty densely written chapters in standard editions, is China's oldest work of narrative history. Its entries provide a year-by-year, often month-by-month, account of happenings in the various feudal states that made up the China of the time for the period from 722 to 468 B.C. The narratives focus primarily on political, diplomatic, and military affairs, but contain considerable information on economic and cultural developments as well.

The period is a highly significant one, when the more powerful feudal states were annexing their feebler neighbors in the process that would lead to eventual unification under a single rule, and agencies of government in the larger states were evolving in the direction of increasing complexity and specialization. In addition, the closing years of the period saw the appearance of Confucius (511–479 B.C.), one of the most influential figures in all of Chinese cultural history.

The *Tso chuan* represents almost the only written source for the history of this crucial period, and is especially valuable for the light it throws upon the society in which Confucius and his disciples lived and out of which the Confucian school of thought emerged. At the same time, the *Tso chuan* has long been recognized as a masterpiece of the early prose tradition, and as such has had an immense influence on later Chinese literature and historiography. From the first century on, it was numbered among the texts of the Confucian canon, and constituted one of the cornerstones of a traditional education both in China itself and in nearby countries such as Korea and Japan that were within the Chinese cultural sphere.

Two texts whose contents may be called historical predate the *Tso chuan.*

One is the *Shu ching* or *Book of Documents,* sometimes referred to as the *Book of History,* which constitutes one of the Five Confucian Classics. It is a collection of documents, mainly speeches, attributed to various rulers and ministers of high antiquity. The documents contain almost no information concerning the circumstances under which they were composed, and there is no narrative relating one document to another. The work hence resembles a collection of source materials rather than a connected history.

The second work is the year-by-year chronicle known as the *Ch'un ch'iu* or *Spring and Autumn Annals,* also one of the Five Classics. This is a record of events in the various feudal states of China for the period from 722 to 481 B.C., which is consequently known as the Spring and Autumn period. The phrase "spring and autumn" is an abbreviation of "spring, summer, autumn, winter" and was used in the state of Lu, where the chronicle was compiled, to designate such a season-by-season record of events. Similar chronicles were compiled in the other feudal states of the time, though they were often known by other designations.

The entries in the *Spring and Autumn Annals,* though of undoubted historical importance, are extremely brief and laconic in style, consisting of notices of accessions to rule, marriages, deaths, diplomatic meetings, wars, and other events in the lives of the rulers of Lu and the other feudal states of the time, along with notations on unusual occurrences in the natural world such as earthquakes, comets, droughts, plagues of insects, and so forth. There is no attempt to weave the entries together into a connected narrative or to inject any comment whatsoever. An early tradition, mentioned first in the writings of the Confucian philosopher Mencius,[1] claims that Confucius compiled the present text of the *Spring and Autumn Annals* on the basis of records preserved in his native state of Lu, and that the text is consequently invested with profound moral meaning, though in fact it is uncertain whether he had anything at all to do with the work.

Because it was believed that Confucius had compiled the *Spring and Autumn Annals* and had attached deep significance to its contents, early followers of the Confucian school understandably took a great interest in the chronicle and its interpretation. This led to the compilation of various commentaries that purported to relate the historical background of the events touched upon in the chronicle and to discuss the moral significance that Confucius attached to them. Two such commentaries, the *Kung-yang Commentary* and *Ku-liang Commentary,* will be referred to from time to time in the notes to the translations that follow. Both were in existence by early

1 *Meng Tzu* III B, 9; IV B, 21. Mencius was active in the latter part of the fourth century B.C.

Han times and were included in the Confucian canon in the reign of Emperor Wu (140–87 B.C.). Both concentrate upon explaining the "lessons" that Confucius was supposed to have intended to convey by the notations in the chronicle or the particular wording employed; they contain a relatively small amount of historical background.

The *Tso chuan* or *Tso shih chuan,* which means "The Commentary of Mr. Tso," takes its name from its putative author, Tso Ch'iu-ming or Tso-ch'iu Ming, who has sometimes been identified with a man of that name praised by Confucius in *Analects* V, 24. In fact, however, nothing is known of who Mr. Tso was, when or where he lived, or what connection he had with the work that bears his name.

The word *chuan* in the title reflects the fact that the text was from early times treated as a commentary on the *Spring and Autumn Annals.* Whether it was originally compiled for that purpose is uncertain. But because it covers almost the same period as the *Annals* and contains detailed accounts of the events referred to in the latter, it can easily be adapted to that end, though its entries do not always jibe exactly with those of the *Annals.* By later Han times, it had been accepted into the Confucian canon, where it joined the *Kung-yang* and *Ku-liang* commentaries to make up the so-called three commentaries on the *Spring and Autumn Annals.*

We do not know what the original form of the *Tso chuan* was. Quite possibly its narratives were grouped by states, as are the narratives in the *Kuo yü* or *Conversations from the States,* a historical text that covers roughly the same period as the *Tso chuan* and often closely parallels it in content. But at some point the *Tso chuan* appears to have been broken up and appended to the year-by-year entries of the *Annals* so as to function more effectively as a commentary on that text. This may have been done as late as the third century A.D., when a scholar named Tu Yü (222–284), drawing on two earlier commentaries on the *Tso chuan,* compiled the earliest extant commentary on the *Tso,* the *Ch'un-ch'iu ching-chuan chi-chieh,* which was completed around A.D. 280. Or it may have been done somewhat earlier by the scholar and statesman Liu Hsin (50 B.C.–A.D. 23), who enthusiastically advocated the use of the *Tso chuan* as a commentary on the *Annals* and urged that it be accepted as part of the Confucian canon.

During the nineteenth century in China a theory was put forward, mainly with the purpose of lending greater glory to the *Kung-yang Commentary,* that Liu Hsin actually forged the present text of the *Tso chuan.* Liu may in fact have made certain additions to the work, as may other redactors or commentators who worked over the text. Passages in the *Tso chuan* which explicitly refer to the entries in the *Annals,* or the moralizing comments introduced in the text from time to time, are particularly suspect. But it is impossible to believe that the bulk of the *Tso* text did not exist in something like its present form from at least the early years of the Han dynasty. The Han historian Ssu-ma Ch'ien (145?–90?), when he came to compile the chapters on the Spring and Autumn period for his *Shih chi* or *Records of the Historian,* clearly drew extensively upon it, and he mentions it by name among his sources.[2] Moreover, linguistic studies of the historical sections of the *Tso chuan* by Bernhard Karlgren have shown that they observe certain grammatical rules and distinctions that would have been unknown to a man of Liu Hsin's time.[3]

Scholars today generally agree that the *Tso chuan* is in the main a genuine work of late Chou times, though no method has so far been found to pinpoint the date of its compilation with absolute surety. The *Han Fei Tzu* and *Lü-shih ch'un-ch'iu* appear to be the earliest works that quote directly from the *Tso* text, and since both these works date from the latter part of the third century B.C., we may suppose that the *Tso chuan* was already in existence by that time. Current scholarly opinion places its compilation somewhere in that century.[4]

As noted earlier, we will probably never know just what motives originally led the author or authors of the *Tso chuan* to compile their work. Likewise we will probably never know the methods they used in compiling it. Certainly they must have drawn upon earlier chronicles such as the *Spring and Autumn Annals* that were preserved in the archives of the various feudal states, since they appear well informed on happenings in all the different parts of the Chinese cultural domain, though regrettably the *Tso* itself nowhere comments on the sources it is based upon or the methods employed in its compilation.

A glance at the *Spring and Autumn Annals* and the few other examples of such local chronicles that have survived suggests, however, that they were at best very lean and uncolorful accounts, containing almost no historical background concerning the events they record and no passages of direct speech whatsoever. To arrive at the kind of vivid, detailed, and speech-laden narrative that characterizes the *Tso chuan* as a whole, the compilers must

2 See *Shih chi* 14, preface to The Chronological Table of the Twelve Feudal States, where he refers to it as *Tso-shih ch'un-ch'iu* or "Mr. Tso's Spring and Autumn."

3 Bernard Karlgren, *On the Authenticity and Nature of the Tso Chuan,* (Göteborg: Elanders, 1926; rpt., Taipei, Taiwan: Ch'eng-wen Publishing Co., 1968).

4 Kamata Tadashi, for example, in vol. 1, p. 13 of his *Shunjū Sashi den* (*Shinyaku kambun taikei,* 4 vols.; Tokyo: Meiji shoin, 1971–77), opines that it was written around 320 B.C. Yang Po-chün, in vol. 1, p. 43 of his *Ch'un-ch'iu Tso-chuan chu* (4 vols.; Beijing: Chung-hua shu-chü, 1981), examines various prophecies in the text and on this basis concludes that it dates from somewhere between 403 and 389 B.C.

have had to supplement such material by drawing heavily upon other written sources, oral tradition, or their own fertile imaginations. We are probably safe in assuming that all three of these sources contributed to the final product, though in just what proportions we will unfortunately never know.

To give some idea of the role played by chroniclers and historians in the period depicted in the *Tso chuan,* and to suggest the general view of the function of history that prevailed at the time—or at least at the time of the compilation of the *Tso*—I would like to quote two passages, the first from the *Tso chuan,* the second from the text that so closely resembles it in style and content, the *Kuo yü* or *Conversations from the States.* Both passages are in the form of remonstrances or "lessons from history," and depict rulers being lectured by their ministers on the need to heed advice and remonstrance. Both cite lists of persons such as court historians and musicians whose duty it was to admonish the ruler and enlighten him with examples from the past.

The first passage is from the *Tso chuan,* Duke Hsiang 14th year, which corresponds to 559 B.C. In this year, Duke Hsien, ruler of the state of Wei, was forced to flee from his domain because of his misdeeds and the hatred he had aroused among his ministers. In the following passage, Duke Tao of Chin, the ruler of a neighboring state, discusses this event with Shih K'uang or Music Master K'uang, one of his court musicians.

> Shih K'uang was attending the ruler of Chin. The latter said, "The people of Wei have driven out their ruler—what a terrible thing!"
>
> Shih K'uang replied, "Perhaps it was the ruler himself who did terrible things. When a good ruler goes about rewarding good and punishing excess, he nourishes his people as though they were his children, shelters them like Heaven, accommodates them like the earth. And when the people serve their ruler, they love him as they do their parents, look up to him like the sun and moon, revere him like the all-seeing spirits, fear him like thunder. How could they drive him out?
>
> "The ruler is host to the spirits and the hope of the people. But if he exhausts the people's livelihood, deprives the spirits, skimps in the sacrifices to them, and betrays the hopes of the populace, then he ceases to be the host of the nation's altars of the soil and grain, and what use is he? What can one do but expel him?
>
> "Heaven gave birth to the people and set up rulers to superintend and shepherd them and see to it that they do not lose their true nature

as human beings. And because there are rulers, it provided helpers for them who would teach and protect them and see that they do not overstep the bounds. Hence the Son of Heaven has his chief officers, the feudal lords have their ministers, the ministers set up their collateral houses, gentlemen have their friends and companions, and the commoners, artisans, merchants, lackeys, shepherds, and grooms all have their relatives and close associates who help and assist them. If one does good they praise him, if he errs they correct him, if he is in distress they rescue him, if he is lost they restore him.

"Thus from the sovereign on down, each has his father or elder brother, his son or younger brother to assist and scrutinize his ways of management. The historians compile their documents, the blind musicians compose poems, the musicians chant admonitions and remonstrances, the high officials deliver words of correction, the gentlemen pass along remarks, the commoners criticize, the merchants voice their opinions in the market, and the hundred artisans contribute through their skills.

"Hence the 'Documents of Hsia' says: 'The herald with his wooden-clappered bell goes about the roads, saying, "Let the officials and teachers correct the ruler, let the artisans pursue their skills and thereby offer remonstrance." ' In the first month, the beginning month of spring, this was done so that people might remonstrate against departures from the norm.[5]

"Heaven's love for the people is very great. Would it then allow one man to preside over them in an arrogant and willful manner, indulging his excesses and casting aside the nature Heaven and earth alloted them? Surely it would not!"

This, as one can see, is a highly enlightened sermon on the responsibilities of rulership and the need for all groups in society to seek advice and correction from their kin and associates. Whether any such counsel was actually delivered to Duke Tao of Chin in 559 B.C., or to any other Chinese ruler at that time, we cannot say. But that it is precisely the kind of homily that would be set forth by Confucian-minded thinkers writing around the end of the fourth or the beginning of the third century B.C., that is, the time of Mencius and Hsün Tzu, there can be no doubt.

5 The quotation is from some unknown work purporting to describe the government of the Hsia dynasty in high antiquity. It was later incorporated into the short text entitled *Yin cheng,* one of the spurious sections of the *Book of Documents* that were put together in the third century A.D.

The second passage, from the opening chapter of the *Kuo yü* (*Chou yü* 1), purports to deal with a considerably earlier period, depicting an interview between the evil King Li of the Chou dynasty, who came to the throne in 878 B.C., and his chief minister, the duke of Shao. Though the setting is entirely different, the reprimand itself, here delivered directly against the ruler himself, is so similar in parts to that in the *Tso chuan* passage just quoted that the two would almost certainly seem to be related, though in just what way it would be difficult to say.

> King Li behaved in a tyrannical manner and the people of the kingdom criticized him. The duke of Shao reported this to the king, saying, "The people cannot endure their fate!"
>
> The king, enraged, employed the shamans of Wei to search out those who voiced criticisms, and the persons they reported he put to death. The people of the kingdom no longer dared speak, but eyed one another meaningfully when they met in the road.
>
> The king was pleased and announced to the duke of Shao, "I have succeeded in silencing the criticisms. Now no one dares to speak out!"
>
> The duke of Shao said, "You have merely dammed them up. But stopping up the mouths of the people is more dangerous than stopping up a river. When a river is blocked and then breaks through, many persons are bound to be injured, and it is the same with the people. Therefore, one who desires to control a river will leave an opening where the water can be drawn off. And one who would control the people should do likewise, encouraging them to speak.
>
> "Therefore when the Son of Heaven listens to affairs of government, he causes his high ministers and others on down to the ranks of gentlemen to present poems, the blind musicians to present musical compositions, the historians to present their documents, the teachers to admonish, the pupilless blind to recite, the dim-pupilled blind to chant, the hundred artisans to remonstrate, the commoners to pass along remarks, the close attendants of the ruler to offer unlimited correction, the ruler's parents and kin to assist and scrutinize, the blind musicians and historians to instruct and correct, and the venerable elders to put these various admonitions into order. After that, the king examines and applies them. In this way, affairs can be carried out without miscarriage."

The word translated as "historian" in these two passages is *shih,* a term which originally denoted officials who appear to have had charge of sacrifices and matters pertaining to divination. Because the latter duties required a knowledge of reading and writing, such officials in time came to act as secretaries to the rulers and to compile records of state affairs such as the chronicles mentioned earlier. According to two somewhat later texts, the *Li chi* or *Book of Rites,* section 13, and the *Han shu* or *History of the Former Han, chuan* 30, rulers in ancient times were regularly attended by two such officials, one of whom kept a record of the ruler's actions, while the other kept a record of his words.[6]

The *shih* are frequently mentioned in the *Tso chuan* in connection with matters of divination and court records, and because of their knowledge of the past they were in an ideal position to counsel the ruler on the proper course of action. In the passages just quoted, they are shown actually presenting their *shu* or "documents" for his perusal as a form of remonstrance.

Both passages quoted above also mention that poems are to be presented to the ruler as a type of admonition. That poetry was in fact employed to this end is well attested by actual poems preserved in the oldest anthology of Chinese poetry, the *Shih ching* or *Book of Odes,* which is numbered among the Five Confucian Classics. Works in the division of the anthology known as *Hsiao ya* or "Lesser Odes" in particular contain stinging criticisms of the ruler and his government, and are sometimes "signed," the writer in the closing lines of the poem stating his name and the reasons that compelled him to set forth his complaint.[7]

It is impossible to say just what sort of words of advice would have been delivered by the various kinds of blind musicians mentioned in the two passages, but we may surmise that, as in so many cultures, their blindness was associated with unusual mnemonic powers and that they commanded a large body of oral lore which they could draw upon to tutor the king.

From what has been said thus far, it should be evident that the early Chinese looked upon the function of history as didactic, and therefore that when the compilers of the *Tso chuan* came to select, order, and perhaps expand their material, they did so in ways that would serve to emphasize the didactic element. This didactic aim should be kept constantly in mind in approaching the *Tso chuan,* for it helps explain why the compilers seem

6 For the period covered by the *Tso chuan,* one might well translate the term *shih* simply as "clerk" or "recorder." I have preferred the translation "historian," however, because the same term was later used to designate true historians such as Ssu-ma Ch'ien and Pan Ku, and these men clearly looked back to the *shih* of the *Tso chuan* as their spiritual ancestors.

7 See, for example, the poems *Chieh nan shan,* Mao no. 191, and *Hsiang Po,* Mao no. 200.

never to tire of dwelling on certain political questions, such as how inferiors can most effectively counsel their superiors in government, or how the true motives and character of a person in public life can be appraised. If, as Joseph Brodsky asserts, "Tragedy is history's chosen genre"[8]—and the *Tso chuan* surely appears to bear that out—the Chinese would have us at least learn some lesson from its grim pages, extract some wisdom from its chronicle of woe.

The historical and philosophical texts of late Chou, Ch'in, and Han times suggest that there was a considerable body of anecdotal material in existence at that time relating to certain outstanding figures of the Spring and Autumn period, such as the rulers Duke Huan of Ch'i and Duke Wen of Chin, or the statesmen Kuan Chung, Yen Ying, and Wu Tzu-hsü. Some material of this nature is to be found in the *Tso chuan,* notably in the section devoted to the career of Duke Wen of Chin (r. 636–628). Duke Wen, whose personal name was Ch'ung-erh or Double Ears, was forced to flee his native state because of charges that he was plotting treason. He spent the following nineteen years wandering from state to state with a small band of faithful followers before returning to Chin to claim the rulership, and the *Tso chuan* chronicles this period of youthful trial and adversity in considerable detail.

But Duke Wen represents something of an exception in the *Tso chuan* in the amount of attention paid to his early years, to his distinctive physical features, and to the assortment of wives that he acquired in the course of his odyssey. By contrast, the *Tso chuan* has relatively little to say about Duke Huan of Ch'i or his famous prime minister Kuan Chung, although later evidence suggests that they were the focus of an extensive body of legends comparable to those that centered around Duke Wen of Chin. Similarly, another figure who is conspicuous in later legend and romance, the fifth century B.C. Ch'u statesman Wu Yün or Wu Tzu-hsü, is accorded only limited space in the pages of the *Tso.*

Whether the full body of legends that came eventually to surround these figures had not yet come into existence at the period when the *Tso* was compiled, or whether its compilers deliberately chose to ignore much of that material, it is impossible to say. It would seem, however, that the authors of the *Tso* were on the whole not interested in tales that were merely curious or colorful, regardless of whose name might be associated with them. Thus in the *Tso,* as pointed out by Ronald Egan, we are given

8 Joseph Brodsky, *Less Than One: Selected Essays* (London: Penguin Books, 1987), p. 271.

extensive accounts of the public or political views and activities of the leaders of the time, but seldom a glimpse of their private lives.[9] Likewise, though we see them on occasion leading their armies into combat, we seldom observe them performing the kind of feats of strength or daring that characterize the heroes of Greece, Rome, or medieval Europe. Also conspicuously absent from their stories is any mention of the type of amatory interests that so often set in motion the protagonists of Western romance. On the whole, the *Tso chuan* alludes to sexual attraction only in connection with transgressions of the moral code such as adultery or incest, or as a force disruptive of political harmony and stability.

The aim of the *Tso chuan,* then, is not to amuse or entertain, but to edify, and its lessons are overwhelmingly political and moral in nature. This is hardly surprising, since politics and morality—the two concepts are scarcely separable in the thought of the period—were the primary concerns of early Chinese philosophy as a whole.

Many of these lessons are set forth in the form of speeches delivered by ministers or advisers to the rulers, as in the passages quoted above. Some of these utterances are terse or even brusque in tone, though more often the style is formal and rather long-winded. The more formal speeches make frequent use of the sorites, parallelisms, and other rhetorical devices characteristic of the philosophical writings of the time. Another trait they share with the works of the philosophers is that of rounding off an argument with a quotation from the Confucian Classics, usually the *Book of Odes* or *Book of Documents.* Most of these quotations are to be found in the present texts of those works, though some are from poems or documents that are now lost or were never included in the standard versions of the *Odes* and *Documents.*

We have already seen an example of the formal type of oration in the admonitions of the Music Master K'uang quoted above. Here is an example of one of the pithier speeches. It was delivered in 573 B.C. (Duke Ch'eng 18th year), when the high ministers of the state of Chin, after putting to death the willful Duke Li, called to the throne of Chin a distant member of the ruling family, a boy of fourteen named the ducal son Chou-tzu, who is posthumously known as Duke Tao (r. 572–558). He addressed the ministers in these words:

"I never wanted it to come to this. Nevertheless it has, which can only be the work of Heaven. In general, men seek a ruler so they can have him issue orders. But if, after they have set him up, they fail to obey him, what

9 Ronald C. Egan, "Narratives in *Tso Chuan,*" *Harvard Journal of Asiatic Studies* (December 1977), 37 (2):323–352.

use is the ruler? If you gentlemen plan to use me, begin today! If not, begin today! Join together in obeying your ruler and the gods will send good fortune!"

According to the text, the ministers replied, "That is what we desire. Would we dare do otherwise than heed your orders?"

Succinct and to the point, the speech serves with great effectiveness to arrest the reader's attention and impress upon him that here is a young man from whom one may expect important things.

Since we have no way of knowing just what sources the compilers of the *Tso chuan* drew upon, we of course cannot determine to what extent these speeches are genuine. The *Book of Documents,* as noted earlier, contains numerous didactic speeches attributed to the rulers and ministers of antiquity, so the idea of employing the speech form as a vehicle for lessons on political wisdom was already old in Chinese culture. We may note, however, that although the *Tso chuan* covers a period of some 250 years, its moralizing speeches, whether attributed to figures who lived early in the period or later, are generally uniform in style and express the same philosophical outlook, which suggests that if they were not actual inventions of the compilers, they were at least heavily reworked and regularized by them.

Another device utilized repeatedly in the *Tso chuan* to point a moral is the prophecy. Someone, for example, will observe the course of action being pursued by a ruler, a government official, or the head of an influential family and, on the basis of the ethical implications of the individual's conduct, predict his future success or failure. Usually the observer goes on to give some logical explanation for his prediction. These predictions or prophecies serve as guideposts to the reader, leading him through the maze of facts and indicating to him the threads of causation that link one fact to another. Since the compilers themselves, in a process known in Chinese as *chang-pen* or "laying the groundwork," have in most cases erected these signposts in the text, they seldom point awry, and what is predicted in due course comes about. In this way the laws of moral cause and effect are made clear, and history, at least in the view of the compilers, yields up its true meaning.

I will quote a brief episode from the *Tso chuan* to illustrate how this type of prophecy works. The passage appears in the narrative dealing with Duke Ai 7th year, or 488 B.C., a time when the southeastern state of Wu, with its capital in the area of modern Suchow, was exercising great power and imposing its will upon the other states. In that year, Duke Ai of Lu met with the ruler of Wu, King Fu-ch'a or Fu-ch'ai (r. 495–473). At the time of the meeting the Wu ruler demanded that the state of Lu provide a hundred *lao* or sets of sacrificial animals as provender for him and his party.

The officials of Lu considered this demand outrageous and commented on it as follows:

> In the summer, Duke Ai of Lu met with the ruler of Wu at Tseng. Wu sent a man to demand that its party be entertained with a hundred *lao*.[10]
>
> The Lu official Tzu-fu Ho replied, "The kings of former times never had any such entertainments!"
>
> But the man from Wu said, "The state of Sung entertained us with a hundred *lao*. Surely Lu cannot do less than Sung! Moreover, Lu entertained the Chin official with over ten *lao*.[11] Why should the king of Wu not receive a hundred *lao*?"
>
> Tzu-fu Ho said, "Shih Yang was greedy and disregarded the rites. He used his position as an official of a major state to intimidate us, and therefore we gave him eleven *lao*. Now if your ruler intends to abide by the rites in issuing commands to the other feudal lords, then there are fixed numbers to be observed. If you disregard the rites, you will simply go to excess.
>
> "When the Chou kings came to the throne, they decreed that entertainments for the most exalted persons should not exceed twelve *lao*. This is the maximum number decreed by the Son of Heaven. But of course if you intend to disregard the rites of Chou and insist upon a hundred *lao*, we will do as your authorities dictate."
>
> The man of Wu refused to listen to these arguments. Tzu-fu Ho said, "Wu will be destroyed! It disregards Heaven and turns against its own roots.[12] But if we do not give it what it wants, it will undoubtedly try to vent its wrath on us!" So Lu gave Wu its hundred *lao*.

Here, in the words of the Lu official Tzu-fu Ho, we are given the prophecy, "Wu will be destroyed!" and the reason, "It disregards Heaven and turns against its own roots," which summarizes the arguments that have been presented by Tzu-fu Ho in the preceding speech. Though the fulfillment of the prophecy is only briefly noted in the *Tso chuan* itself, we will not be surprised to learn that the state of Wu was attacked and

10 A *lao* denotes a set of sacrificial animals, usually an ox, a sheep, and a pig for a "big *lao*," and a sheep and a pig for a "little *lao*," though apparently deer were sometimes included in the set. Whatever the exact meaning, Wu is demanding that its men be treated to a very lavish feast.

11 When the Chin official Shih Yang came on a state visit to Lu in 521, he was entertained with a seven-*lao* banquet. He complained that this was incommensurate with the dignity of his state, whereupon the Lu officials out of fear increased the number to eleven *lao*. See Duke Chao 12th year.

12 The Wu ruling family traced its lineage back to the founders of the Chou dynasty. Hence in disregarding the rites laid down by the Chou, it was turning against its own ancestors.

completely wiped out by its nearby rival, Yüeh, in 473 B.C., at which time King Fu-ch'ai committed suicide.

The passage quoted above is also noteworthy because it illustrates another important characteristic of the *Tso chuan,* its intense occupation with the concept of *li,* a term I have usually rendered as "rites" or "propriety." In the passage just quoted, at issue is a very specific question of ritual behavior, that is, how many animals should be provided by the ruler of a feudal state for an official visitor from another state. As usual in such questions, appeal is made to custom and precedent. Anyone who attempts to defy precedent is felt to be disrupting the social order and pursuing a course that can lead only to disaster. In other instances, the *Tso* narrative is less concerned with specific details of ritual behavior than with the basic moral principles that underlie correct conduct.

The moralizing passages of the *Tso* refer frequently to the concepts of *jen* (benevolence), *yi* (righteousness), or *te* (virtue) that figure so importantly in the *Analects* and the writings of Mencius and Hsün Tzu. But above all it is the concept of *li* that dominates the ethical outlook of the *Tso.* Though the word often refers to the specific rules of conduct that govern religious and social ceremonies, in other passages it is expanded in scope until it comes to designate a comprehensive moral standard that embraces all phases of human behavior and extends even to the natural and supernatural worlds. Thus under Duke Chao 25th year we read: "Ritual *(li)* is the constant principle of Heaven, that which is right for the earth, the proper course of the people. . . . Ritual determines the relations between high and low; it is the warp and woof of Heaven and earth and that by which the people are enabled to live."

A correct understanding of ritual, both in its detailed manifestations and in its underlying attitudes, therefore, is the basis of all correct action and the key to success. In the *Tso,* to characterize someone as *wu li,* or lacking in a proper sense of ritual or propriety, is to say that the person is ignorant, evil in action, and doomed to certain failure.[13]

The period dealt with in the *Tso chuan* was a dark one, marked by almost incessant political turmoil and attacks by one feudal state upon another. Not surprisingly, we encounter in the pages of the *Tso* many figures who reject these calls for adherence to the principles of ritual or propriety, or who scorn the other traditional virtues enjoined by the ancient texts such as the *Odes* and *Documents.* Thus we encounter militarists who celebrate the

13 For further discussion of the concept of *li* in the *Tso chuan,* see the section on the *Tso* in my *Early Chinese Literature* (New York: Columbia University Press, 1962), pp. 40–66.

glories of warfare, cynics who deny the value of morality in government, or fatalists who would shift all responsibility for human failure to Heaven or the gods. In addition, the *Tso* contains frequent references to baleful spirits, prophetic dreams, and consultations with shamanistic mediums—elements reflecting the popular beliefs of the time that have often distressed Confucian-minded admirers of the *Tso chuan* in later ages. One may recall in this connection that, according to *Analects* VII, 21, Confucius never discussed matters pertaining to prodigies, feats of strength, disorder, or supernatural beings.

Despite the presence of such elements, however, the *Tso* narratives as a whole, and particularly the moralizing speeches and judgments strewn throughout them, are marked by an attitude of underlying rationalism and humanism. As the events of the somber chronicle unfold, a variety of observers and commentators on the action warn against the violation of moral principles, predicting that disaster will befall the violator. And if we read far enough, we see these prophecies fulfilled. Through such warnings and judgments, and through the ordering of their material as a whole, the compilers of the *Tso* seem to be urging us to recognize that it is the moral actions of men, particularly the men in positions of leadership, that primarily determine the course of history. Supernatural forces play little or no part in its unfolding except perhaps as responses to, or reinforcements of, the good or evil deeds of human beings themselves. Whether such a belief was actually characteristic of the historical personages who are shown exemplifying it we are hardly in a position to say. But clearly this is the lesson that the *Tso chuan* itself would have us garner from our reading.

THE WORLD OF THE *TSO CHUAN*

In 722 B.C., when the *Tso chuan* begins its narrative, the area of northern and central China was divided into some 120 feudal states of varying size. A few were almost the dimensions of a modern province, though many consisted of little more than one or two walled towns and the farmland in the immediate vicinity. The states acknowledged allegiance to the Chou king, the Son of Heaven, who had his court at Lo-yang in the Yellow River valley.

The Chou dynasty was founded by King Wu of the state of Chou, who overthrew the last ruler of the Shang or Yin dynasty. Traditional accounts picture this as the result of a decisive battle that took place in 1122 B.C., though in fact the conquest was probably a lengthy process extending over a number of years. The Shang had been preceded, according to tradition, by a dynasty known as the Hsia. These three, the Hsia, Shang, and Chou, constitute the so-called Three Dynasties of Chinese antiquity. There is abundant archeological evidence for the existence of the Chou and the Shang, but so far none of incontrovertible nature for the Hsia.

In the early years of the dynasty, the Chou capital was situated in the Wei River valley in the area of the present-day city of Hsi-an, where the Chou state originated, far to the west of Lo-yang. Internal troubles and invasion by non-Chinese tribes, however, forced the Chou rulers to abandon this capital in 771 B.C., bringing to an end the era known as the Western Chou. The capital was then moved east to Lo-yang, initiating the period known as the Eastern Chou, which lasted until the final abolishment of the Chou court in 256 B.C.

The Chou rulers belonged to a family that bore the surname Chi, and many of the ruling families in the feudal states were of the same Chi family, having been enfeoffed in their territories at the time of the Chou conquest. Among the important Chi clan states were Chin, Cheng, Wei, and Lu, stretching in a line west to east in the area of the Yellow River and flanking the Chou capital at Lo-yang. Other major states in the northern area were Ch'i in the Shantung Peninsula, ruled by the Chiang family, which had aided the founders of the Chou at the time of the conquest and was closely allied with the Chou ruling family by marriage; and Sung in eastern Honan, ruled by descendants of the Shang royal family. (It was thought inauspicious to abolish a former ruling family altogether and thus cut off the sacrifices to its ancestors, and therefore the descendants of former rulers were granted fiefs, such as was done in the case of Sung, so that they could carry on their sacrifices.)

In addition to these major states ruled over by families of ancient and distinguished lineage, there were several important outlying states that were looked upon by the Chinese people of the time as semibarbarian in descent or culture. The most noteworthy of these states were Ch'in, ruled by the Ying family, in the Wei River area of the old Chou capital; Ch'u, ruled by the Mi family, in the central Yangtze River valley; and later the states of Wu and Yüeh in the Suchow and northern Chekiang area respectively. The rulers of the state of Wu, who had their capital at Suchow, claimed to be descended from an ancestor of the Chou kings, and thus to belong to the Chi clan, a claim that was apparently accepted by the Chinese of the time.

Surrounding all these states, and often living interspersed with them in the more rugged or remote areas, were the *ssu-i* or Four Barbarian Tribes, non-Chinese peoples whose languages were probably unintelligible to the Chinese and who doubtless differed from them in custom and perhaps in race, though little is known of them.[14] The Four Barbarians comprised the Jung and Ti tribes living to the west and north, with whom, as we shall see, the Chinese sometimes intermarried; the Yi peoples in the Shantung Peninsula and along the eastern coast; and the Man people to the south. As the Chinese opened up new lands for cultivation, these tribes, who were probably mainly hunting and gathering peoples, were constantly being pushed out of their customary territories, and frequently retaliated by invading or raiding the Chinese settlements.

In the earlier and more flourishing years of the dynasty, the Chou rulers had presumably possessed the power to resist such foreign incursions, as well as to punish any of the Chinese states that defied their authority or were lax in fulfilling obligations to the throne. But by the start of the Spring and Autumn period, when the *Tso chuan* begins its account, the Chou kings had lost all real power and were allowed to go on occupying the throne only because of their religious significance as heads of the ruling Chi clan and because they continued to be acknowledged as holders of the all-important Mandate of Heaven that legitimized their rule.

To fill the vacuum created by their decline from power, one or another of the leaders of the major feudal states came forward to exercise authority in the ruler's name and undertake to guard the Chinese empire from foreign invasion and maintain order within its borders. Such leaders were known as *pa,* a word variously translated as "hegemon," "overlord," or simply "leader." There were reported to have been five of them who rose to prominence in succession, though lists of the five do not always agree. Duke Huan of Ch'i (r. 685–643) and Duke Wen of Chin (r. 636–628), the two most famous, are included in all lists. Other rulers who are frequently mentioned among the five are Duke Mu of Ch'in (r. 659–621) and King Chuang of Ch'u (r. 613–591), both of whom figure prominently in the translated excerpts that follow.

Traditional accounts of the early centuries of Chou rule picture the dynasty as commanding widespread respect and insuring peace and stability to China as a whole, though this may be no more than a later idealization

14 See *Tso,* Hsiang 14 (559 B.C.), the speech of the leader of the Chiang Jung people to the men of Chin, in which he says: "We Jung do not have the same food, drink, or clothing as the Hua (Chinese), we do not exchange gifts and offerings with you, we do not understand your language. . . ."

fabricated by Confucian-minded writers who looked back to the Western Chou period as one of the golden ages of antiquity. By contrast, the age of the *Tso chuan* is an era of almost ceaseless warfare and social strife. The contrast is made doubly striking by the fact that, though we have only the sketchiest accounts of the centuries before the beginning of the Spring and Autumn period—even the dates for events prior to 841 B.C. cannot be fixed with any certainty—the *Tso chuan* confronts us with a recital of military clashes and political intrigues and machinations that is painfully explicit in its detail.

The greatest single source of the internal troubles that plagued China at this time was undoubtedly the numberless succession disputes that erupted in the Chou royal house and the ruling houses of the feudal states. Though the principle of primogeniture was apparently thought to be proper, it was by no means universally observed in the Spring and Autumn period. In actual practice, it was left to the ruler or head of a powerful family to decide which of his sons by his wife or concubines he wished to be regarded as his *t'ai-tzu* or heir. This inevitably led to much scheming for favor and precedence among the various sons and their mothers, and the ruler was constantly being importuned to make haste in naming his heir, or to reconsider his choice if he had already done so.

Once the heir had been designated, the other sons were frequently assigned to fiefs or posts in the outlying regions, presumably to remove them from the immediate vicinity of the heir. There they were tempted to build up local power bases and in time to contest the ruler's decision through a recourse to arms. And even if they resisted such temptation and remained unswervingly loyal, they often faced charges of treason that had been trumped up for the purpose of removing them from the scene. To avoid execution or enforced suicide, they were in many cases obliged to flee the state entirely, taking refuge at the court of a nearby ruler. There they would amass a body of followers and plan for the day when they could return to their native state and press their claim to the throne. The ruler hosting their sojourn abroad was usually happy enough to aid them in their endeavors because of the opportunities it afforded him to meddle in the affairs of his neighbor.

This pattern of dissension within a ruling house over the question of succession, flight abroad of one or more of the contestants, and eventual resort to military action, is one we will see repeated again and again in the narratives that follow. It was a malady that appeared to attack all the ruling houses at one time or another, and its seemingly irremediable nature represented perhaps the gravest problem besetting the society of the period.

In view of the nearly incessant hostilities that mark the era, it is hardly surprising that the *Tso chuan* should be renowned for its battle descriptions, which are among the most vivid in all of Chinese historical literature. The selection that follows includes translations of the passages dealing with the so-called Five Great Battles of the *Tso chuan,* plus several other battles or military operations that were of special note.

In times of combat, the rulers of the various feudal states and their kinsmen usually headed their own armies, riding into the fray in war chariots drawn by teams of four horses. Three men rode in a single chariot: the chariot commander, who stood on the left side and was armed with a bow; the driver, who stood in the middle; and a right-hand attendant who wielded a *ke* or halberd and was often a man noted for his outstanding strength. Both the driver and the right-hand attendant were customarily men of distinguished social rank, and the *Tso chuan* takes care to list their names along with that of the commander of the chariot. The chariots appear to have been rather clumsy to maneuver, and in the narratives that follow we often see them overturning, breaking down, or having to be pushed out of holes. Each chariot was accompanied by seventy-two soldiers on foot, probably recruits from the peasantry, who ran alongside. Since in the period depicted in the *Tso chuan* warfare was still one of the approved pursuits of the aristocracy, however, the *Tso* narrative customarily ignores these humble foot soldiers to concentrate upon the exploits and deeds of daring executed by the patrician riders in the chariot.

The *Tso* battle narratives tend to follow a rather stereotyped pattern, beginning with speeches for and against the battle, prophetic dreams and utterances, and divinations on the outcome of the battle, followed by the actual hostilities, often conveyed in choppy scenes of single combat or confrontation, and concluding with notations on the number of severed heads and prisoners taken and the disposition of spoils. The battle descriptions themselves, with their emphasis upon the aristocratic code of valor and military honor, hold a place of special importance in the history of Chinese literature. In the centuries that followed the composition of the *Tso chuan,* when Confucian ideals came to dominate the Chinese upper classes, such deeds of violence and physical daring were frowned upon and ceased to occupy a place in the literature of the gentry, though they reappear many centuries later in popular works such as the *San-kuo yen-i* or *Shui-hu chuan.* The *Tso chuan* thus in effect gives us our only opportunity to glimpse the ancient Chinese counterparts of the warrior heroes of the Greek or Indian epics.[15]

15 For a detailed discussion of the battle scenes and tactics in the *Tso,* particularly the Battle of Ch'eng-p'u, see Frank A. Kierman, Jr., "Phases and Modes of Combat in Early China," in Frank

The cities of the period, at least those that functioned as the capital or seat of power for the ruling family of the state, were protected by thick earthen walls surrounding the palaces and ancestral temples of the aristocrats. City gates were often fitted with a heavy portcullis that could be raised and lowered by pulleys. Artisans, merchants, and farmers probably lived in the area just outside the wall, at times with an outer wall around the area to protect them. The *Tso chuan* contains numerous accounts of sieges launched against these walled citadels, with scenes of the scaling of walls and storming of gates that are reminiscent of the tales of medieval European warfare.

The following brief vignette, though not a depiction of combat, will give some idea of the importance of these walled cities for the defense of the state, as well as conveying the atmosphere of ruthless aggression that characterized the period. It concerns a small state called Chü in the southern part of the Shantung Peninsula. The time is 583 B.C. (Duke Ch'eng 8th year).

> The ruler of Chin sent Wu-ch'en, the duke of Shen, on a mission to the state of Wu. To reach his destination, Wu-ch'en borrowed passage through the state of Chü.
>
> Standing by the moat around the city wall of Ch'ü-ch'iu, one of the cities of Chü, and talking with the ruler of Chü, he remarked, "The wall has gotten into very bad repair!"
>
> The ruler of Chü said, "A tiny out-of-the-way state situated among the Yi tribes—who would give a thought to us?"
>
> Wu-ch'en replied, "What country is without its crafty fellows who scheme of ways to extend the boundaries of their state and bring profit to its altars of the soil and grain? That is precisely why we have so many big states! One person schemes, another is lax in taking precautions. A brave man keeps his house doors tightly shut—how much more so should a state!"

The following year, 582, Chü was attacked by its powerful neighbor to the south, Ch'u. Because the walls around Ch'ü-ch'iu and the capital city were in poor condition, it was conquered and swallowed up.

In addition to warfare, and the elaborate hunts that served as military exercises in the brief intervals of peace, another important occupation of the aristocracy was the carrying out of the complex rituals and religious ceremonies that were believed necessary to the preservation and proper function-

Kierman and John K. Fairbank, eds., *Chinese Ways in Warfare*, pp. 27–66 (Cambridge, Mass.: Harvard University Press, 1974).

ing of the social order. The Chou king conducted sacrifices to his ancestors and to Heaven and the important nature deities on behalf of the empire as a whole. But within the individual feudal domains, the local rulers were responsible for carrying out sacrifices to their own ancestors and to the mountain and river deities within their realm. In addition, they watched over the *she-chi* or altars of the soil and grain which symbolized the existence of the state. The rulers and heads of families conducted their sacrifices in person, since there was no class of professional priests in ancient China, though it appears that male and female shamans at times played a role in religious observances. The usual sacrifices were domestic and wild animals, fish, grain, and alcoholic beverages. At several points, the *Tso* narrative suggests that prisoners of war were used on rare occasions as human sacrifices, but discussion of this question will be reserved for the notes to the translation.

Much of the time of the feudal leaders was taken up with the elaborate rites and entertainments that governed social intercourse in ancient China. The states, in an effort to insure their safety and further their interests, entered into alliances with one another. One important succession of alliances was made up of northern states which banded together to block the expansion of the state of Ch'u. Ch'u retaliated by welding together its own group of confederates that would lend it military support and help to further its aims. Because of the rapidly shifting military and diplomatic climate of the time, the exact composition of these various confederations changed quite often, and it was necessary for the participants to come together to renew old alliances or swear new ones at frequent intervals.

To conclude such alliances, as well as to arrange marriages among the ruling houses and report on important births, accessions, and deaths within their own domain, the rulers or their envoys traveled back and forth on state visits. These visits entailed elaborate receptions and entertainments, as well as, in the case of the swearing of alliances, solemn ceremonies of oath-taking in which the participants smeared their lips with the blood of a sacrificial animal.

The banquets that accompanied these diplomatic meetings ordinarily included musical entertainment, and it was customary for the host to order his musicians to perform a selection from the *Book of Odes,* the particular poem he chose being employed to pay a graceful compliment to his guest or to hint at where his own preferences lay in the questions of policy under consideration. The guest would then request the musicians to reply with a poem of his own selection, thereby responding to the compliment or conveying his own inclinations in the matter. At such times it was of course imperative that the rulers and their guests be thoroughly versed in the *Odes* and the requirements of etiquette so that they might play their role correctly, or, lacking that, be aided by assistants who were so versed. This in time opened the way to advancement for men such as Confucius and the followers of his school who were experts in ancient literature and ritual.

At the start of the Spring and Autumn period, as we have seen, there were around 120 feudal states in existence. When the *Tso chuan* comes to a close in 468 B.C., some two and a half centuries later, only about 40 of these survived. Thus the tendency for the more powerful states to swallow up their smaller neighbors was marked throughout the period. This tendency continued in the Warring States period that followed, when China was divided among 7 states, and reached its logical conclusion when one of these, Ch'in in the northwest, overthrew the others and united all of China under a single rule, a process that reached its conclusion in 221 B.C.

Another tendency clearly discernible in the period is the gradual shift of ruling power from one group in society to another. We have noted earlier how all real exercise of power passed from the Chou kings to their barons, the leaders of the various feudal states. In the Spring and Autumn era this same process is observable within the individual states. Thus in Lu, the native state of Confucius, for example, power passed from the ducal house, the hereditary rulers of the state, to three collateral houses, the so-called Three Families descended from three sons of Duke Huan of Lu. When Duke Chao (r. 541–510) attempted to reverse the process, he found himself forced into exile. Similarly, in the state of Chin authority passed into the hands of six prominent ministerial families, leaving the ruling house impotent. In the years following the end of the Spring and Autumn period, three of the six succeeded in eliminating their rivals and eventually overthrew the state entirely, creating the three new states of Han, Wei, and Chao in its place. An analogous situation obtained in Ch'i, where the ruling Chiang family was toppled from power and replaced by the ministerial family known as Ch'en or T'ien.

But these same tides of change that undermined the power of the ruling houses eventually eroded the power of the ministerial families as well. Just as the Chou kings had been replaced in authority by the leaders of the feudal states, and those leaders replaced by the heads of the ministerial families, so the last were in time replaced by men of the next lower order in society, the *shih* or knights, the lowest rank in the nobility. This came about when the rulers of the feudal states, in a bid to regain personal control of their governments, succeeded in gradually abolishing the hereditary rights that had enabled the members of the upper nobility to fill high government posts generation after generation, making such posts appointive instead. This move enabled the rulers to fill these posts with capable and well-trained men from the *shih* class who, less encumbered by clan loyalties than were the members of the great families of the upper nobility, would be more faithful to the interests of the ruler. This process had only just begun in the period covered by the *Tso chuan* and cannot be discussed in detail here, but it led in time to the creation of complex bureaucracies staffed by men chosen for their ability and education rather than their social standing, and eventually, many centuries later, to the creation of the famous civil service examination system.

The *Tso chuan,* then, presents us with a picture of a society in transition. The men and women of the time believed they could look back to an earlier age when a divinely-sanctioned Son of Heaven commanded unquestioning loyalty among his nobles and the empire was well governed by a system of carefully observed rites and social distinctions. But they were acutely aware that the old rites and distinctions no longer enjoyed such widespread support, and that new loyalties and modes of behavior were evolving to take their place.

The *Tso* preserves for us a remarkably detailed account of the people who lived through this troubled transitional period of warfare and social ferment. The record focuses mainly upon the rulers of the feudal states and their immediate associates, with only an occasional glance at the Chou Son of Heaven in his court in Lo-yang. Not surprisingly, the narrative is concerned almost entirely with the doings of the aristocracy, the only class in society whose activities were thought to be worth recording in detail. We occasionally catch sight of traveling merchants as they go from state to state with their wares, but learn almost nothing of the lives and activities of the artisans and peasants. The women of the aristocracy, living sheltered and closely circumscribed lives, are most of the time hidden away from male eyes in carefully guarded quarters of their own. But because of the important role they exercise in family affairs, particularly when they are older and can invoke the ideal of filial piety to exact obedience from their sons, they figure frequently in the history of the time. Women who attempt to play a role in politics, however, are not likely to be accorded sympathetic treatment by the compilers of the *Tso chuan.* As a result, the *Tso* being primarily a recital of political happenings, the women who appear in its pages are seldom of the exemplary type.

The Chinese have cherished the *Tso chuan* and elevated it to a place among the Confucian Classics first of all because of the light it throws upon the life and times of Confucius and the society that gave birth to him and his ideals, and upon the *Spring and Autumn Annals,* the work that he was believed to have compiled. And in a broader sense, they have prized it because they felt it preserved a truthful account of an important era of the past, albeit a dark and disordered one. If the other Classics are largely normative in nature, depicting men and women as they ought to be, the *Tso chuan* reveals them as they actually are, or were in one period of history. In this sense, its value has traditionally been thought to be chiefly cautionary.

In addition to preserving an invaluable picture of an era that would otherwise be largely unknown, the *Tso chuan* is important in the history of Chinese culture for another reason. As the earliest narrative history in the language, it has played a key role in shaping the patterns and motifs that were to characterize later works of historical literature. Because the *Tso chuan* was part of the Confucian canon and the chief commentary on the *Spring and Autumn Annals,* young men receiving a traditional education customarily made a thorough study of the work, and in many cases committed the entire text to memory. Later in their lives, if they produced works of history or historical romances of their own, they tended to shape their materials in terms of the patterns and concerns that had been inculcated in them by their study of the *Tso.* As a result, we find certain motifs and themes that appear first in the *Tso chuan* recurring again and again in the literature of later ages.

To give an example, in the very first of my selections from the *Tso chuan* there appears a motif that might be labeled The Filial Diner: someone is offered food and sets part of it aside for an absent parent. In this particular episode, the border guard Ying puts aside part of the meal given him by Duke Wu of Cheng so that he can take it to his mother, and in doing so awakens in the duke feelings of remorse over his own unforgiving treatment of his mother.

The same motif appears again later in the *Tso chuan* itself, in the section under Duke Hsüan 2d year, as seen in my translation on p. 78, and often in later works of history and literature. We encounter it, for example, in the biography of Lu Chi of Wu in the *San-kuo-chih* chapter 57, which relates how Lu Chi, when only a small boy, was served oranges by a host and surreptitiously stuffed three of them in the breast of his robe to take home to his mother, only to have them roll out incriminatingly when he made his parting bows.

At some far-distant time in the dawn of Chinese history the setting aside of a portion of food for an absent parent may have been done as a purely spontaneous act of thoughtfulness. But once the motif had been enshrined in a text included in the Confucian canon, the action became a kind of cultural stereotype, at times perhaps to be deliberately performed by those who wished to signal their outstanding filial piety, or at least to be attributed to persons who were being depicted in works of history or fiction as paragons of filialness.

Another recurring pattern of behavior found in the *Tso chuan,* though not in the excerpts translated here, might be called The Enumeration of Crimes, in which an accuser, usually in an act of direct confrontation, lists a series of offenses which he believes the other party to be guilty of. The offenses are numbered "first crime," "second crime," and so forth, and often the action is described by the verb *shu,* "to number," used in a special sense meaning to accuse or confront someone with a list of offenses. By my count, the pattern appears three times in the *Tso chuan* (Duke Hsüan 15th year, Duke Hsiang 14th year, Duke Chao 2d year), as well as in the *Kuo yü* or *Conversations from the States, Chin yü* 3. A famous later example of the same motif is found in the eighth chapter of the *Shih chi* or *Records of the Historian* when, in 203 B.C., the military leader Hsiang Yü challenges his rival Liu Pang, the founder of the Han dynasty, to personal combat. Liu Pang declines to accept the challenge and instead delivers a lengthy harangue in which he "confronts" *(shu)* Hsiang Yü with a list of ten crimes.

Other motifs occurring in the *Tso chuan* that have been of great significance in the literature of China, and of countries like Korea and Japan that have been under strong Chinese influence, include the minister who places loyalty to his ruler over loyalty to members of his own family; the follower who impersonates his lord in order to allow the latter to escape danger; the lord who remembers (or forgets) to reward his followers who were faithful to him in time of trouble; and the son who strives to avenge the death of a parent. Of course only a careful cataloging of these various topoi and a study of their recurrence in later works can fully define the nature and extent of the *Tso chuan*'s influence. My remarks here are intended simply to draw attention to the phenomenon and suggest it as a subject for investigation.

When Hsiao T'ung (501–531) came to compile his famous anthology of early Chinese literature, the *Wen hsüan* or *Anthology of Literature,* he excused himself for omitting excerpts from the Confucian Classics by explaining in his introduction that it is impossible to "cut and slice up" works of such brilliance and profundity. In the case of my own work, I might perhaps have avoided the kind of cutting and slicing that Hsiao T'ung deplored by going to the opposite extreme and offering a complete translation of the text. However, the *Tso chuan* is an extremely long and complex work, and a complete English translation would have demanded a far greater expenditure of time and effort than I am capable of giving at this point. Moreover, though the *Tso chuan* contains passages of great beauty and power, there are frequent arid stretches in between, and it is not at all certain that an uncut translation would answer the needs of all types of readers.[16]

The present selection is designed for persons who do not feel inclined to work their way through the entire text but wish to familiarize themselves with its most famous and influential narratives and get some sense of its style and principal ideas. I have naturally attempted to select passages that form a more or less complete entity or deal with a single train of events, such as a military campaign or a political revolution. I have added notes to identify the source of quotations in the text and wherever else I felt they were necessary to assist readers in following the thread of the narrative, but I have not attempted to discuss the numerous problems in the social, economic, and cultural history of ancient China that are raised by the text. It may be noted that archeological excavations being carried out in China at the present time are throwing new and unexpected light on the history of the period, so that opinion on many such problems is at the moment in a state of flux.[17] All excerpts are arranged in chronological order except those in the very last section, "Attitudes Toward the Supernatural," in which I have grouped a number of short passages culled from different places in the text that illustrate the attitude of rationalism and humanism that pervades the *Tso chuan* as a whole.

The *Tso* is famous for the denseness and extreme economy of its style, and readers of the original require the aid of commentaries in order to follow the narrative and keep track of the large number of persons mentioned. To assist readers of the translation, at the beginning of the selections, and sometimes at other points along the way, I have provided passages outlining the background of the events described and the principal personages. In the translations themselves, I have tried to stick as closely to the wording of the original as possible, though even so, classical Chinese being the highly concise language it is, there are countless places where one or two characters in the original have had to be expanded into an entire clause or more in order to be intelligible in English. It is regrettable that this should be so, since it slows down the narrative markedly, but considerations of compre-

16 Japanese sinologues have traditionally employed the term *Kikō Saden* or "Duke Hsi *Tso chuan*" to describe the performance of readers who approach the work with every intention of reading it from cover to cover, but whose good intentions desert them by the time they reach Duke Hsi, the fifth of the twelve dukes of Lu whose reigns are covered by the text, or about one-sixth of the way through.

17 For a summary of what recent archeological finds reveal about the period, see Li Xueqin, *Eastern Zhou and Qin Civilizations*, K. C. Chang, tr. (New Haven: Yale University Press, 1985).

hensibility must take precedence over those of pace. Occasionally I have added a brief identifying phrase such as "the Ch'u official" before the name of an individual in order to cue the reader in as to the person's identity. Such phrases are based on information in the standard Chinese commentaries on the text.

In addition to conciseness, the *Tso* is noted for the fact that it frequently refers to a single individual by a bewildering variety of personal names, family or fief names, official titles, or posthumous titles. Such a multiplicity of names may have been quite intelligible to persons of the period, but for readers many centuries removed from the world of the text, it places a great burden upon patience and comprehension. I have therefore attempted to ease the burden by fixing upon one or at most two names by which to refer to a given individual throughout. Though certain nuances of tone in the original may be thereby obscured, I hope the increase in clarity will be felt to justify such a liberty.

I have taken one other notable liberty in the translation, one that experts will perhaps bridle at. The Chou was an intensely hierarchical-minded era and employed a carefully defined system of titles and ritual prescriptions to distinguish the different grades in the feudal nobility. Thus the Chou ruler alone was authorized to employ the title *wang* or "king" in referring to himself, while the other members of the nobility were granted lesser titles such as *kung, hou, po,* and so on, titles that have by longstanding custom been rendered in English by the words "duke," "marquis," "earl," and so forth. Regardless of what title the ruler of a feudal state might hold while he was alive, however, when he died he was referred to by the term *kung,* customarily translated as "duke," often preceded by the posthumous name that had been bestowed upon him and by which he is known in history. As a result, the *Tso* may refer to a particular ruler in a variety of different ways. If the translator sticks to the exact wording of the Chinese, he is therefore in the position of asking his English readers to understand that the individual called a marquis or an earl in one sentence is the same as the one called a duke in the next. When English readers are already under considerable strain because of the large number of look-alike place and personal names in the translation, is it reasonable to make such a demand?[18]

To further complicate matters, rulers at times usurped titles which, according to the protocol of the Chou court, they were not authorized to

18 One might get around the difficulty by translating *kung* not as "duke" but as "lord" or "sire," which is probably what it meant in such contexts. See C. N. Tay, "On the Interpretation of *Kung* (Duke?) in the *Tso-chuan,*" *Journal of the American Oriental Society* (1973), 93(4):550–555. But the practice of rendering it as "duke" has been so consistently followed in translations of early texts and writings in English on early China that a change at this point seems to me hardly feasible.

use. Thus the rulers of the southern states of Ch'u and Wu regularly referred to themselves as kings, though the older states in the north naturally disapproved of the practice and in their own records persisted in referring to such rulers as viscounts. The chaos that practices of this sort create in the terminology of the text is easily imaginable. To avoid continual bracketing and to spare the reader as much obfuscation as possible, I have not attempted to render all these various noble titles in English, but have referred to the individuals in most cases simply as "the ruler of ____." To determine the feudal rank held by such rulers, the reader should refer to the table of principal states following this introduction, which lists the main feudal states mentioned in the text along with the surname and feudal title of the ruling family.

Since the *Tso chuan* was valued from early times for the light in throws on the events recorded in the *Spring and Autumn Annals,* and in time was recognized as part of the Confucian canon, the text has come down to us in very good condition. There are few important textual variants, and few places where the text appears to be faulty or unintelligible. The translator of the *Tso chuan* is thus in a much happier position than someone struggling to make sense out of a philosophical text such as the *Chuang Tzu* that dates from approximately the same period but is rife with textual knots and gnarls.

This does not mean, however, that there are not places where interpretations of the text may reasonably differ, particularly in cases where the subject of a verb is unexpressed and hence open to doubt. In the notes to the translations that follow, I will on occasion be mentioning alternative interpretations or indicating which of the numerous commentaries on the text I have followed.

The only complete English translation of the *Tso chuan* is that done by James Legge over a hundred years ago, *The Ch'un Ts'ew, with the Tso Chuen,* published as volume five of *The Chinese Classics* in London in 1872 (Taiwan reprint 1985). Unfortunately, Legge's main attention is focused upon the *Spring and Autumn Annals (Ch'un Ts'ew),* and the translation of the *Tso chuan* is relegated to the notes, printed in very small type, and mixed in with the translator's own notes, making it extremely difficult to read. Legge's style, sonorously Biblical in places and always remarkably faithful to the wording of the original, is now largely out of date, though the translation as a whole remains a highly impressive achievement. In my own translation I have aimed at a strictly contemporary style as most appropriate in rendering the harshly realistic tone of the original.

Among the various works I have consulted in making my translation, I am particularly indebted to the Kamata and Yang works cited in note 4 above, as well as the Japanese translation by Kaizuka Shigeki and others, *Shunjū Sashi den* (*Sekai koten bungaku zenshū* 13; Tokyo: Chikuma shobō, 1970), and the modern Chinese translation by Shen Yü-ch'eng, *Tso-chuan i-wen* (Beijing: Chung-hua shu-chü, 1981).

In addition to the Egan article cited in note 9 above, readers who wish to read further in English on the *Tso chuan* should consult John C. Y. Wang, "Early Chinese Narrative: The *Tso-chuan* as Example," in Andrew H. Plaks, ed., *Chinese Narrative: Critical and Theoretical Essays,* pp. 3–20 (Princeton: Princeton University Press, 1977).

I would like to thank Moss Roberts, professor of Chinese at New York University, for reading the manuscript of this work and making numerous helpful suggestions. Needless to say, he is not responsible for any of the shortcomings that remain. I also wish to thank my friends Miwa Kai and John Meskill of Columbia University for helping me to get hold of needed material.

TABLE OF

PRINCIPAL STATES

NAME OF STATE	NAME OF RULING FAMILY	RANK OF RULING FAMILY
Ch'en	Kuei	marquis *(hou)*
Cheng	Chi	earl *(po)*
Chi	Ssu	duke *(kung)*
Ch'i	Chiang	marquis
Chin	Chi	marquis
Ch'in	Ying	earl
Chou	Chi	king *(wang)*
Chu	Ts'ao	viscount *(tzu)*
Ch'u	Mi	viscount
Chü	Ying	viscount
Hsü	Chiang	baron *(nan)*
Hsüeh	Jen	marquis
Lu	Chi	marquis
Sung	Tzu	duke
T'eng	Chi	marquis
Ts'ai	Chi	marquis
Ts'ao	Chi	earl
Wei	Chi	marquis
Wu	Chi	viscount
Yüeh	Ssu	viscount

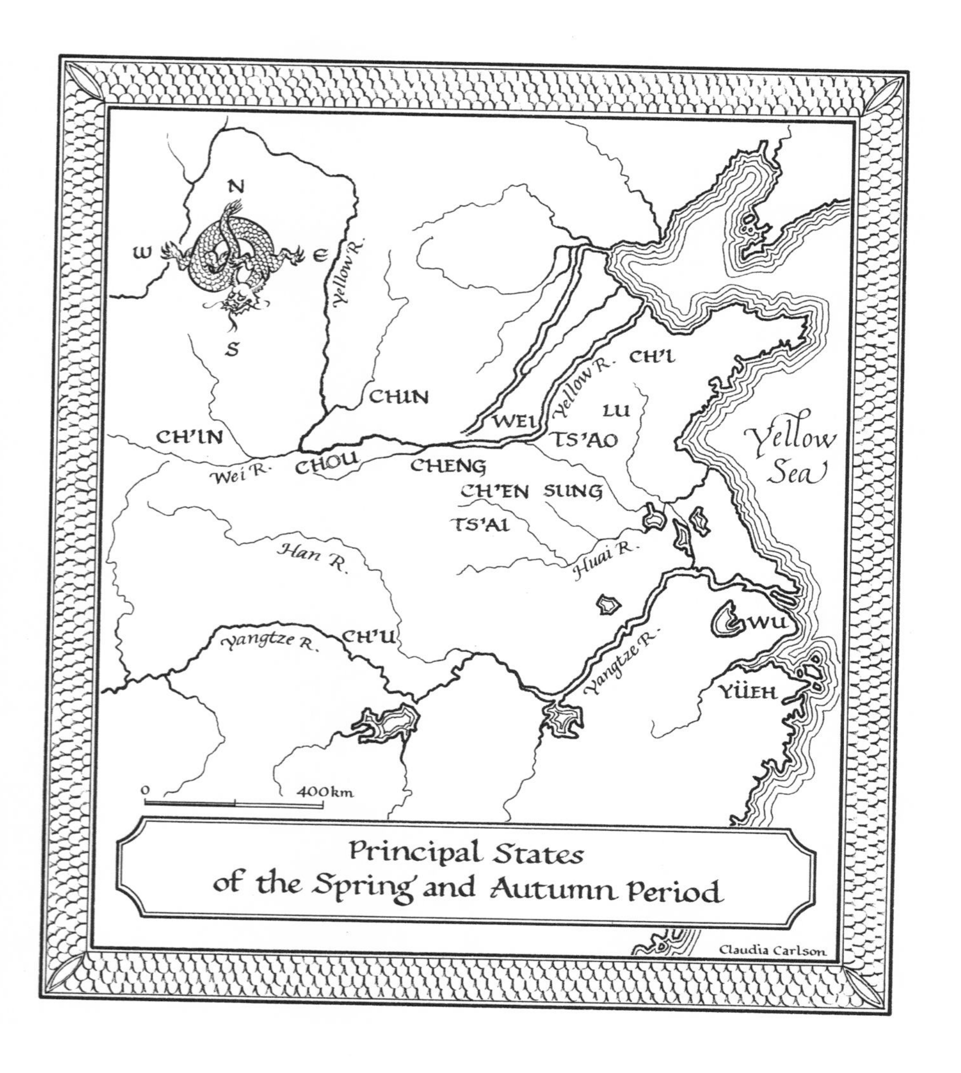
N
W
E
S
Yellow R.
CHIN
CH'IN
Wei R.
CHOU
CHENG
WEI
Yellow R.
CH'I
LU
TS'AO
CH'EN
SUNG
TS'AI
Han R.
Huai R.
Yellow Sea
CH'U
Yangtze R.
Yangtze R.
WU
YÜEH
0
400km
Principal States
of the Spring and Autumn Period
Claudia Carlson

The Tso chuan

TRANSLATIONS FROM THE ORIENTAL CLASSICS

O N E

Two Brothers of Cheng and the Mother Who Doted on the Younger

THE FOLLOWING IS THE FIRST EXTENDED NARRATIVE IN THE *Tso chuan* and one of the most famous in the entire text. The episode illustrates the extremely compressed style of the *Tso.*

The story begins with a theme common in folklore, the infant who startles or disgusts its mother by some unusual appearance or manner of birth. This is followed by a section in which an older brother, ruler of the feudal state of Cheng, tolerates a series of increasingly outrageous moves by his younger brother, despite advice from his ministers to take a firmer stand, until the proper moment for action comes at last.

The older brother, having sworn in a moment of anger never to see his mother again, in time regrets his vow. He is given advice on how to circumvent the vow without actually breaking it by a minor official who is himself a model of filial piety. The episode ends in a brief burst of laconic verse, one of the relatively few examples of original poetry to be found in the *Tso chuan.*

DUKE YIN 1ST YEAR (722 B.C.)

In the past, Duke Wu of Cheng had taken a bride from the state of Shen, known as Lady Chiang of Duke Wu.[1] Lady Chiang gave birth to the future

1 Shen was ruled by a branch of the Chiang family, hence the bride was referred to as Lady Chiang.

Duke Chuang and to his brother, Tuan of Kung. Duke Chuang was born wide awake and consequently greatly startled Lady Chiang.[2] Therefore she named him Born Awake and came to hate him. But she loved his younger brother Tuan and wished to have him declared heir to the throne of Cheng. Repeatedly she begged Duke Wu to do so, but he would not agree.

Later, when Duke Chuang became ruler of Cheng (743 B.C.), Lady Chiang asked him to assign the city of Chih to his younger brother Tuan. But the duke replied, "Chih is a strategic city, the place where Kuo Shu met his death.[3] Any other city you have only to ask for."

She then requested that Tuan be given the city of Ching, and he was accordingly sent to reside there. He came to be called the T'ai-shu or Grand Younger Brother of Ching City.

Chai Chung, a high official of Cheng, said to the duke, "If any of the major cities have walls exceeding a hundred *chih* in length, they pose a danger to the capital.[4] According to the regulations of the former kings, even the largest cities should not exceed one third the size of the capital, while middle-sized cities should be one-fifth and small cities one-ninth. Now the city of Ching does not fit these dimensions and violates the regulations. You may find yourself unable to endure the consequences!"

The duke said, "Lady Chiang would have it that way—how can I avoid the danger?"

"There is no end to what Lady Chiang would have!" replied Chai Chung. "Better tend to the matter at once and not let it grow and put out runners, for runners can be hard to control. If even plants that have put out runners cannot be rooted out, how much more so the favored younger brother of a ruler!"

The duke said, "If he does too many thing that are not right, he is bound to bring ruin on himself. I suggest you wait a while."

After some time the T'ai-shu ordered that the western and northern border regions acknowledge fealty to him as well as to the duke. The ducal son Lü,[5] an official of Cheng, said to the duke, "The state cannot tolerate a

2 The phrase *wu-sheng,* translated here as "born wide awake," is also interpreted to mean born just as his mother was waking up, or born feet first. Ssu-ma Ch'ien in *Shih chi* ch. 42, the account of the state of Cheng, adds, in order to help explain the mother's loathing for the child, that the birth was a difficult one.

3 A ruler of the nearby state of Kuo who made his capital at Chih and behaved evilly until overthrown by Cheng. Duke Chuang fears his younger brother will do likewise.

4 According to commentators, one *chih* represents a section of city wall one *chang* in height and three *chang* (or, according to another theory, five *chang*) in length. One *chang* is said to equal ten feet.

5 *Kung-tzu,* "ducal son," is a designation used for sons of feudal rulers; *kung-sun,* "ducal grandson," is used for grandsons; descendents in the next generation were given a surname of their own. Both Kung-tzu and Kung-sun later became surnames.

system of double fealty! What do you intend to do? If you sanction what the T'ai-shu has done, then I beg leave to serve him rather than you. If you do not intend to sanction it, then I urge you to do away with him before he stirs up the hearts of the people!"

"No need," said the duke. "He will bring on his own downfall."

The T'ai-shu proceeded to take over the cities that had previously acknowledged double fealty and make them his own, extending his control as far as Lin-yen. The ducal son Lü said, "Now is the time to act! If he expands his territory, the people will go over to his side."

The duke replied, "If he acts wrongly, no one will side with him.[6] Though he expands his territory, he will face ruin."

The T'ai-shu completed the building of his walls, called together his men, mended his armor and weapons, equipped his foot soldiers and chariots, and prepared for a surprise attack on the capital of Cheng. Lady Chiang was to open the city to him. When the duke learned the date planned for the attack, he said, "Now is the time!" He ordered the ducal son Lü to lead a force of two hundred chariots and attack Ching. Ching turned against the T'ai-shu Tuan, who took refuge in Yen. The duke attacked him at Yen, and on the day *hsin-ch'ou* of the fifth month, the T'ai-shu fled the state and went to Kung.[7]

In the end the duke confined his mother, Lady Chiang, in Ch'eng-ying and took a vow, saying, "Not until we reach the Yellow Springs shall we meet again!"[8]

Later he regretted the vow. Ying K'ao-shu, a border guard of Ying Valley, hearing of this, presented gifts to the duke, and the duke in turn had a meal served to him. He ate the meal but set aside the meat broth. When the duke asked him why, he replied, "Your servant has a mother who shares whatever food he eats, but she has never tasted your lordship's broth. I beg permission to take her some."

"You have a mother to take things to. Alas, I alone have none!" said the duke.

"May I venture to ask the meaning of that?" said Ying K'ao-shu.

The duke explained why he had made the remark and confessed that he regretted his vow.

"Why should your lordship worry?" said the other. "If you dig into the

6 Or, following Tu Yü's interpretation, "He is acting wrongly and in an unbrotherly manner."

7 At this point there appears a passage explaining the wording of the *Spring and Autumn Annals* entry pertaining to these events. In the present translation passages of this type have been omitted.

8 Yellow Springs, meaning the springs within the yellow earth, is a term for the land of the dead.

earth until you reach the springs, and fashion a tunnel where the two of you can meet, then who is to say you have not kept your vow?"

The duke did as he suggested. As the duke entered the tunnel he intoned this verse:

> Within the great tunnel,
> genial, genial is my joy!

When Lady Chiang emerged from the tunnel she intoned this verse:

> Outside the great tunnel,
> far-flung, far-flung is my joy!

So in the end mother and son became as they had been before.

The gentleman remarks:[9] Ying K'ao-shu was a man of utmost filial piety. He loved his mother, and succeeded in inspiring a similar feeling in Duke Chuang. Is this not what the *Book of Odes* means when it says:

> While filial sons are unslacking,
> forever shall be given you good things.[10]

9 The *Tso chuan* frequently introduces didactic comments on the events of its narrative in this fashion. Though it has been asserted that "the gentleman" refers to Confucius, this is clearly impossible in many cases and these remarks are presumably judgments made by the author or authors of the *Tso chuan*, though some may have been added by later hands. There are eighty-four such passages in the *Tso chuan*.

10 "Greater Odes," *Chi-tsui*, Mao no. 247.

TWO

The Revolt of the Ducal Son Chou-hsü in Wei

AS MENTIONED IN THE INTRODUCTION, A GREAT MANY OF THE narratives in the *Tso chuan* deal with succession struggles or usurpations in the ruling houses of the various feudal states. The following is an account of one such usurpation, this one in the small northern state of Wei carried out by the ducal son Chou-hsü. Chou-hsü, whose name may also be read Chou-yü, was a son of Duke Chuang (r. 757–735) of Wei by a concubine and was much favored and pampered by his father, although Shih Ch'üeh, a high minister of Wei, warned the duke against such favoritism. Some years after Duke Chuang died and was succeeded by his heir, Duke Huan (r. 734–719), Chou-hsü assassinated Duke Huan, his half brother, and replaced him as ruler of Wei. He was aided by Shih Hou, son of Shih Ch'üeh, though Shih Ch'üeh himself strongly disapproved of the usurper.

Chou-hsü proved to be a cruel and unwise ruler and as a result failed to win the allegiance of his people. Accompanied by his supporter Shih Hou, he journeyed to a neighboring state in hopes of gaining an audience with the Chou king in order to lend legitimacy to his rule. But Shih Ch'üeh arranged for the execution of both Chou-hsü and his own son Shih Hou while they were abroad. In doing so, Shih Ch'üeh demonstrated that he placed duty to the state above concern for his own son.

DUKE YIN 3D YEAR (720 B.C.)

Duke Chuang of Wei married the younger sister of Te-ch'en, the heir apparent of the state of Ch'i. Known as Lady Chiang of Duke Chuang, she was beautiful but bore no sons.[1] For her the people of Wei composed the poem "Stately Lady."[2] The duke also took a wife from the state of Ch'en named Li Kuei; she bore Hsiao-po, who died early. Her younger sister Tai Kuei bore the duke a son who later became Duke Huan. Lady Chiang raised him as though he were her own son.

Chou-hsü was a son of the duke by a concubine. He enjoyed great favor with the duke and was fond of arms. The duke denied him nothing, but Lady Chiang hated him.

Shih Ch'üeh reprimanded the duke, saying, "I have heard that if one loves a son, he will teach him righteous ways and not lead him into error. Arrogance, luxury, license, and dissipation are the source of error. When these four appear, it is because favor and bounty have been excessive. If you intend to establish Chou-hsü as your heir, you should settle the matter clearly. If you leave it unsettled, you tempt him to disaster. To enjoy favor and yet not become arrogant, to be arrogant and yet able to submit to others, to submit to others and not feel resentment, to be resentful and yet able to restrain oneself—these are rare indeed!.

"The humble obstructing the worthy, the junior overbearing the senior, the distantly related causing dissention among the closely related, the new alienating the old, the petty overpowering the great, the licentious destroying the righteous—these are called the six perversities. The ruler righteous, the minister carrying out his righteousness, the father kind, the son filial, the elder brother loving, the younger brother respectful—these are called the six compliances. To depart from compliancy and act with perversity will serve only to hasten disaster. As a ruler of men, you do not strive to depart from disaster, but on the contrary hasten it! How can this be right?"

The duke did not heed him. Shih Ch'üeh's son Shih Hou spent much time in Chou-hsü's company. His father forbade him to do so, but the son refused to listen. When Duke Huan came to the throne of Wei (734 B.C.), Shih Ch'üeh retired from office on grounds of old age.

1 Ch'i, like the state of Shen in the preceding episode, was ruled by a branch of the Chiang family.

2 "Airs of Wei," *Shih jen,* Mao no. 57. The poem describes the great beauty of a lady who was a "Daughter of the ruler of Ch'i, / wife of the ruler of Wei, / younger sister of the heir apparent," which surely fits Lady Chiang. The poem is traditionally supposed to express the pity which the people of Wei felt for the unfortunate lady.

DUKE YIN 4TH YEAR (719 B.C.)

In the spring Chou-hsü of Wei assassinated Duke Huan and set himself up as ruler.

The ruler of Lu and the ruler of Sung were planning to meet, intending to renew their former alliance, but before the date of the meeting arrived, men from Wei came to Lu to report the rebellion in Wei.

When Duke Shang of Sung became ruler (720 B.C.), his cousin, the ducal son P'ing, fled from Sung to Cheng. The men of Cheng wished to assist P'ing to return to Sung and claim the throne. Later, when Chou-hsü set himself up as ruler of Wei, he hoped to take revenge on Cheng for what it had done to the former ruler of Wei,[3] and at the same time seek to win favor with the other feudal lords so as to gain the support of his own people. He therefore sent an envoy to announce to the ruler of Sung, "If you are planning to attack Cheng to wipe out your enemy P'ing, then you might act as leader of the expedition and I would contribute my humble forces along with those of Ch'en and Ts'ai to assist you. This is what the state of Wei desires."

The men of Sung agreed to this plan. At this time Ch'en and Ts'ai were on friendly terms with Wei. Therefore the ruler of Sung, the ruler of Ch'en, and the men of Ts'ai and Wei attacked the capital of the state of Cheng, laying siege to its eastern gate, but after five days they went home.

The duke of Lu questioned Chung Chung, a high official of Lu, saying, "This Chou-hsü of Wei—will he succeed?"

Chung Chung replied, "I have heard of gaining the support of one's people through virtue, but I have never heard of doing so through violence. To try to do so through violence is like trying to straighten out threads by further tangling them. Now Chou-hsü relies on military force and is quite ready to resort to cruelty. Relying on military force, he has few followers;

3 Cheng had attacked Wei two years previously.

ever ready to resort to cruelty, he has few allies. Anyone whose followers turn against him and whose allies desert him will find it difficult to accomplish anything!

"Military force is like fire—if it is not kept in check, it will end by consuming the user. Chou-hsü has assassinated his sovereign and used his people tyrannously. And yet now he makes no attempt to practice true virtue but hopes to achieve success through violence—he will never escape!"

Since Chou-hsü had still been unable to gain the support of his people, Shih Hou asked his father Shih Ch'üeh how one might help to strengthen the position of the new ruler.

Shih Ch'üeh replied, "If he were to obtain an audience with the king, that would do it."[4]

"And how could he gain such an audience?"

"Duke Huan of Ch'en is at present in great favor with the king. Ch'en and Wei are now on friendly terms. If he paid a visit to the court of Ch'en and persuaded Ch'en to ask on his behalf, he could surely obtain an audience."

Shih Hou thereupon accompanied Chou-hsü on a visit to Ch'en. Shih Ch'üeh meanwhile sent an envoy to Ch'en to report, saying, "Wei is a small and insignificant state, and I am an old man—I myself can do nothing. The fact is that these two men have assassinated my lord, the ruler of Wei. May I ask you to take care of them for me?"

The men of Ch'en seized Chou-hsü and Shih Hou and requested Wei to supervise the matter.

In the ninth month the men of Wei dispatched Ch'ou, superintendant of the right, to supervise the execution of Chou-hsü at P'u. Shih Ch'üeh dispatched his house steward Nou Yang-chien to supervise the execution of his son Shih Hou in Ch'en.

The gentleman remarks: Shih Ch'üeh was a minister of utmost fidelity. He hated Chou-hsü, and his son Hou was allied with Chou-hsü. Is this not what is meant by the saying, a larger duty cancels out the bonds of kinship?

4 The Chou king or Son of Heaven, nominally sovereign over all the feudal states at this time. Though he wielded little actual power, his prestige was still very great.

THREE

A Quarrel Over Precedence

CHINA IN THE PERIOD DEPICTED IN THE *TSO CHUAN* WAS A complex patchwork of feudal domains, some as large as a modern province, others no more than tiny city-states. Some had apparently been in existence since long before the founding of the Chou dynasty, while others had been assigned to kin or allies of the Chou conquerors when the dynasty was established around 1100 B.C. or thereafter. All acknowledged fealty to the Chou king, and their relations with him and with one another were governed by an elaborate code of *li* or rules of ritual or propriety. Disputes often arose as to just what rules applied in what situation, however, and in the following brief episode we see one such dispute between leaders of two small states who had come to visit the court of the ruler of the state of Lu in present-day Shantung. One is the lord of T'eng, a small state in Shantung whose ancestor, a son of King Wen, one of the founders of the Chou dynasty, was enfeoffed in the time of King Wen's son, King Wu. The other is the ruler of Hsüeh, a small state in Shantung near T'eng whose ruling family, surnamed Jen, was said to have descended from the Yellow Emperor and to have been enfoeffed in the time of the Hsia dynasty many centuries before the founding of the Chou.

DUKE YIN 11TH YEAR (712 B.C.)

Eleventh year, spring: the ruler of T'eng and the ruler of Hsüeh came to the court of Lu. They quarreled over precedence.

The Hsüeh ruler said, "My ancestors were enfeoffed first!"

"But my ancestor was chief diviner for the house of Chou!" said the T'eng ruler. "Hsüeh's ruling family is not even of the royal clan. It is impossible that I should go after!"

The duke of Lu dispatched his relative Yü-fu to speak on his behalf to the ruler of Hsüeh and request him to step aside. "You and the lord of T'eng have graciously come to call upon me and inquire about my well-being," he said. "Now there is a Chou proverb that goes:

> Mountains have trees,
>   and the carpenter fells them.
> Guests have propriety,
>   they do as the host tells them.

When drawing up an alliance, the house of Chou first records the rulers of its own surname, and those of other surnames come after. If I were to pay a visit to the court of Hsüeh, I would not venture to take rank with persons of the Jen surname.[1] If you will be so kind as to do me this favor, I would like to ask you to let the lord of T'eng go first."

The Hsüeh ruler consented, and the T'eng ruler accordingly took first place.

1 The ruler of Lu belongs to the same Chi family as the royal house of Chou and the ruler of T'eng.

F O U R

A Wife's Dilemma

THE RULERS AND HIGH MINISTERS OF THE SPRING AND AUTUMN period, whose intrigues and predatory strikes kept the society of the time in such perpetual turbulence, may be said to have brought upon themselves the sufferings that ensued. But often their wives and daughters as well, though in most cases innocent of any part in the planning of such exploits, were fearfully embroiled in the consequences. Sometimes, as in the episode below, they were confronted with agonizing conflicts of loyalty. At other times they were wrested from their husbands and summarily carried off as part of the spoils of war. A famous example of the latter type was Lady Kuei, wife of the ruler of the tiny southern state of Hsi. King Chuang (r. 740–690) of the nearby state of Ch'u, having heard reports of her beauty, attacked and overthrew the state of Hsi and carried Lady Kuei back with him to Ch'u. But though she bore him two sons, for years she refused to speak to him out of shame over the fate she had been subjected to. (Duke Chuang 14th year.) Another and somewhat gaudier victim of the disordered times, the beautiful Lady Hsia, originally the wife of the ruler of Ch'en, was abducted or handed about by such a succession of husbands and lovers that the list becomes quite dizzying. (Hsüan 9, Ch'eng 2 and 7, Hsiang 26.) In view of the callous treatment so often accorded these women of the aristocracy, we should not be surprised at the cynical attitude expressed by one of their number in the passage below. Chai Chung, the powerful minister of the state of Cheng, has appeared earlier, in chapter 1.

DUKE HUAN 15TH YEAR (697 B.C.)

Chai Chung monopolized power, much to the distress of the ruler of Cheng. The latter ordered Chai Chung's son-in-law, Yung Chiu, to kill Chai

Chung, inviting him to a banquet in the suburbs of the capital in order to do so.

Yung Chiu's wife was aware of the plot [against her father] and said to her mother, "Which is dearer, a father or a husband?"

Her mother replied, "All men are potential husbands, but you have only one father. How could there be any comparison?"

In the end she informed her father, saying, "Yung is deliberately forego-ing his own house and holding the banquet in the suburbs. I have told you because I am suspicious of the arrangement."

Chai Chung killed Yung Chiu and threw his corpse into the Chou family pond. The ruler of Cheng loaded the corpse on his carriage and fled from the capital, saying, "He told even his wife about the plot—no wonder he died!"

F I V E

Two Half Brothers Who Hurried to Their Death

THE FOLLOWING EPISODE TELLS OF TWO HALF BROTHERS OF Wei, one of whom faced death rather than disobey his father's orders, the other of whom tried to spare his brother by dying in his place. Following the highly compressed *Tso chuan* version of the tale, I give the story as it was rewritten by the historian Ssu-ma Ch'ien in order to show how Ssu-ma Ch'ien adapted and expanded material from the *Tso*. Finally I give a poem from the *Book of Odes* that was traditionally believed to refer to the brothers.

DUKE HUAN 16TH YEAR (696 B.C.)

Earlier, Duke Hsüan of Wei committed incest with his father's concubine Yi Chiang, and from this union was born Chi-tzu. He was entrusted to the Ducal Son of the Right. A bride was brought for him from the state of Ch'i, but because she was beautiful, Duke Hsüan took her for himself. From this union were born Shou-tzu and Shuo. Shou-tzu was entrusted to the Ducal Son of the Left. Yi Chiang committed suicide by strangling herself.

Duke Hsüan's bride from Ch'i plotted with her son Shuo to do away with Chi-tzu. As part of the plot, Duke Hsüan ordered Chi-tzu to go on a mission to Ch'i and arranged for robbers to lie in wait at Hsin and kill him.

Shou-tzu informed his half brother Chi-tzu of the plot and urged him to flee, but Chi-tzu refused, saying, "Who would have any use for a son who disobeys his father's orders? In a country where there are no fathers, such behavior might be acceptable."

When the time for departure came, Shou-tzu gave Chi-tzu wine to drink and then, placing Chi-tzu's banner on his own carriage, he set out ahead of Chi-tzu. The robbers accordingly killed him.

When Chi-tzu arrived, he said, "I'm the one you want—what fault has he committed? Please kill me!" The robbers killed him as well.

The following is Ssu-ma Ch'ien's version of the story as found in *Shih chi* 37, The Hereditary House of Wei K'ang-shu. Whether the details added in Ssu-ma Ch'ien's version derive from some text or texts now lost, from oral tradition, or from Ssu-ma Ch'ien's imagination, it is impossible to tell.

Earlier, Duke Hsüan had made love to Lady Yi Chiang, and Yi Chiang gave birth to a son named Chi. Chi was designated heir to the duke. The Ducal Son of the Right was assigned to be his tutor.

The Ducal Son of the Right arranged for the heir to take a bride from the ruling house of the state of Ch'i. But before the marriage could be carried out, Duke Hsüan saw that his son's prospective bride was beautiful and, pleased with her, appropriated her for himself and arranged for the heir to take another bride. After Duke Hsüan had taken the woman of Ch'i into his entourage, she gave birth to Shou and Shuo. The Ducal Son of the Left was assigned to be their tutor. Meanwhile, the heir's mother died.

Duke Hsüan's wife from Ch'i plotted with her son Shuo to slander and speak evil of the heir, Chi. Duke Hsüan, having snatched away the heir's bride, hated him in his heart and wanted to remove him. When he heard the evil reports of him, he was enraged and ordered Chi to go on a mission to the state of Ch'i. Meanwhile, he commanded robbers to block Chi's way at the border and kill him. He gave the heir a white banner and told the robbers at the border, "When you see someone bearing a white banner, kill him!"

Chi was about to set out when Shuo's older brother Shou, the younger brother of Chi by a different mother, knowing that Shuo hated Chi and that the ruler planned to have Chi killed, said to him, "There are robbers at the border who will kill you when they see your white banner. You'd better not go!"

But the heir replied, "One must not disobey his father's orders in hopes of saving his own life." Then he made ready to set off.

When Shou saw that he could not stop his brother, he stole the white banner and started out ahead of him, galloping to the border. The robbers, spotting the signal they had been told to look for, accordingly killed him.

After Shou had been killed, the heir Chi arrived on the spot and said to the robbers, *"I'm* the one you should have killed!" The robbers killed him as well and reported to Duke Hsüan.

At the end of the chapter, in the section devoted to personal comments on the narrative, Ssu-ma Ch'ien has this to say:

The Grand Historian remarks: When I read the narratives of the hereditary houses, I come to the story of how Duke Hsüan's heir Chi was put to death because of a woman, and how his younger brother Shou attempted to spare him by dying in his place. The story is like that of Shen-sheng, the heir of the state of Chin, who did not dare to expose the misdeeds of Lady Li.[1] Both Chi and Shen-sheng hated to go against their father's will, and so in the end they died. How moving!

1 For the story of Shen-sheng and Lady Li, see pp. 21–24 below.

From at least Han times, the legend of the two half brothers of Wei has been associated with the following poem from the *Book of Odes,* "Airs of Pei," *Erh tzu ch'eng chou,* Mao number 44, which was believed to have been written by the people of the state of Wei in memory of the ill-fated brothers. The poem is in two stanzas.

Two boys aboard a boat—
drifting, drifting, its shadow.
Longingly I think of them,
my heart restless, so restless!

Two boys aboard a boat—
drifting, drifting, it departs.
Longingly I think of them,
may they come to no harm!

Some commentators take the boat to be merely symbolic of the uncertainty and danger that faced the brothers on their journey. But one version of the legend preserved in the *Hsin hsü, Chieh-shih* chapter, by Liu Hsin (d. A.D. 23) states that the brothers actually boarded a boat at one stage in their trip. According to this version of the story, the poem was written by their wet-nurse, who saw them off.

SIX

The Deaths of Duke Huan of Lu and Duke Hsiang of Ch'i

THE FOLLOWING NARRATIVES DESCRIBE FIRST THE SORDID murder of Duke Huan of Lu (r. 717–694) by Duke Hsiang of Ch'i (r. 697–686), and the subsequent murder of Duke Hsiang at the hands of rebels. The two deaths are eerily related through the figure of the strong man P'eng-sheng. Duke Huan's consort Wen Chiang was a half sister of Duke Hsiang of Ch'i. An incestuous relation between Duke Hsiang and his half sister had begun before her marriage to Duke Huan and, as described here, was resumed on the occasion of her visit to Ch'i.

DUKE HUAN 18TH YEAR (694 B.C.)

Duke Huan of Lu met with the ruler of Ch'i, Duke Hsiang, at the Lo River. After that, he and his consort Wen Chiang proceeded to the capital of Ch'i. The ruler of Ch'i committed incest with Wen Chiang. When Duke Huan upbraided her, she reported the matter to the ruler of Ch'i.

Summer, fourth month, the day *ping-tzu:* the ruler of Ch'i entertained Duke Huan at a banquet. He ordered P'eng-sheng, a ducal son, to lift the duke into his carriage. The duke expired in the carriage.[1]

1 According to the *Kung-yang Commentary,* Duke Chuang 1st year, P'eng-sheng, a man of unusual strength, crushed the duke's ribs as he lifted him into the carriage, and in this way brought about his death.

The men of Lu reported to Ch'i: "Our lord, fearful of your lord's might, did not dare to rest easy until he had journeyed to your state to renew old bonds of friendship. But once the rites were completed, he was unable to return. There is no place to lay the blame for this outcome, and it makes us look bad in the sight of the other feudal lords.[2] We request that you wipe out the shame of this act by doing away with P'eng-sheng."

The men of Ch'i accordingly put P'eng-sheng to death.

In this passage on the death of Duke Hsiang of Ch'i, famous for its swift and highly compressed style, there is a suggestion that the ghost of the murdered P'eng-sheng has appeared in the form of a wild pig in order to take revenge on the ruler of Ch'i, though it is unclear whether the author or authors of the *Tso chuan* believe in the existence of the ghost.

DUKE CHUANG 8TH YEAR (686 B.C.)

Duke Hsiang, the ruler of Ch'i, ordered Lien Ch'eng and Kuan Chih-fu to garrison Kuei-ch'iu. It was melon time when they went, and the duke said, "When the melons come ripe again, I will relieve you." Their year of garrison duty went by, however, and no word came from the duke.

The two men requested to be relieved, but the duke refused permission, and for that reason they plotted rebellion.

Yi Chung-nien, a younger brother of Duke Hsiang's father, Duke Hsi, had a son named the ducal grandson Wu-chih who enjoyed great favor with Duke Hsi. In matters of clothing, ritual, and rank he was treated the same as the duke's heir. When Duke Hsiang succeeded his father as ruler of Ch'i, he deprived Wu-chih of these privileges. Lien Ch'eng and Kuan Chih-fu accordingly joined with Wu-chih in starting a revolt.

Lien Ch'eng had a female cousin who was in the service of Duke Hsiang

2 Out of fear or deference, the men of Lu speak in a deliberately vague and circuitous manner.

but did not enjoy his favor. They used her to spy on the duke, saying, "If we succeed, we'll see that you become the wife of Lord Wu-chih."

Winter, the twelfth month: the ruler of Ch'i went on an outing to Ku-fen and then proceeded to hunt at Shell Hill. He saw a large pig.

His attendant said, "It's the ducal son P'eng-sheng!"

The duke was enraged. "Would P'eng-sheng dare show himself?" he said and shot at it. The pig stood up like a man and wailed.

The duke, terrified, fell down in his carriage, injured his foot and lost his shoe.

When he returned home, he berated his attendant Pi, demanding the shoe, and when he failed to get it, he beat Pi till he had drawn blood.

Pi dashed out of the palace and encountered the rebels at the gate. They seized him and bound him, but Pi said, "How would I dare try to stop you?" Then he doffed his robe and showed them the wounds on his back, whereupon the rebels trusted him.

Pi asked to be allowed to go in ahead of them. When he had done so, he concealed the duke and then went outside to attack the rebels. He died fighting in the middle of the gate.

Shih-chih Fen-ju died at the foot of the stairs.[3]

The rebels finally entered the palace and killed Meng-yang in bed. But when they looked at him, they said, "This is not the duke! They look nothing alike!" Then they spied the duke's feet under the door and eventually assassinated him. They set up Wu-chih as ruler of Ch'i.

Earlier, when Duke Hsiang first became ruler of Ch'i, he failed to follow any regular procedure. Pao Shu-ya said, "The ruler treats his people in an arbitrary manner—I'm afraid a rebellion will break out." Accordingly he fled to the state of Chü with the ducal son Hsiao-po. When the rebellion broke out, Kuan I-wu and Shao Hu fled with the ducal son Chiu to Lu.[4]

3 Shih-chih Fen-ju was evidently a minor official or servant of Ch'i who remained loyal to the duke, as was Meng-yang, mentioned in the next sentence. Meng-yang had taken the duke's place in bed and was attempting to deceive the rebels. It is typical of the *Tso chuan* to introduce names in this fashion without giving any indication of who the persons are.

4 Both Chiu and Hsiao-po were sons of Duke Hsi by concubines and hence half brothers of Duke Hsiang. Hsiao-po put an end to these internal troubles by becoming ruler of Ch'i in 685, continuing to rule until his death in 643. Posthumously known as Duke Huan of Ch'i, he is the first of five *pa* or hegemons and is noted for having frequently called together the other feudal lords for meetings and imposed his will on them. Kuan I-wu, who originally supported Hsiao-po's rival Chiu, is Kuan Chung, the famous high minister who served under Duke Huan and helped him to govern effectively. According to *Shih chi* 32, he died in 645. As mentioned in the introduction, the *Tso chuan* has relatively little to say about the details of Duke Huan's reign, and even less concerning Kuan Chung's role as prime minister, which is rather surprising in view of the fact that Kuan Chung is mentioned frequently in the *Analects, Mencius, Hsün Tzu,* and other philosophical works of the late Chou, and is the central figure of one such work, the *Kuan Tzu,* which purports to describe his economic and political policies. Possibly these early pages of the *Tso chuan,* or the materials on which they are based, were put together before the Kuan Chung legend had fully taken shape.

Earlier, Lord Wu-chih had treated Yung Lin, a Ch'i official, with harshness.

DUKE CHUANG 9TH YEAR (685 B.C.)

Yung Lin murdered Wu-chih.

SEVEN

Duke Hsien of Chin and Lady Li

THE FOLLOWING NARRATIVE, WHICH DEALS WITH THE WIVES and sons of Duke Hsien of Chin (r. 676–651), begins the saga of his famous son Ch'ung-erh or Double Ears, posthumously known as Duke Wen of Chin, the most memorable figure in the *Tso chuan*.

DUKE CHUANG 28TH YEAR (666 B.C.)

Duke Hsien of Chin took a bride from the state of Chia but she bore no sons. He had a clandestine affair with Lady Chiang of Ch'i, the concubine of his father, Duke Wu, and from this liaison were born the daughter who later became the wife of Duke Mu of Ch'in and the son, Shen-sheng, who became Duke Hsien's designated heir. He also took two brides from the Jung people, Hu-chi or Lady Hu of the Greater Jung, who bore him Ch'ung-erh, and a daughter of the Lesser Jung, who bore him I-wu.[1] When the state of Chin attacked the Jung people of Li, the ruler of the Li Jung gave his daughter Li-chi or Lady Li to the duke. The duke took her home with him and she bore him a son named Hsi-ch'i. Her younger sister, who accompanied her, bore him a son named Cho-tzu.

Lady Li enjoyed great favor with the duke and hoped to have her son Hsi-

1 The Jung were non-Chinese peoples living along the northern and western borders of the Chinese states at this time. Chin, situated on the northern border in the area of present-day Shansi, was frequently troubled by incursions of the Jung. The Greater Jung used the Chinese surname Chi, claiming descent from T'ang-shu, the founder of the ruling family of Chin. The Li Jung, mentioned in the next sentence, also bore the surname Chi, and their ruler held the title of *nan* or baron.

ch'i appointed heir. She accordingly bribed two ministers who also enjoyed the duke's favor, Liang Wu and Tung-kuan Wu, and had them speak to the duke as follows: "Ch'ü-wo is the site of our lord's ancestral temple, while P'u and Ch'ü are on the frontier of our lord's realm. They must not be left without proper overseers. If the city of the ancestral temple lacks an overseer, the people will not view it with awe; and if the frontier stations lack overseers, the Jung tribes will be tempted to harbor ambitions. If the Jung harbor ambitions and the people of Chin look with contempt on their government, the state will suffer injury. We suggest that the heir apparent, Shen-sheng, be appointed overseer of Ch'ü-wo, and Ch'ung-erh and I-wu be made overseers of P'u and Ch'ü respectively. Then you can awe the people, put fear into the Jung, and at the same time make a display of the ruler's merit."

The two men were further instructed to say: "Since the lands of the barbarians are so broad and vast, Chin should make P'u and Ch'ü into cities of importance. Chin will thus be broadening its territory—would that not be wise?"

Duke Hsien was pleased.

In the summer he ordered the heir to take up residence in Ch'ü-wo, Ch'ung-erh to reside in the city of P'u, and I-wu to reside in Ch'ü. The remainder of his sons were all sent to outlying areas. Only the two sons of Lady Li and her younger sister remained in the capital city of Chiang. Thus the two ministers Liang Wu and Tung-kuan Wu joined with Lady Li in slandering the other sons of the duke and working to have Hsi-ch'i set up as heir. The men of Chin referred to this as "the teamwork of the two Wus."

Shen-sheng, the eldest son and nominal heir of Duke Hsien of Chin, was appointed leader of one division of the army and accorded other marks of honor. But there were indications that he himself was very uneasy about his position and his chances for ever succeeding to the throne of Chin, and there were predictions by those around him that in fact he would be overtaken by disaster. In the *Tso chuan,* prophecies of this type have an uncanny way of coming true, and in the following section we witness the realization of Shen-sheng's worst fears. With the death of

Shen-sheng, a figure tragically paralyzed by the dictates of filial piety, the way is cleared for a struggle for power among his four younger half brothers, Ch'ung-erh, I-wu, Hsi-ch'i, and Cho-tzu.

DUKE HSI 4TH YEAR (656 B.C.)

Earlier, when Duke Hsien of Chin wished to take Lady Li for a wife, he divined by the tortoiseshell and the answer was "unlucky." Then he divined by the milfoil stalks and the answer was "lucky."

The duke said, "I will follow the milfoil stalks."

The diviner said, "The milfoil stalks are short on authority, the tortoise is long. Better follow the long one. Moreover, the words of the oracle were: 'Persist and there'll be turnabout, they'll steal the duke's ram.[2] One stalk fragrant, one stalk fetid: ten years and still the stink remains.' Under no circumstances must you do this!"

But the duke refused to listen and established Lady Li as his wife. She bore him Hsi-ch'i, and her younger sister bore him Cho-tzu.

Later, when Lady Li was hoping to have Hsi-ch'i declared heir to the duke, she first plotted with one of the officials in charge of palace internal affairs on how to carry out the move. She said to the heir, Prince Shen-sheng, "Our lord has dreamed of your mother, Lady Chiang of Ch'i. You must make haste and sacrifice to her spirit!"

The prince accordingly performed the sacrifice at his fief in Ch'ü-wo and brought the sacrificial meat and wine to the duke's palace. The duke was out hunting at the time and Lady Li stored the offerings in the palace.

Six days later, when the duke returned from hunting, Lady Li put poison in the offerings and then presented them to the duke. The duke poured some of the sacrificial wine on the ground, whereupon the ground boiled up. He gave some of the meat to one of the dogs and the dog died. He gave some to a petty servant and the servant too died.

Lady Li, weeping, said, "Traitors are in league with the heir!"

Shen-sheng fled to the New City, his fief at Ch'ü-wo. The duke had Shen-sheng's tutor Tu Yüan-k'uan put to death.

Someone said to the prince, "If you explain the matter, your father is certain to understand."

But the prince replied, "Without Lady Li, my father cannot rest in

2 Though the wording is deliberately obscure, this can be taken as a reference to the downfall of Shen-sheng.

comfort, cannot eat his food with satisfaction. If I try to excuse myself, the blame will fall on Lady Li. My father is an old man—I could never be happy with such a course of action."

"Then why don't you run away?"

The prince said, "My father will never make clear where the true guilt lies. If I were to go abroad charged with this crime, who would give me shelter?"

On the day *mou-shen* of the twelfth month, he hanged himself in the New City.

Lady Li then proceeded to slander the other two older sons of the duke, saying, "They both knew about this!" Ch'ung-erh fled to his fief in P'u, I-wu to his fief in Ch'ü.[3]

The following episode deals with the walling of the cities assigned earlier by Duke Hsien of Chin to his sons Ch'ung-erh and I-wu, and the flight of Ch'ung-erh from the state after the death of Shen-sheng.

DUKE HSI 5TH YEAR (655 B.C.)

Earlier, the ruler of Chin had assigned Shih Wei, a high official of Chin, to supervise the walling of the two cities P'u and Ch'ü, which had been assigned to his sons Ch'ung-erh and I-wu respectively. Shih Wei took little pains with the job, and had brushwood mixed in with the earth used for the walls.

I-wu complained about this, and Duke Hsien had Shih Wei upbraided for such conduct.

Shih Wei, appearing before the duke and bowing his head to the ground, said, "I have heard that if one laments when there has been no loss, trouble

3 For some of the scenes from the story of Lady Li as it is found in the parallel passages in the *Conversations from the States,* see my *Early Chinese Literature* (New York: Columbia University Press, 1962), pp. 69–73.

is certain to appear; and if one walls his cities when there is no military threat, his enemies in the end are certain to occupy them. And if the cities are to be occupied by villainous enemies, then why should one take pains in walling them? If in carrying out my duties I do not abide by orders, then I am guilty of lack of respect. But if I help to strengthen the fortresses of your enemies, I am guilty of lack of fidelity. If I must choose between lack of fidelity and lack of respect, how can I serve my ruler properly?

"The *Odes* says:

> Embrace virtue, your safeguard;
> let your heirs be your fortress.[4]

I would urge you, my lord, to cultivate virtue and strengthen the position of your heirs! Why worry about the walling of cities? Three years from now you will be calling out your armies. What use will you have then for carefully walled cities?"

When Shih Wei retired from the duke's presence, he composed a poem that went:

> Fox furs frayed and ragged,
> in one state, three rulers—
> who am I to follow?[5]

Later, when the trouble of the heir Shen-sheng occurred, the duke dispatched the eunuch P'i to attack the city of P'u. Ch'ung-erh said, "The commands of my father, the ruler, must not be resisted!" Then he circulated an order among his men, saying, "Anyone who resists is my enemy."

Ch'ung-erh himself climbed over the wall and fled. P'i succeeded in slicing off the cuff of his robe, but in the end he escaped and fled to the territory of the Ti tribes.

4 "Greater Odes," *Pan,* Mao no. 254.

5 Fox furs are the dress of aristocrats, so the first line perhaps refers to the worn-out condition of the state's nobility. In the second line, "three rulers" may refer to Duke Hsien and his sons Ch'ung-erh and I-wu, or may simply indicate a plurality of persons contending for power.

E I G H T

Duke Hui of Chin

DUKE HSIEN DIES AND CHIN, AFTER A SERIES OF DEATHS, acquires a new ruler, Duke Hui.

DUKE HSI 9TH YEAR (651 B.C.)

In the ninth month Duke Hsien of Chin died. Li K'o and P'i Cheng, high officials of Chin, wanted to call Ch'ung-erh home from abroad and make him ruler. They therefore joined with the allies of Shen-sheng, Ch'ung-erh, and I-wu in fomenting revolt. . . .

Later, when Li K'o was preparing to kill Duke Hsien's son Hsi-ch'i, he first announced his intentions to Hsi-ch'i's tutor Hsün Hsi, saying, "The allies of the three older sons of the duke are about to rise up in revolt. If the people of Ch'in and Chin support them, what will you do?"

"I'll kill myself."

"That is pointless!" said Li K'o.

Hsün Hsi said, "I promised the late ruler. I can't go back on my word. And if it is necessary in order to carry out my word, why should I regret giving up my life? Though it may be pointless, how can I avoid it? But I know that other people are trying to do what is right just as I am. My aim is not to go back on my promise, but I would never try to tell others to desist from the course they have chosen." [1]

1 That is, though Hsün Hsi himself, out of loyalty to Duke Hsien, intends to do what he can to protect Hsi-ch'i and Cho-tzu, he does not necessarily disapprove of Li K'o's efforts to do away with them.

In the winter, the tenth month, Li K'o murdered Hsi-ch'i in the place of mourning. . . .

Hsün Hsi was about to take his own life when someone said, "It would be better to set up the ducal son Cho-tzu as ruler and support him."

Hsün Hsi accordingly set up Cho-tzu as ruler and carried out the burial of Duke Hsien.

In the eleventh month Li K'o murdered the ducal son Cho-tzu in the court. Hsün Hsi committed suicide.

The gentleman remarks: The *Odes* says:

> A flaw in a white jade baton
> can still be polished away.
> But a flaw in one's words—
> nothing can be done about that![2]

This applies to Hsün Hsi. . . .

Hsi Jui, an official of Chin, sent word to I-wu advising him to give generous gifts to the state of Ch'in and solicit its help in returning him to his native state. Hsi P'eng of Ch'i led his forces to a rendezvous with the forces of Ch'in and together they escorted I-wu, posthumously known as Duke Hui, into the state of Chin.

I-wu, having assumed the rulership of Chin, proceeds to do away with Li K'o, the high minister of Chin who cleared the way for I-wu's rise to power.

DUKE HSI 10TH YEAR (650 B.C.)

The ruler of Chin ordered the death of Li K'o in order to make up for Li K'o's earlier actions. When he was about to give the order, he sent a

2 The poem quoted is "Greater Odes," *Yi*, Mao no. 256. Hsün Hsi's "flaw in words" was his unfortunate promise to Duke Hsien to support and protect Hsi-ch'i.

messenger to Li K'o saying, "Without you, I could not have arrived where I am. Nevertheless, you have assassinated two rulers of Chin and brought about the death of one of its high ministers. It would be hard to be a ruler with a subject like you!"

Li K'o replied, "If those people had not been done away with, how could the present ruler have risen to power? But if he wishes to place the blame on me, he can no doubt find excuses to do so. I know what is expected of me."

Thereupon he fell on his sword and died.

The following is the type of ghost story for which the *Tso chuan* is famous, or, in the eyes of rational-minded Confucian scholars who deplore such attention to the supernatural, infamous. According to ancient Chinese belief, the spirits of the dead are sustained by the sacrifices of their heirs, and if the sacrifices are cut off, the spirits perish. Only sacrifices offered by one's own descendants are efficacious, hence the great emphasis placed upon the continuation of the family line. Note that in the story that follows, the ghost himself seems very poorly informed on such rules of the spirit world and has to be given instructions by a living man, his former carriage driver Hu T'u, who presumably encounters him in a dream.

The ruler of Chin had the body of the late heir, Prince Kung [Shen-sheng], moved to a new grave.

In the autumn Hu T'u, Prince Shen-sheng's former carriage driver, was on his way to one of the lesser towns [Ch'ü-wo], when he encountered the late prince. The prince ordered him to climb up into his own carriage and had him act as charioteer.

The prince announced to Hu T'u, "I-wu has no concern for ritual! I have asked the Emperor of Heaven to punish him. Heaven will hand the state of Chin over to Ch'in. Ch'in is going to carry on the sacrifices to me!"

Hu T'u replied, "I have heard that the spirits do not accept sacrifices from those who are not of their own kind, and the people do not offer sacrifices to those who are not of their own clan. [If the ruling house of Chin is destroyed,] then how can the sacrifices to you fail to be cut off? Moreover, what fault have the people of Chin committed? You propose to inflict punishment on persons who do not deserve it and to wipe out your own sacrifices, but I think you had better reconsider the matter!"

The prince said, "All right. I will go and ask the Emperor once more. Seven days from now there will be a shaman in the western outskirts of the New City. You can meet with me through him."

Hu T'u agreed to this, whereupon the prince disappeared. When the time came, Hu T'u went to the designated place. The prince announced, "The Emperor has given me permission to punish the guilty party. He will meet defeat at Han."

N I N E

The Battle of Han

THE FOLLOWING EXTENDED NARRATIVE DEALS WITH THE Battle of Han, an encounter between the forces of Duke Mu of Ch'in and I-wu or Duke Hui of Chin which took place in Chin in 645 B.C.. This is not one of the so-called Five Great Battles of the *Tso chuan,* descriptions of which will be given later, but is often lumped with them to form the Six Great Battles.

The actual battle scene is quite brief and ends in the ingnominious capture of Duke Hui of Chin. The remainder of the narrative deals with the aftermath of the battle, when Ch'in took the captured duke back to its own territory and pondered what to do with him. The situation was greatly complicated by the fact that the wife of the victor, Duke Mu of Ch'in, was the elder sister of the captured ruler of Chin, and indicated that she would kill herself and her children if any harm came to her brother.

After considerable debate, the defeated ruler was returned to his own territory and an uneasy peace established between the states of Ch'in and Chin.

DUKE HSI 15TH YEAR (645 B.C.)

When I-wu was assisted by the forces of Ch'in to return to his own state, his elder sister, the wife of Duke Mu of Ch'in, asked him to see to the welfare of Lady Chia [the widow of Prince Shen-sheng]. She also said, "Make sure that all the late duke's sons are allowed to return to Chin."

But I-wu carried on a clandestine affair with Lady Chia, and he did not permit the other sons of Duke Hsien to return to Chin. For this reason the wife of Duke Mu of Ch'in was enraged at him.

In addition, I-wu had earlier promised to give gifts to certain of Chin's high ministers if he were allowed to return to the state, but later he went back on all these promises. He also agreed to give to the ruler of Ch'in five cities south of the Yellow River, the territory to extend east all the way to the borders of Kuo, south to Mount Hua, and north of the Yellow River to the city of Hsieh-liang. But later he failed to hand over the territory. Finally, when Chin was suffering from a famine, Ch'in sent shipments of grain, but when Ch'in in turn was afflicted by famine, Chin refused to export its grain to Ch'in. As a result of all this, the ruler of Ch'in decided to attack Chin.

T'u-fu, the diviner of Ch'in, divined with the milfoil stalks and the outcome was "lucky." But the prediction said that "after crossing the river, the ruler's carriage will be wrecked."[1].

When the ruler of Ch'in demanded to know how such a prediction could be considered lucky, the diviner replied, "Ah, but this means great luck! After three defeats, you are bound to capture the ruler of Chin. The hexagram indicated by the divination is *ku.* The explanation says: 'A thousand chariots three times depart. After three departures, they will 'capture the male fox.' Now the fox is a *ku* or pest, so this must refer to the ruler of Chin.

"The lower part of the hexagram is the trigram for wind, while the upper is the trigram for mountain. The year is now in the season of autumn. If we knock down their fruit and make off with their timber, that means we will be victorious. And if Chin's fruit falls to the ground and it loses its timber, what other outcome could this be but defeat?"[2]

The Chin forces suffered three defeats and retreated as far as Han. The Chin ruler said to his minister Ch'ing Cheng, "How far the invaders have pushed into our territory! What's to be done?"

Ch'ing Cheng replied, "It was you, my lord, who caused them to come this far. There's nothing to be done!"[3]

"Impudent fellow!" exclaimed the duke.

The duke divined to see if Ch'ing Cheng should be his right-hand attendant when he mounted his war chariot, and the response was "lucky," but because of what Ch'ing Cheng had said, he refused to employ him. Instead, Pu Yang acted as driver of the chariot and Chia P'u-t'u was the attendant on the right. The chariot was drawn by the Little Team of Four, horses that had been presented by the state of Cheng.

1 The wording is deliberately ambiguous. The word translated "wrecked" can also mean "defeated."

2 Though the predictions somewhat resemble those found in the *Book of Changes* under the hexagram *ku,* the diviner is clearly either following some other work of divination or improvising.

3 In 646, Ch'ing Cheng had strongly urged the Chin ruler to send supplies of grain to Ch'in to relieve the famine there but, as we have seen, the Chin ruler rejected the advice.

Ch'ing Cheng said, "In the old days when one embarked on important military undertakings, the chariots were always drawn by horses that were native to the state. Born and raised in the midst of the state's lands and waters, they understood the hearts of the people, were at home with their commands, and were fully accustomed to the roads. Therefore one had only to guide them and they would do whatever one wished.

"But if one employs foreign-bred horses to carry out military operations, when they are frightened, they will become excited and will go against the commands of the driver. In their confusion they will grow unruly, the blood in their inner areas will rush throughout their bodies, and their veins will swell and stand out. From the outside they will appear powerful, but inside their strength will be exhausted. One cannot make them advance or retreat properly, nor swerve or wheel them about as one wishes. You are bound to regret your decision, my lord!"

The duke gave no heed to this advice.

In the ninth month the Chin ruler decided to meet the Ch'in forces in battle and dispatched his minister Han Chien to look the enemy over.

When Han Chien returned, he reported, "Their army is fewer in number than ours, but they have twice as many spirited fighters!"

"Why do you say that?" asked the duke.

Han Chien replied, "When you were abroad, you relied on Ch'in's resources; when you returned to your own state, you did so through the good offices of Ch'in; and when you were starving, you ate its grain. Three kindnesses, and you have repaid none of them! That is why they have come, and now they are about to attack you. Our forces are listless, theirs are in a rage. When I said they had twice as many spirited fighters, that was perhaps too modest an estimate."

"One cannot endure to be treated with contempt by a single individual, much less by a whole state!" said the duke.

He sent his messenger to request that hostilities begin, saying, "I am a man of no ability, capable of calling my forces together but not of dispersing them. If you refuse to withdraw from my territory, I will have no course but to accept your challenge to battle."

The ruler of Ch'in dispatched the ducal grandson Chih to reply, saying: "Before you had returned to your state, I was fearful for you, and after you had returned but had not yet firmly established your position, I fretted. But now if your position is firmly established, how would I dare refuse to accept your command to battle?"

When Han Chien withdrew from the interview, he remarked, "I will be lucky if I am taken prisoner in the battle!"

On the day *jen-hsü* the two armies fought in the plain of Han. The Chin ruler's war horses swerved in the mud and floundered to a stop. The ruler called out to Ch'ing Cheng, but Ch'ing Cheng said, "You rejected my admonitions and went against the results of divination. You have brought defeat upon yourself! How can you hope to escape?" With this he abandoned the duke.

Meanwhile, Liang Yu-mi was acting as carriage driver for Han Chien and Kuo She was his attendant on the right, and they confronted the Ch'in ruler and were on the point of forcing him to a halt. But Ch'ing Cheng distracted them by calling out for someone to rescue the duke of Chin. As a result the Ch'in ruler was able to escape capture. Instead, the Ch'in forces captured the ruler of Chin and took him back to Ch'in with them.

The high ministers of Chin, unbinding their hair and camping in the fields at night, followed after their captured ruler. But the ruler of Ch'in sent someone to try to persuade them to desist, saying, "Why do you gentlemen grieve so? The reason I am escorting your lord to the west is simply that I may put an end to the ominous dreams of the state of Chin. How would I dare do anything more drastic?"[4]

The ministers of Chin bowed their heads to the ground three times and replied, "You, my lord, plant your feet upon the earth and bear the heavens above you. August Heaven and Sovereign Earth have heard the words you have just spoken and will hold you to them. We, your servants, likewise stand humbly to the side and listen to them."[5]

When the wife of Duke Mu of Ch'in heard that [her younger half brother] the ruler of Chin was being brought to Ch'in, she took her eldest son, the heir Ying, her younger son Hung, and her daughter Chien-pi, and together they ascended a terrace and stationed themselves on piles of brushwood.[6] The wife of Duke Mu had her servant dress them all in mourning caps and mourning garments of hemp and in this way prepared to greet the arrival of the two rulers. She addressed her children, saying, "Heaven on high has sent down misfortune, making it impossible for our two rulers to meet in a friendly exchange of jades and silks, but instead to rush into battle. If the

4 Tu Yü and other commentators take the phrase "ominous dreams" to refer specifically to Hu T'u's dream of Shen-sheng's revenge described on p. 28 above, though it is hard to see how the ruler of Ch'in would have had knowledge of that incident. More likely the phrase "ominous dreams" simply refers to the nightmarish succession of events that had occurred in Chin following the downfall of Shen-sheng.

5 The ministers of Chin were naturally fearful that their lord was being taken to Ch'in to be killed. Ssu-ma Ch'ien, in his version of the incident in *Shih chi* 5 and 39, says that the ruler of Ch'in intended to sacrifice the Chin ruler to the Lord on High but was dissuaded from this by the intervention of the Chou king.

6 An indication that they were prepared to immolate themselves.

ruler of Chin arrives in the morning, we will die at evening; if he comes at evening, we die the next morning. It is up to the ruler of Chin to decide."

The Chin ruler was lodged at the Spirit Terrace.[7] The officials of Ch'in asked that he be brought to the capital, but the duke of Ch'in replied, "When I captured the ruler of Chin, I supposed that I would be coming home in triumph. But if I am to come home to a funeral, what profit is there in that? And you, my lords—what have you to gain from such a course?

"Moreover, the men of Chin are grieved and perplexed and hold me responsible for the welfare of their ruler, and Heaven and earth count on me to keep my promise. If I do not consider the fears of the men of Chin, I will only double their hatred, and if I fail to keep my promise, I will be turning against Heaven and earth. Doubling hatred only makes one's own course more difficult, and turning against Heaven is an ill-omened act. We must allow the lord of Chin to return to his own state."

The ducal son Chih said, "Better to kill him so he cannot store up enmity against us!"

The ducal grandson Chih said, "Send him home but keep his heir here as a hostage. That way you are certain to reach an overall settlement. It is too soon to think of wiping out the state of Chin. If you kill its ruler, you are certain to stir up hatred. Moreover, the historian Yin Yi[8] voiced these words: 'Never initiate misfortune. Never exploit disorder. Never double hatred.' Doubling hatred makes one's own course more difficult, and abusing others is ill-omened."

The ruler of Ch'in thereupon agreed to make peace with the state of Chin.

The ruler of Chin dispatched Hsi Ch'i to report this to Hsia-lü I-sheng and have the latter come to Ch'in. When he arrived, he advised the duke to announce to his subjects that he, the ruler, wished them to assemble at court so that Hsia-lü I-sheng could hand out awards in the ruler's name. He also advised the duke to say: "Although I am returning home, I have disgraced my country's altars of the soil and grain. Let divination be made to determine whether my son Yü should replace me as ruler."

When the people of Chin heard this last announcement, they all wept.

The state of Chin thereupon opened up the so-called changed fields.[9]

7 Said to be the site of a terrace dating back to the time of King Wen, one of the founders of the Chou dynasty. It was outside the Ch'in capital, so the wife of Duke Mu had not yet had occasion to carry out her suicide threat.

8 A court historian of early Chou times. The *shih* or historians in ancient times were also involved in matters of divination.

9 The manner of marking off the fields or of collecting taxes from them was changed in some way—

Hsia-lü I-sheng said to the people, "When our lord was abroad, he did not let that fact distress him; his only worry was for us, his subjects. He acted with the utmost beneficence.[10] What do you think of such a ruler?"

The people said, "How shall we go about repaying him?"

Hsia-lü I-sheng replied, "We can raise funds to use for armaments and in that way assist his young son. When the other feudal lords hear of this, they will realize that, though we have lost one ruler, we have gained another in his place, that harmony and accord prevail among the people, and that the state has ever-increasing supplies of arms and armor. Then those who favor us will encourage us in our efforts, and those who hate us will be fearful. Would this not be beneficial?"

The people were pleased. Chin thereupon initiated the system of regional weaponry.[11]

Years before, Duke Hsien had divined by the milfoil stalks to see whether he should give his daughter in marriage to Duke Mu of Ch'in. The results of the divination indicated the hexagram *kuei-mei* or "the marriageable maiden," which transformed into the hexagram *k'uei* or "the estranged."

The historian Su, called upon to divine the outcome, pronounced it "unlucky" and explained: "The interpretation reads: 'A man stabs a sheep but there is no blood. A woman holds a basket but there is no gift.'[12] A western neighbor's blaming words cannot be recompensed. 'Marriageable maiden' changing to 'the estranged,' and still there's no helpmate. *Chen* (thunder) changing to *li* (fire), *li* changing to *chen:* there'll be thunder, there'll be fire, there'll be Yings overthrowing Chis.[13] Chariots lose their axle thongs, fire burns their flags, no profit if the army advances, defeat at the Ancestral Hill.[14] Marriageable maiden, estranged, is lonely; the enemy stretches his bow. The nephew attends his aunt, six years and he runs away, flees homeward to his native state, there abandons his family. The next year he dies in the wasteland of Kao-liang."[15]

---

commentators disagree on the details—so that revenues went to the officials. These are the "awards" mentioned earlier as slated to be handed out in the ruler's name.

10 The word translated as "beneficence" is *hui,* which in fact was the posthumous name bestowed on I-wu, who is known as Duke Hui of Chin.

11 Once again, commentators disagree on the nature of the system. According to one theory, the population was divided into units of 2,500 families each, called *chou,* which had their own stores of armaments.

12 The diviner is quoting from the last section of explanation for the hexagram *kuei-mei* in the *Book of Changes*. The "western neighbor" in the next line is the state of Ch'in.

13 *Chen* and *li* are the names of the trigrams in the upper parts of the hexagrams *kuei-mei* and *k'uei* respectively. Ying is the surname of the ruling family of Ch'in, Chi the surname of that of Chin.

14 Ancestral Hill (Tsung-ch'iu) is another name for the plain of Han.

15 These pronouncements, which seem to be based at least in part on an analysis of the trigrams that make up the two hexagrams, are said to refer to the fact that Duke Hui's son Yü, after being held hostage in Ch'in for some years under the care of his aunt, fled home to Chin in 638, became ruler of Chin the following year, and was killed at Kao-liang in 636.

Later, when Duke Hui had been taken captive and was in Ch'in, he said, "If my father, the former ruler, had only heeded the divination indicated by historian Su, I would not have ended up like this!"

Han Chien, who was attending him at the time, said, "The tortoiseshell divination employs patterns, while that by milfoil stalks employs numbers. After creatures are born, they begin to assume patterns. Later they begin to flourish, and after they have begun to flourish, they appear in numbers. But the ill-considered deeds of the late ruler—they were too manifold to be numbered! What difference does it make that he failed to heed the divination? The *Odes* says:

> Calamities of the people below—
> they do not descend from Heaven.
> Chattering, babbling—hatred behind one's back—
> this constant contention is the work of men! [16]

In the tenth month [before the ruler of Chin had returned to his state], Hsia-lü I-sheng of Chin met with the ruler of Ch'in at Wang-ch'eng in Ch'in to conclude an agreement between the two states.

The ruler of Ch'in asked, "Is there harmony in the state of Chin?"

Hsia-lü replied, "There is no harmony. The ordinary people are ashamed that their ruler was captured and mourn for the kin they lost in battle. They do not begrudge spending funds on armaments because they want to make Yü their ruler, saying, 'We must have vengeance on our enemy, even if it should mean serving the Jung and Ti barbarians!' [17]

"The gentlemen, on the other hand, love their ruler, but they know he was at fault. They do not begrudge spending funds on armaments but they await orders from Ch'in, saying, 'We must requite its kindness—though it may mean death, we will never be false-hearted!' Because of this, there is no harmony in the state."

The Ch'in ruler said, "What do they think will happen to their ruler?"

Hsia-lü replied, "The ordinary people grieve for him but say he will never escape harm. The gentlemen put themselves in Ch'in's place and surmise that he will be allowed to return. The ordinary people say, 'We have treated Ch'in venomously—why would Ch'in return our ruler?' The gentlemen say, 'We have acknowledged our fault—surely Ch'in will return our ruler! Our ruler acted falsely and they seized him. Now he has acknowl-

16 "Lesser Odes," *Shih-yüeh-chih-chiao,* Mao no. 193.

17 According to another interpretation, the words "Jung and Ti" are a derogatory reference to the state of Ch'in, which was regarded as a semibarbarian state, and the latter part of the utterance should read: "How could we ever serve that country of Jung and Ti?"

edged his fault, they will let him go. No kindness could be more admirable, no punishment more awesome. From now on, those who acknowledge their faults will know how to appreciate such kindness, and those who act falsely will know enough to fear punishment. As a result of this one military action at Han, Ch'in can rise to the position of hegemon among the feudal states. However, if Ch'in returns the ruler but fails to make certain that his position is firmly established, or if it deposes the ruler but makes no provision to set up another, the gratitude it has won by its kindness will turn to hatred. But I cannot believe Ch'in would do that!"

The ruler of Ch'in replied, "These are my feelings exactly."

Ch'in had the ruler of Chin shifted to a new lodging and provided him with seven sets of *lao* animals for sacrifice.[18]

[Back in Chin,] O Hsi said to Ch'ing Cheng, "Why don't you flee from the state?"

Ch'ing Cheng replied, "I was the one who brought about my lord's defeat and capture. Having brought on his defeat, I then failed to die. If I should also make it impossible for him to punish me, I would be no proper minister. A minister who is no minister—where could he go and expect to gain acceptance?"

In the eleventh month the ruler of Chin returned to his own state. He had Ch'ing Cheng put to death on the day *ting-ch'ou,* and after that he entered the capital.

This year the state of Chin was once more troubled by famine, and the ruler of Ch'in once more sent supplies of grain. He said, "Though I hate its ruler, I pity its people. Moreover, I have heard that when T'ang-shu was first enfeoffed in the region of Chin, Chi Tzu remarked, 'His heirs will surely prosper!'[19] How can one hope to overthrow the state of Chin? Better to treat it with kindness for the time being and wait until some competent ruler appears."

Thereupon the state of Ch'in for the first time began collecting taxes from the area of Chin east of the Yellow River, and established officials there to oversee the operation.[20]

18 One *lao* sacrifice usually consisted of an ox, a sheep, and a pig, which were cooked for consumption after being sacrificed. Ch'in is in effect providing the Chin ruler with a sumptuous banquet which, along with the change in residence, represents a marked improvement in its treatment of him.

19 T'ang-shu was a younger son of King Wu, one of the founders of the Chou dynasty. Chi Tzu was a minister of the preceding Yin dynasty who was active at the Chou court.

20 That is, Ch'in received the grant of Chin territory that had been promised earlier; see p. 31 above.

TEN

The Brief Career of Yü or Duke Huai of Chin

IN THE PASSAGE ON THE BATTLE OF HAN, WHEN DUKE MU OF Ch'in was debating what to do with the captured ruler of Chin, he was urged by one of his advisers to "Send him home but keep his heir here as a hostage." This was in fact the course of action decided upon. The following two brief episodes deal with Yü, the heir of Duke Hui of Chin, who was for some years detained as a hostage in the state of Ch'in, where he was under the surveillance of his aunt, the wife of Duke Mu of Ch'in. In the second episode, we see him planning to escape from Ch'in and return to Chin, an action that he carried out in 638. The following year his father, I-wu or Duke Hui, died, and Yü succeeded him as ruler of Chin. He was killed at Kao-liang two years later, and is known by the posthumous name Duke Huai of Chin.

DUKE HSI 17TH YEAR (643 B.C.)

In the summer the Chin heir apparent Yü became a hostage in the state of Ch'in. The ruler of Ch'in returned the Chin territory east of the Yellow River that he had received earlier, and he gave his daughter to Prince Yü for a wife.

Earlier, when Yü's father, Duke Hui of Chin, fled to the state of Liang, the ruler of Liang gave Duke Hui his daughter for a wife. The daughter, of the Liang branch of the Ying family, became pregnant, but the time for her delivery passed and no child was born.

The Liang diviner Chao-fu and his son divined by the tortoiseshell with regard to the matter. The son announced, "She will bear one son and one daughter."

The father Chao said, "Yes, but the son will be a manservant and the daughter will be a maidservant."

For this reason the son was named Yü or Groom, and the daughter was named Ch'ieh or Maidservant.[1] Later, as it turned out, Yü was sent west to be a hostage in Ch'in, and Ch'ieh became a waiting-woman in the same state.

DUKE HSI 22D YEAR (638 B.C.)

Yü, the heir apparent of the state of Chin, was being held hostage in the state of Ch'in. When he was preparing to flee from Ch'in and return to his own state, he said to his wife, the daughter of Duke Mu of Ch'in, "Shall I take you with me?"

She replied, "You are the heir of Chin and have been humiliated by being detained in Ch'in. It is only right that you should want to go home. But my father ordered me to become your wife and wait on you with towel and comb in order to make certain you would remain here. If I accompanied you on your return to Chin, I would be disregarding my father's commands. I would not venture to accompany you. But neither would I venture to speak of this to anyone."

In the end Yü fled from Ch'in and returned to his own state.

1 By openly acknowledging an unfavorable prediction in this manner, it was believed one could avert its bad effects.

ELEVEN

Ch'ung-erh: The Years of Wandering

IN THE DESCRIPTIONS OF THE DOWNFALL AND SUICIDE OF Prince Shen-sheng of Chin, we had a glimpse of Shen-sheng's younger half brother Ch'ung-erh or Double Ears as he fled to his fief in P'u and then from his native state altogether. The following narrative focuses on the history of Prince Ch'ung-erh during his years of wandering abroad, where he acquires an assortment of wives. Like many heroes in romance, he is accompanied by a small band of faithful attendants and is subjected to various ordeals.

DUKE HSI 23D YEAR (637 B.C.)

When the troubles accompanying the death of Prince Shen-sheng occurred, the men of Chin attacked the Chin ducal son Ch'ung-erh at his walled city of P'u. The men of P'u wanted to fight, but Ch'ung-erh refused permission. "Through the kind command of my father the ruler I have received a stipend to insure my living, and in this way have gathered these men around me. If, having acquired followers, I should use them to resist my father, I could be guilty of no greater crime! I had far better flee!"

He thereupon fled to the territory of the Ti barbarians.[1] He was accom-

1 Non-Chinese tribes who, like the Jung people mentioned earlier, lived along the northern border of the Chinese states at this time.

panied by Hu Yen, Chao Ts'ui, Tien Hsieh, Wei Wu-tzu, and the minister of works Chi-tzu.

The Ti people attacked the Ch'iang-kao-ju and seized Shu Wei and Chi Wei, the two daughters of their leader.[2] They handed them over to Prince Ch'ung-erh. Ch'ung-erh took the younger, Chi Wei, for his wife, and she bore him two sons, Po-ch'ou and Shu-liu. He gave Shu Wei to his follower Chao Ts'ui to be his wife, and she bore him a son named Chao Tun.

When Ch'ung-erh was about to leave the territory of the Ti and journey to the state of Ch'i, he said to his wife Chi Wei, "Wait for me twenty-five years. If I don't return by that time, then remarry."

Chi Wei replied, "I am twenty-five now. If I am to wait that long before remarrying, I'll be laid in my grave! With your permission, I'll just wait."

Ch'ung-erh remained among the Ti for twelve years before moving on.

As he was passing through the state of Wei, Duke Wen of Wei failed to treat him with courtesy. When Ch'ung-erh was leaving the state by way of Wu-lu, he begged one of the peasants to give him something to eat. The peasant gave him a clod of earth.

The prince, enraged, was about to whip the man, but his attendant Hu Yen said, "Heaven presents this to you!"[3] The prince thereupon bowed his head, accepted the clod of earth, and placed it in his carriage.

When he reached the state of Ch'i, Duke Huan of Ch'i gave him one of his daughters for a wife, along with twenty carriages and eighty horses to pull them.

The prince was content to stay in Ch'i, but his followers, convinced it was wrong to do so, gathered under a mulberry tree to plot how they could bring about his departure. A serving woman was up in the tree gathering mulberry leaves, and she reported what she overheard to the prince's wife, the daughter of Duke Huan of Ch'i. The wife had the woman killed.

His wife said to the prince, "I know your ambition is to roam to the four directions. Someone overheard this, but I have had her killed."

The prince said, "I have no such ambition!"

His wife replied, "Just go! Too much concern for comfort and the ties of affection will undo your fame!"

2 According to commentators, the Ch'iang-kao-ju were a branch of the Ti people.

3 The clod of earth was an omen that the prince in time would become the ruler of a state. During these wanderings, Ch'ung-erh is being tested to see if he has the qualities of mind and character needed to make him a worthy ruler. At the same time, the rulers of the various states through which he passes are being tested to see how wisely they respond to his presence.

When the prince declined to leave, his wife plotted with Hu Yen and together they contrived to get him drunk and send him off in a carriage. When he sobered up, he chased after Hu Yen with a halberd.

When the prince visited the state of Ts'ao, Duke Kung of Ts'ao, having heard that the prince's ribs were all grown together, wanted to catch a glimpse of him naked.[4] When the prince took a bath, therefore, he peered in through the curtain.[5]

The wife of Hsi Fu-chi, a minister of Ts'ao, said to her husband, "I have observed the followers of the prince of Chin, and all are worthy to serve as chief minister of a state. If they continue to assist him, he is bound in time to return to his own state. Once he returns to his state, he will be able to do as he pleases with the other feudal lords, and when he can do as he pleases, he will surely punish those who failed to show him the proper courtesy. And Ts'ao will be the first to feel it! Why don't you hurry and do something to show you regard him differently from the others!"

Hsi Fu-chi accordingly sent the prince a supper heaped on a platter, and placed a jade disk in with the food. The prince accepted the supper but returned the jade.

When the prince passed through Sung, Duke Hsiang of Sung sent him off with a gift of eighty horses.

When he reached Cheng, Duke Wen of Cheng, like some of the other rulers, failed to treat him courteously. Shu Chan remonstrated with the duke, saying, "I have heard that when Heaven is opening up the way for a man, others cannot touch him! There are three proofs that this ducal son of Chin is such a man. Heaven, it would seem, intends to make him a ruler. You would do well to treat him with courtesy!

"Ordinarily, when a man and woman of the same surname marry, their offspring do not prosper. Yet this prince of Chin, though born of a mother of the Chi surname, has been able to come this far.[6] This is the first proof. He has had the misfortune to wander abroad, and yet Heaven has not in the meantime brought peace to the state of Chin, no doubt because it intends

4 The *Chin yü* chapters of the *Kuo yü* or *Conversations from the States* contain an account of the career of Ch'ung-erh that roughly parallels this, though the two often differ considerably. Neither the *Tso chuan* nor the *Kuo yü,* however, gives any details on this physical peculiarity, *p'ien-hsieh* or "linked ribs," which is said to be a sign of great strength. It is of course one of the marks of a hero that he should have some unusual physical feature.

5 Or, according to another interpretation, "he pressed forward in order to get a better look."

6 Ch'ung-erh's mother, though a daughter of the Greater Jung people, bore the same surname, Chi, as the ruling family of Chin. Chinese custom was generally very strict in prohibiting marriage between persons of the same surname.

to open the way for him there. This is the second proof. He has three gentlemen with him capable of ranking above others, yet they consent to be his followers.[7] This is the third proof.

"Chin and Cheng are of equal rank. If even a younger son of the Chin ruling house were passing through, you should surely treat him courteously, to say nothing of one for whom Heaven is opening the way!"

The duke ignored this advice.

When the prince visited Ch'u, the ruler of Ch'u[8] entertained him at a banquet. "If you return to the state of Chin, Prince, what will you give me as a reward for this?" he asked.

The prince replied, "Men and women, jewels, silks—all these you have, my lord. Feathers, furs, tusks and hides—these your own land produces, and what is more than enough for you overflows and reaches as far as the state of Chin. What could I give you as a reward?"

The ruler of Ch'u said, "Be that as it may, how will you reward me?"

The prince replied, "If, due to your kind assistance, I am able to return to Chin, and if Chin and Ch'u should take up arms and meet on the plain of battle, then for your sake I will withdraw my forces for a distance of three days' march.[9] If, having done that, you fail to command your troops to withdraw, however, then I will seize my whip and bow in my left hand, take my arrow case and bow case in my right, and I will go round and round with you!"[10]

Tzu-yü Te-ch'en of Ch'u begged to be allowed to kill the prince. But the ruler of Ch'u said, "This prince of Chin is broad-visioned and disciplined, refined and courteous, and his followers are respectful and generous, loyal and of great strength and ability. The present ruler of Chin[11] is without allies; those inside and outside the state alike hate him. I have heard it said that the family of the Chi surname, the descendants of T'ang-shu, will be the last to wane in power. This must be because of this prince of Chin. When Heaven is about to raise a man up, who can put him down? To oppose Heaven can only lead to grave consequences!"

So in the end the Ch'u ruler sent off the prince to the state of Ch'in.

7 Tu Yü, citing evidence from the *Kuo yü,* identifies the three men as Hu Yen, Chao Ts'ui and Chia T'o, though it is by no means certain just who is intended here.

8 King Ch'eng (r. 671–626). Though in theory only the Chou ruler was entitled to employ the title *wang* or king, the rulers of the southern state of Ch'u, which in some ways considered itself outside the Chinese cultural sphere, had for several centuries been calling themselves kings.

9 One day's march was said to be 30 *li,* or about 10 miles.

10 This would seem to be a somewhat unwieldy handful of weapons and implements, and commentators suggest that the words "whip" and "bow case" be "read lightly."

11 I-wu, Duke Hui of Chin.

When the prince arrived in Ch'in, the ruler of Ch'in, Duke Mu, assigned five of his daughters to wait on him, among them the wife of Yü.[12] She waited on him with a washbasin while he washed his hands. When he had finished, he flicked the water off his hands and spattered her.

The daughter of the Ch'in ruler, angered at this, said, "Ch'in and Chin are equals—why do you treat me so rudely!"

The prince, alarmed, removed his upper garment and bowed in the humble posture of a prisoner.

Another day the duke of Ch'in invited the prince to a banquet. Hu Yen said to the prince, "When it comes to polite accomplishments, I am no match for Chao Ts'ui. I beg you to let Chao Ts'ui accompany you to the banquet."

At the banquet the prince recited the poem "River Water."[13]

The duke responded with the poem, "Sixth Month."[14]

Chao Ts'ui said, "Ch'ung-erh gratefully accepts the gift [of this poem]." The prince thereupon bowed his head to the ground.

The duke of Ch'in descended a step and indicated he was unworthy of such obeisance.

Chao Ts'ui said, "My lord, you have referred to Ch'ung-erh as one capable of 'assisting the Son of Heaven.'[15] How would he dare fail to make obeisance?"

12 The son of Ch'ung-erh's younger brother, I-wu, the ruler of Chin. He was a hostage in Ch'in at this time.

13 No such poem is found in the present text of the *Odes*. Tu Yü says it describes how the waters of the rivers all flow into the sea. The prince was implying that in like manner the feudal lords all pay homage to the ruler of Ch'in. According to one theory, the title *Ho-shui* ("River Water") is simply an error for *Mien-shui* ("Swelling Water"), "Lesser Odes," Mao no. 183, a poem that begins "Swelling is that flowing water; it goes to pay court to the sea." This is probably where Tu Yü derived his description of the lost poem "River Water."

14 "Lesser Odes," *Liu yüeh*, Mao no. 177, a poem that praises the military leader Chi-fu for assisting King Hsüan of Chou to win victory over the barbarian tribes. The duke is comparing Ch'ung-erh to the military leader Chi-fu.

15 Chao Ts'ui is quoting from the poem "Sixth Month." One of course needed a thorough understanding of the *Odes* in order to know how to respond to such implied compliments, which is why Hu Yen urged the prince to take Chao Ts'ui with him to the banquet.

TWELVE

Ch'ung-erh:
The Return to Chin

I-WU, CH'UNG-ERH'S YOUNGER BROTHER, POSTHUMOUSLY known as Duke Hui of Chin, died in the ninth month of 637 and was succeeded by his son Yü, posthumously known as Duke Huai. At this point, Ch'ung-erh judged the time was right for him to return to Chin and make his bid for the rulership. He did so in the first month of 636, aided by the support of Duke Mu of Ch'in. The following narrative describes his return to his native land after twenty years of wandering abroad and the steps he took to defeat the opposition of Yü's supporters and gain control of the government.

DUKE HSI 24TH YEAR (636 B.C.)

In the first month the Ch'in ruler assisted Prince Ch'ung-erh to return to his state.

When the prince was about to cross the Yellow River into Chin, his retainer Hu Yen returned the jade disk he had been keeping for the prince, saying, "I have held the tether of your horse and accompanied you on your journeys throughout the world. The faults I have committed are many indeed. Even I know it, and you of course know it even better than I. I beg herewith to take my leave."

The prince replied, "Uncle, if from now on I fail to be of one heart with you, may the bright waters of this river bear witness against me!" Then he threw the jade disk into the river.[1]

Having crossed the river, the prince surrounded Ling-hu, entered Sang-chüan, and seized control of Chiu-ts'ui.

In the second month, on the day *chia-wu,* the Chin army encamped at Lu-liu. The Ch'in ruler sent the ducal son Chih to negotiate with the Chin army, and as a result the army withdrew and encamped at Hsün.

On the day *hsin-ch'ou,* Hu Yen concluded a pact with the high ministers of Ch'in and Chin at Hsün.

On the day *jen-yin,* Prince Ch'ung-erh took command of the Chin army; on the day *ping-wu* he entered Ch'ü-wo; and on the day *ting-wei* he paid his respects at the ancestral temple of his grandfather, Duke Wu, in the capital. On the day *mou-shen* he had Duke Huai put to death at Kao-liang.

Duke Huai's supporters Hsia-lü I-sheng and Hsi Jui, fearful that they would be attacked, planned to set fire to the ducal palace and do away with the new ruler of Chin. The eunuch P'i [aware of this] requested an interview with the duke.

But the duke sent someone to berate him and refuse the interview, saying, "At the time you attacked me at the city of P'u, my father gave you orders to attack on the following day, but you launched your attack immediately! And later, when I was accompanying the chief of the Ti people and hunting along the Wei River, you came on behalf of Duke Hui and attempted to kill me. At that time you had been ordered to attack after three nights in the field, but you attacked after only two nights! Granted that you were acting on orders from the ruler, why were you in such a hurry? And I still have the cuff of the robe that you cut off in your attack![2] You had better be on your way!"

The eunuch replied, "I thought, since you had returned to the state, that you would understand how to go about things. If you do not, I am afraid you will meet once again with difficulties. When one is acting on orders from the ruler, there are no two ways to the matter. This is the rule from ancient times. To do away with anyone who threatens the ruler—that is all one works for! The men of P'u, the men of Ti—what did I care about them?

"Now, however, you have assumed the position of ruler yourself, and can

1 Hu Yen was the brother of Ch'ung-erh's mother. The prince threw the jade disk to the god of the Yellow River as a gesture to seal his oath.

2 See p. 25 above.

you hope to be without your own 'men of P'u and Ti' who threaten your power? Duke Huan of Ch'i employed Kuan Chung as his prime minister, though earlier Kuan Chung had shot an arrow that struck the buckle of the duke's sash.[3] If you intend to act differently from Duke Huan, then I will not trouble you to give the order, but will leave at once. And there will be many others who will leave as well, not only this one victim of the penal law!"[4]

The duke agreed to see him, and the eunuch reported the plot against the duke.

In the third month the duke met in secret with the ruler of Ch'in at Wang-ch'eng.

On the day *chi-ch'ou,* the last day of the month, the ducal palace burned, but Hsia-lü I-sheng and Hsi Jui did not succeed in entrapping the duke in the fire. They fled to Ho-shang, where the ruler of Ch'in drew them into a trap and had them killed.

The duke of Chin sent word for his wife, the daughter of Duke Mu of Ch'in, to come to Chin. The Ch'in ruler had her escorted to Chin with a guard of three thousand men, all stalwart fellows of the most outstanding type.[5]

Earlier, the duke of Chin had a servant named T'ou-hsü who was in charge of the duke's storehouse. When the duke left Chin and went abroad, the man stole the contents of the storehouse and ran away, though in fact he used all the resources in an effort to bring about the duke's return to Chin.

After the duke came back to Chin, the man requested an interview, but the duke refused, saying that he was busy washing his hair.

The man said to the duke's valet, "When one washes one's hair, one's mind is upside down, and when one's mind is upside down, then one's thinking is backwards. It is just as well that I do not get to see him. Those who stayed behind in Chin were guarding the state's altars of the soil and grain, and those who went abroad with him were servants who held the tether of his horse. Both groups did right. Why must he blame those of us who stayed at home? If the ruler of the state is going to treat even ordinary men like myself as his enemies, a great many people are certain to be filled with fear!"

3 Kuan Chung originally supported Duke Huan's brother in the struggle for control of Ch'i, but was later pardoned and appointed to high office by Duke Huan. On this aspect of Kuan Chung's career, see Eric Henry, "The Motif of Recognition in Early China," *Harvard Journal of Asiatic Studies* (June 1987), 47 (1): 5–30.

4 A reference to the fact that in the past he had been condemned to castration.

5 Duke Mu of Ch'in was apparently fearful of opposition from dissident elements in the state of Chin.

The valet reported to the duke what the man had said, and the duke hurriedly granted him an interview.[6]

The Ti people sent the duke's wife, Chi Wei, to Chin, but asked permission to keep his two sons.[7]

The duke gave his own daughter to his retainer Chao Ts'ui for a wife and she bore him three sons, Chao T'ung, Chao K'uo, and Chao Ying-ch'i. Chao's wife, the daughter of the duke, asked permission to send for Shu Wei, the wife Chao had taken when he was among the Ti people, and her son Tun.

Chao Ts'ui refused to grant the request, but she said, "If, having found someone who pleases you, you forget those you used to know, how can you be worthy to command others? You must send for your wife and son by all means!"

Because she persisted in her request, Chao gave his permission. When Tun and his mother arrived in Chin, Tun proved to be very talented. Chao's later wife repeatedly pleaded with the duke to recognize Tun as Chao Ts'ui's legitimate heir and to relegate her own three sons to an inferior position. She also requested that Shu Wei be made Chao Ts'ui's principal wife and she herself be demoted to a lower rank.[8]

When the ruler of Chin was handing out rewards to the followers who had accompanied him in his wanderings, Chieh Chih-t'ui did not ask for any emolument, and hence was not given any.[9]

Chieh Chih-t'ui said, "Duke Hsien had nine sons, but only this one remains alive today. Dukes Hui and Huai had no allies; everyone inside and outside the state rejected them. But Heaven did not bring an end to the state of Chin, so it must intend for it to have a ruler of some kind. And if

6 The duke evidently was unaware that the man had worked on his behalf and perhaps thought that he had requested an interview so he could excuse himself for having made off with the contents of the storehouse. This episode, like the one above concerning the eunuch P'i, is designed to show how the duke responded to situations that tested his ability to forgive past faults and to judge men's characters.

7 Or perhaps the meaning is "asked what to do about his two sons." The anecdote breaks off abruptly and we are not told what became of the sons. There is no parallel passage in the *Kuo yü* or the *Shih chi*.

8 Her behaviour was thus the exact opposite of that of most of the women described in the *Tso*, who do all they can to work themselves and their sons into positions of power.

9 *Chuang Tzu* ch. 29 says of Chieh Chih-t'ui, whom it calls Chieh Tzu-t'ui: "He was a model of fealty, going so far as to cut a piece of flesh from his thigh to feed his lord, Duke Wen. But later, when Duke Wen overlooked him, he went off in a rage, wrapped his arms around a tree, and burned to death." There are many different versions of the Chieh Chih-t'ui legend, but all agree that he failed to be justly rewarded and retired into hiding. According to most versions, the duke set fire to the forest in an effort to drive him out of hiding, but he chose to die in the flames. The *Han-shih* or Cold Food festival, held 105 days after the winter solstice, when cooking fires are put out and only cold food is eaten, a custom that dates back at least to the Later Han, is said to commemorate the death by fire of Chieh Chih-t'ui.

this man is not to be the ruler and carry on the sacrifices of the state, then who is?

"Heaven in fact has put him where he is, and yet these two or three followers of his believe that he has become ruler because of their own efforts. What blasphemy! If you steal a man's goods, you're called a robber. And what of men who have the presumption to try to take claim for Heaven's work and say it is due to their own efforts! Those in inferior position put a righteous face on their faults, and their superior rewards them for their felony. Superior and inferior delude one another! I cannot keep company with such as these!"

Chieh's mother said, "Why don't you ask him for some reward? If you die without ever speaking up, then who have you got to blame?"

Chieh replied, "Having condemned others, if I were then to do the same, my blame would be even greater than theirs. Moreover, I have already voiced my resentment against the duke—I could not in good conscience accept his support."

His mother said, "Why don't you at least let him know how you feel?"

Chieh replied, "Words are the adornment of the person. But when a person is about to go into hiding, what need does he have to adorn himself? To do so would be merely to seek recognition."

His mother said, "If you have really made up your mind to this, then I will join you and we will go into hiding together."

Chieh thereupon went into hiding and in time died. The ruler of Chin attempted to discover his whereabouts but could not do so. He then set aside the area of Mien-shang as fields [to be used to support sacrifices to Chieh's spirit] saying, "I do this to commemorate my error and honor a good man."

THIRTEEN

The Battle of Ch'eng-pu

THE BATTLE OF CH'ENG-P'U, THE FIRST OF THE *TSO CHUAN*'S Five Great Battles, took place in 632 at Ch'eng-p'u in the state of Wei. On one side were the troops of the powerful southern state of Ch'u, led by its *ling-yin* or prime minister, Tzu-yü Te-ch'en. Opposing him were the armies of Chin, led by Ch'ung-erh or Duke Wen of Chin, and the forces of his allies. The battle resulted in a disastrous defeat for Ch'u, and Duke Wen as a result was granted recognition by the Chou king as a *pa* or hegemon of the feudal rulers.

As is often the case in the *Tso chuan,* the description of the battle itself is relatively brief, the greater part of the narrative being devoted to preparations, prognostications, the shifts and defections of allied states, the division of spoils, and the swearing of various *meng* or oaths of alliance that were intended to prevent future hostilities but somehow never did. The succession of events that led to the battle began with an attack by the forces of Ch'u upon the small state of Sung that lay to the northeast of it. In the opening section we see the Ch'u forces preparing for this attack.

DUKE HSI 27TH YEAR (633 B.C.)

The ruler of Ch'u, King Ch'eng, was preparing to besiege the capital of the state of Sung. He ordered Tou K'ou-wu-t'u to drill the troops at K'uei. Tou finished the drill before the morning was out and did not discipline a single soldier.[1]

1 Tou K'ou-wu-t'u, whose name K'ou-wu-t'u is said to mean "suckled by a tiger" in the Ch'u dialect, was so called because as an infant he was abandoned in the wilderness and nursed by a tiger. (See Duke Hsüan 4th year.) He became *ling-yin* or prime minister of Ch'u in 664, but in 637 passed the post on to his protégé Tzu-yü Te-ch'en. Here he rushes through the drill so as to give Te-ch'en a chance to shine.

When Te-ch'en drilled the troops again at Wei, however, he kept them at it the whole day, and ordered seven men to be whipped and three to have their ears pierced.[2] The elders of the state all congratulated Tou K'ou-wu-t'u on the performance of his protégé, and he in turn gave them wine to drink.

Wei Chia, who was a young man at the time, arrived late and failed to offer any congratulations. When Tou K'ou-wu-t'u asked why, he replied, "I don't see there is any cause for congratulations. When you handed control of the government over to Te-ch'en, you said you were doing so in order 'to insure peace in the country.' But if you have thereby insured peace within the country but defeat abroad, then what has been gained? And the defeat of Te-ch'en will in a sense have been brought about through your recommendation of him. If your recommendation leads to defeat for the country, what cause is there for congratulation? Te-ch'en is stern and lacking in courtesy—he is incapable of governing the people. Give him a force of three hundred chariots and he will never be able to return home in safety.[3] If by chance he should succeed in doing so, there will be time enough then for congratulations!"

The scene now shifts to Chin and we are given a description of the Chin army and the steps Chin takes to counter Ch'u's attack on Sung, particularly Duke Wen's efforts to instruct his people and ready them for military action.

In the winter the ruler of Ch'u and the other feudal lords surrounded the capital of Sung. The ducal grandson Ku of Sung hastened to the state of Chin to report the crisis.

The Chin general Yüan Chen said, "Here is an opportunity for Chin to

2 A form of punishment used in the army.

3 Each war chariot carried three armed men—the carriage driver who stood in the middle, the chariot leader on the left armed with a bow, and his attendant on the right armed with a halberd—and was accompanied by 72 soldiers on foot. So 300 war chariots would represent a fighting force of 22,500 men.

repay a kindness,[4] relieve a distress, display its might, and play the part of hegemon."

Hu Yen said, "Ch'u has recently succeeded in acquiring Ts'ao as an ally, and has newly concluded a marriage alliance with Wei. If we attack Ts'ao and Wei, Ch'u will surely come to their rescue, and in that case Ch'i and Sung will be spared its attacks."

Duke Wen of Chin thereupon conducted a spring military drill at Pei-lu. Dividing the army into three divisions, he held discussions as to who should be appointed commander of the central army.[5]

Chao Ts'ui said, "Hsi Ku would be appropriate. I have often listened to his words and find that he delights in the rites and music and is well versed in the *Odes* and *Documents*. The *Odes* and *Documents* are the repository of righteousness and the rites and music are the prototypes of virtue. And virtue and righteousness are the root of profitable action. The "Documents of Hsia" says: 'They will set forth, and you will receive, their reports; you will make proof of them severally by their merits; you will confer chariots and robes according to their services.'[6] Your lordship would do well to try him out in the position."

The duke thereupon appointed Hsi Ku to be commander of the central army, with Hsi Chen to assist him. He appointed Hu Yen to command the upper army, but Hu Yen deferred to his elder brother Hu Mao and himself took up the post of assistant. Chao Ts'ui was made a high minister and ordered to head the lower army, but he deferred to Luan Chih and Yüan Chen, and therefore Luan Chih was made commander of the lower army, with Yüan Chen to assist him. Hsün Lin-fu was appointed driver for the duke's war chariot, with Wei Wu-tzu to be the duke's attendant on the right.

When Ch'ung-erh, the ruler of Chin, first returned to his state and began teaching his people, he wanted at the end of two years to use them in a military action. But his minister Hu Yen said, "The people do not yet understand righteousness and have not settled down in their places."

In the field of foreign affairs the duke thereupon took measures to insure that King Hsiang was restored to his throne, and at home worked to profit

4 The kindness shown earlier to Ch'ung-erh or Duke Wen of Chin when he visited Sung in the course of his wanderings. See p. 42 above.

5 In 661 the Chin army had been organized in a two-part division; here it is changed to a three-part one, with the commander of the central army exercising overall control.

6 *Book of Documents, Yi Chi*. The passage describes the ideal government in the time of the sage ruler Yü, founder of the Hsia dynasty; "they" refers to the government officials.

the people.[7]people as a result became attached to their various means of livelihood.

Once more the duke wanted to employ them, but Hu Yen said, "The people do not yet understand good faith and have not clearly perceived what is expected of them."

The duke carried out the attack on Yüan and gave them a demonstration of good faith.[8] After that, when the people bartered for goods, they did not seek undue riches, and they were honest and faithful in their word.

The duke said, "Now is the time!", but Hu Yen said, "The people do not yet understand ritual, they have not yet acquired an attitude of reverence."

The duke then held the spring military drill at Pei-lu to show them the importance of ritual, establishing supervisors to make certain that each person carried out his function correctly. Thereafter the people obeyed orders without confusion and were ready for use.

The duke then drove off the Ch'u troops who were garrisoned at the city of Ku in Ch'i, relieved the siege against Sung, fought one battle with Ch'u, and gained the status of hegemon. Such were the teachings of Wen.[9]

In order to force Ch'u to cease its attack on Sung, Duke Wen of Chin decided to attack one of Ch'u's allies, the small state of Ts'ao. When the state of Wei, which lay between Chin and Ts'ao, refused to allow the Chin armies to pass through its territory, it incurred Chin's anger and was included in the attack.

7 In 635 Duke Wen of Chin dispatched troops to assist the Chou ruler, King Hsiang (r. 651–619), to regain his throne, which had been seized by the king's younger brother. In this way he demonstrated to his people his concern for principles of righteousness or moral duty.

8 Late in 635 he surrounded the little city-state of Yüan, promising his troops that if it did not capitulate within three days he would withdraw. The city failed to surrender and the duke gave the order to lift the siege. Spies from within the city advised him that it was about to capitulate and urged him to persist, but he declared that fidelity to one's word was "the treasure of the state," a prize more important than victory, and withdrew his troops.

9 This last paragraph refers to the battle of Ch'eng-p'u, which did not take place until the following year. It is rare for the *Tso chuan* in this way to refer to future events in plain terms rather than in the cryptic language of prophecy or divination. The last sentence plays on Ch'ung-erh's posthumous title, Duke Wen. The word *wen* can mean patterns or adornments, but also, in a broader sense, literature, learning, moral order, and culture in general.

DUKE HSI 28TH YEAR (632 B.C.)

In the spring the ruler of Chin, who was preparing to attack the state of Ts'ao, asked permission to pass through the territory of Wei. When the men of Wei refused permission, he went roundabout, proceeding through the area south of the Yellow River and crossing from there, invading Ts'ao and attacking Wei. On the day *mou-shen* of the first month he captured the Wei region of Wu-lu.

In the second month the Chin commander Hsi Ku died. Yüan Chen was appointed to replace him as commander of the central army. The minister of works Chi-tzu replaced Yüan Chen as assistant to the commander of the lower army. Yüan Chen was promoted in this fashion in recognition of his merit.

The ruler of Chin concluded a pact with the ruler of Ch'i at Lien-yü in Wei. The ruler of Wei asked to be a member of the pact, but the people of Chin refused to permit this. The ruler of Wei then thought of allying himself with the state of Ch'u, but his own countrymen did not approve, and in fact expelled him from the capital in order to gain favor with Chin. The Wei ruler, driven from his capital, took up residence in Hsiang-niu in Wei.[10]

The ducal son Mai, an official of Lu, was stationed in Wei to protect it from attack,[11] and troops from Ch'u also came to Wei's rescue. But when the latter failed to win a victory, the duke of Lu, fearful of Chin's anger, had the ducal son Mai put to death in order to curry favor with Chin. To justify this action to the men of Ch'u, he claimed that Mai had attempted to leave Wei before his term of office as military commander had expired.

The Chin ruler surrounded the Ts'ao capital, and many of his soldiers stormed the gate and died there. The men of Ts'ao took the bodies of the Chin dead and exposed them on the city wall.

This caused great distress to the ruler of Chin, but adopting a plan put forward by some of his subordinates, he announced that he was going to encamp on the graves of the Ts'ao ancestors, and proceeded to shift his army to the graveyard. The men of Ts'ao, filled with panic and horror, coffined

10 The Wei ruler was Duke Ch'eng of Wei, who became ruler in 634.

11 The states of Lu and Ch'u were allies at this time, and Lu was helping Ch'u to protect Wei by stationing a garrison in Wei.

the Chin dead they had taken and had the bodies carried out of the city. The Chin forces took advantage of this panic to press their attack, and on the day *ping-wu* of the third month entered the city.

The Chin ruler berated the men of Ts'ao for failing to heed the example of Hsi Fu-chi,[12] though the state had some three hundred men of ministerial rank riding in fine carriages who should have known better. "And while I'm at it," he added, "shall I show you how my ribs are shaped?"

The Chin ruler gave orders that no one was to enter the house of Hsi Fu-chi, and exempted all the members of his clan from punitive measures in recompense for the kindness Hsi Fu-chi had shown him.

Wei Wu-tzu and Tien Hsieh were enraged, saying, "Our labors he gives not a thought to![13] What has this man done that he should receive recompense?" Then they burned down the buildings belonging to Hsi Fu-chi's family. In the process, Wei Wu-tzu was wounded in the chest.

The duke of Chin wanted to have him put to death because of his insubordination, but was loath to lose a man of such ability. He therefore sent a messenger to inquire about Wei Wu-tzu's condition and to see how badly he was wounded, saying, "If he is badly wounded, have him put to death."

Wei Wu-tzu bandaged up his chest and received the messenger, saying, "Since my lord is gracious enough to inquire, how could I be anything but well and hearty?" He then leaped forward and clapped his hands three times, then leaped to the side and gave three more claps.

In the end the duke spared him, but he had Tien Hsieh put to death as an example to the army. He appointed Chou Chih-ch'iao to replace Wei Wu-tzu as the right-hand attendant in his war chariot.

The men of Sung, besieged by Ch'u, sent Men Yin-pan on a mission to the Chin army to report the crisis. The duke of Chin said, "The people of Sung have come with their report of distress. If I ignore them, they will break with Chin. If I appeal to Ch'u to raise the siege, however, it will never consent. I would like to engage Ch'u in battle, but Ch'i and Ch'in will not go along with that. What should I do?"

Yüan Chen said, "If you ignore Sung's pleas, then it will give bribes to Ch'i and Ch'in and rely on them to appeal to Ch'u to lift the siege.

12 The minister of Ts'ao who had treated Ch'ung-erh courteously when the latter visited Ts'ao in the course of his wanderings. See p. 42.

13 Wei Wu-tzu and Tien Hsieh, it will be recalled, were members of the band of followers who accompanied Ch'ung-erh in his wanderings. They were no doubt vexed that they had not received more generous treatment after the duke's return to Chin. In the present campaign, Wei Wu-tzu was serving as right-hand attendant in Duke Wen's chariot.

Meanwhile, we can seize the ruler of Ts'ao, divide up the fields of Ts'ao and Wei, and present a portion of them to the men of Sung as a gift. Ch'u, because of its special ties with Ts'ao and Wei, is bound to refuse the request from Ch'i and Ch'in that it lift the siege. Ch'i and Ch'in, pleased with the bribes from Sung and angered by the stubbornness of Ch'u, will in that case undoubtedly be persuaded to join us in the attack on Ch'u."

The duke of Chin, delighted with this plan, seized the ruler of Ts'ao, divided up the fields of Ts'ao and Wei, and handed a portion of them over to the men of Sung.

King Ch'eng, the ruler of Ch'u, disappointed in the course events are taking, decides to abandon the siege against Sung, withdrawing himself and ordering his chief minister Te-ch'en to do likewise. Te-ch'en, however, defies the ruler's orders —Te-ch'en's arrogance and lack of consideration for the welfare of the people is one of the principal themes of the narrative—and the Ch'u ruler in retaliation severely limits the number of troops assigned to Te-ch'en.

The ruler of Ch'u withdrew from Sung and took up residence in the city of Shen [in the Fang-ch'eng mountains of Ch'u]. He sent orders to Shen Shu to abandon the garrisoning of the Ch'i city of Ku.[14]

He also ordered Te-ch'en to abandon the siege of Sung, saying, "Do not try to go after the Chin army! The ruler of Chin has spent nineteen years abroad, and now at last he has succeeded in gaining control of Chin. He has tasted every kind of hardship, trouble, and danger, and knows all about the true feelings and the deceptions of the people. Heaven has lent him abundance of years and has removed those who wished him ill. And when Heaven has placed a man in such a position, who can thrust him aside?

"The Maxims for the Army[15] says, 'When pitted against an equal, better retire.' It also says, 'When you know there are difficulties ahead, withdraw.'

14 Ch'u forces, led by Duke Hsi of Lu, had attacked Ch'i and seized the city of Ku in 634, when Shen Shu was assigned to garrison it.

15 Presumably some lost text on military science.

And it says, 'The man of virtue cannot be opposed.' All three of these maxims apply to Chin."

Te-ch'en, however, dispatched Po Fen to invite the Chin ruler to combat, saying, "It is not that I presume to believe I can win merit in battle, but I want to stop up the mouths of those who speak slander and malice against me!"[16]

King Ch'eng of Ch'u was angered by this defiance of his orders and assigned only a small number of troops to Te-ch'en. Thus Te-ch'en in fact had only the western wing of the army, plus the troops of the heir and the six hundred men in the command of the Jo-ao family, to accompany him in his attack.[17]

Duke Wen of Chin, now evidently confident of victory, decides to deliberately provoke Te-ch'en to attack. But when Te-ch'en does attack, he withdraws his forces for a distance of three days' march, thus honoring the promise he had made earlier to repay the kindness shown him in the past by the ruler of Ch'u.

Te-ch'en of Ch'u sent Yüan Ch'un to deliver the following message to the Chin army: "I request that you restore the ruler of Wei to his position and enfeoff the ruler of Ts'ao once more. I for my part will then lift the siege against Sung."

Hu Yen said to Duke Wen, "Te-ch'en has no respect for ritual! He would have you, the ruler of Chin, receive one advantage, while he, a mere subject, receives two! He must not be allowed to go unpunished!"

But Yüan Chen said, "Agree to his proposal, my lord. The purpose of ritual is to secure men in their position. The state of Ch'u, by giving one word of agreement, thereby insures the continuance of three states [Wei, Ts'ao, and Sung]. But if we on our part give one word of refusal, we thereby

16 Te-ch'en is referring to the remark made by Wei Chia that, given a force of three hundred chariots, he could never return in safety from battle. See p. 51 above.

17 The Ch'u army was divided into two parts, a left or eastern wing, and a right or western wing. Te-ch'en was himself a member of the Jo-ao family and hence was entitled to command its forces.

condemn these three states to destruction. Then we will be the ones who are lacking in ritual, and in that case how can we hope to gain success in battle?

"If we refuse to agree with Ch'u's proposal, we will be abandoning Sung to the mercy of Ch'u. Our original purpose was to rescue Sung, and if now we abandon it, how can we excuse ourselves with the other feudal lords? Ch'u's proposal will confer benefit upon three states; our refusal will arouse enmity in the three of them. If we arouse enmity and create too many foes for ourselves, how can we hope to fight successfully? Better to send word in secret to the rulers of Ts'ao and Wei telling them that you will restore them to their positions, and in that way win them over to our side. At the same time we can forcibly detain Yüan Ch'un so as to anger Ch'u. After we have engaged Ch'u in battle, we can decide what to do about Ts'ao and Wei."

The duke of Chin, pleased with this advice, proceeded to detain Yüan Ch'un in Wei, and meanwhile sent word in secret that he would restore the rulers of Ts'ao and Wei. Ts'ao and Wei accordingly announced that they were breaking off their alliance with Ch'u.

Te-ch'en, enraged by these developments, opened attack on the Chin army, but the Chin forces withdrew. One of the Chin officers exclaimed, "Our lord retires before a mere subject of Ch'u—this is shameful![18] The Ch'u troops are on their last legs—why should we give way to them!"

But Hu Yen said, "If an army follows proper procedure, we say it is in its prime. If it bends the regulations, we say it is on its last legs. It has nothing to do with how long it has been in the field. Were it not for the kindness that Ch'u showed our ruler in the past, how would he have reached his present position? He agreed to withdraw his forces for a distance of three days' march in order to repay that kindness.[19] If he were to ignore that kindness, go against his promise, and instead protect Ch'u's enemy, Sung, then we would be guilty of bending procedures and Ch'u would be in the right. Ch'u's men are obviously well-fed—one could never say they are on their last legs. If we withdraw and Ch'u turns around and goes home, what more could we ask? And if Ch'u declines to turn around and go home, then our 'lord' will have given way and their 'subject' will be the one who is provoking the attack, so the 'bending of procedure' will lie with them."

The Chin army accordingly withdrew three days' march. The Ch'u troops wanted to give up the attack, but Te-ch'en would not hear of this.

18 In addition to the fact of withdrawal, the Chin officer is outraged that, while the Chin forces are commanded by the Chin ruler, Duke Wen, those of Ch'u are under the command of a mere minister or subject of Ch'u, Te-ch'en. The same point is made in Hu Yen's speech that follows.

19 See p. 43 above.

Duke Wen has fulfilled his promise to withdraw before the Ch'u forces, which themselves wish to withdraw without further conflict. But Te-ch'en insists upon forcing the issue.

In the summer, the fourth month, the day *mou-ch'en,* the ruler of Chin, the duke of Sung, the high ministers Kuo Kuei-fu and Ts'ui Yao of the state of Ch'i, and Hsiao-tzu Yin, son of Duke Mu of Ch'in, assembled their forces at Ch'eng-p'u in Wei. The Ch'u army drew up its encampment with its back to the hills of Hsi.

The ruler of Chin, worried about the outcome of the battle, heard the soldiers singing this song:

Lush, lush the fields and gardens:
cast aside the old,
the new—take thought for that!

The duke was wondering what this might portend when Hu Yen said, "Let us fight! If we fight and win, we are bound to gain control over the other feudal lords. If we fail to win, Chin still has the Yellow River for its outer boundary and the mountains in its interior—harm can never come to us!"

The duke said, "What about the kindness Ch'u showed me in the past?"

Luan Chih said, "Ch'u has in fact wiped out all the Chi clan states north of the Han River![20] Rather than remember a little kindness and forget that great shame, it would be better to fight!"

The ruler of Chin dreamt that he was grappling with the ruler of Ch'u, and the Ch'u ruler had forced him down on his back and was sucking out

20 Ch'u, like the other major states, was at this time expanding by swallowing up the smaller states around it. The ruling family of Chin belonged to the same Chi clan as these states along the Han River that had been destroyed by Ch'u.

his brains. The dream terrified him, but Hu Yen said, "Good fortune! You were facing up to Heaven, but Ch'u was bent over, as though being punished for some crime. And your brains would soften him up!"[21]

Te-ch'en dispatched Tou Po to challenge the Chin forces to battle, saying, "We beg to have a wrestling bout with your lordship's officers! Your lordship may lean on the crossbar of your carriage and watch, and I, Te-ch'en, will likewise cast my eyes over the proceedings."

The Chin ruler instructed Luan Chih to reply as follows: "My lord heeds your command. He has not ventured to forget the kindness he once received from the ruler of Ch'u and hence has withdrawn to this position. And if he will withdraw this far for you, a minister of Ch'u, how would he dare to oppose Ch'u's ruler! But since your orders leave him no choice, he begs to trouble this gentleman here to convey word to the various Ch'u commanders and to tell them: Look well to your war chariots, honor your lord's instructions, and let us meet at daybreak tomorrow!"

The seven hundred war chariots of Chin proceeded to tighten the girths and straps of their horses. The Chin ruler climbed up to the site of the capital of Yu-hsin to view his troops.[22] "Young and old conduct themselves according to ritual," he said. "They are fit for use!" Then he ordered the men to cut down trees and use them to supplement their weapons.

On the day *chi-ssu* the Chin army encamped at Hsin-pei.[23] The Chin commander Hsü Ch'en, who was acting as assistant to the leader of the lower army, prepared to oppose the troops of Ch'en and Ts'ai.[24]

On the Ch'u side, Te-ch'en, with the six hundred men of the Jo-ao family, was acting as commander of the central army. "Today, mark my word, Chin will be wiped out!" he said. Tou I-shen was acting as commander of the left wing of the Ch'u army, and Tou Po as commander of the right wing.

Hsü Ch'en, having cloaked his horses in tiger skins, led the attack by striking directly at the troops of Ch'en and Ts'ai. The men of Ch'en and Ts'ai fled, and the right wing of the Ch'u army was thus routed.

Hu Mao [the commander of the Chin upper army] hoisted two pennons and began to retreat, while Luan Chih [commander of the Chin lower army] had his men drag brushwood over the ground to simulate the dust of a

21 Brain matter was believed to have softening properties. Thus pigs' brains were used in tanning to soften the leather.

22 A state of ancient times.

23 That is, Ch'eng-p'u.

24 Small states that were allied with Ch'u.

general rout.[25] The Ch'u forces raced after in pursuit, whereupon Yüan Chen and Hsi Chen, leading the duke's own select troops of the central army, fell upon them from either side. Hu Mao and Hu Yen, leading the upper army, turned about and likewise attacked Tou I-shen from either side, thereby routing the left wing of the Ch'u army. Thus the Ch'u army suffered a resounding defeat. Only Te-ch'en, who had kept his troops back and had not attempted to pursue the enemy, as a result managed to escape defeat.

Following this description of the battle, we are given a number of short notices concerning the disposition of spoils, the tokens of honor granted the victor, Duke Wen, by the Chou Son of Heaven, and the concluding of alliances.

The Chin army occupied the Ch'u encampment for three days and lived off Ch'u's rations. On the day *kuei-yu* it returned to its former position. On the day *chia-wu* it reached Heng-yung in Wei and proceeded to build a palace for the king at Chien-t'u.[26]

Previous to the battle, in the third month, the ruler of Cheng had gone to Ch'u to put his troops at Ch'u's disposal. Later, when the Ch'u army suffered defeat, he became alarmed and dispatched Tzu-jen Chiu to go and make peace overtures to Chin. Luan Chih as a result went to Cheng to arrange an alliance with the Cheng ruler. On the day *ping-wu* of the fifth month the rulers of Chin and Cheng concluded the alliance at Heng-yung.

On the day *ting-wei,* Chin presented the Ch'u prisoners and booty it had taken in battle to the Chou king. These consisted of a hundred four-horse teams of armed war horses and a thousand foot soldiers. At that time the Cheng ruler acted as adviser to the king and the ritual followed was that used in former times by King P'ing.[27]

25 The two pennons were those signifying the presence of the commander of the upper army and his assistant or second in command.

26 King Hsiang of the Chou, who had previously been assisted by Duke Wen of Chin in regaining his throne, had received news of Chin's victory and was planning to visit the Chin army in the field.

27 The ritual said to have been used some hundred years earlier when King P'ing (r. 770–720) of the

On the day *chi-yu* the king presented the Chin ruler with rich wine and commanded him to drink his fill. The king also commanded Yin-shih, along with the royal son Hu and the internal secretary Shu Hsing-fu, to draw up a document proclaiming the ruler of Chin to be the leader of the feudal lords and presenting him with a large ceremonial carriage and its garments and equipage, a war carriage with garments and equipage, a red lacquered bow and set of a hundred red lacquered arrows, ten black lacquered bows and a thousand black lacquered arrows, a jar of fragrant black millet wine, and three hundred tiger-fleet warriors.[28] The document said: "The king speaks thus to his uncle:[29] Reverently obey the king's command, bring peace to the states in the four directions, chastize and drive off the king's foes!"

The Chin ruler declined these honors three times and then, acceding to the king's command, said, "Ch'ung-erh ventures to bow twice, touching his head to the ground, and respectfully accepts and publishes abroad these illustrious, enlightened, and excellent commands of the Son of Heaven." He then accepted the document and withdrew. All in all, he had three audiences with the king.[30]

When the ruler of Wei heard that the Ch'u army had been defeated, he left his state and fled in fear to Ch'u. Eventually he made his way to Ch'en, where he dispatched Yüan Hsüan to wait on Shu-wu and conclude an alliance with the victors.[31]

On the day *kuei-hai* the royal son Hu drew up an oath of alliance which was administered to the various feudal lords in the court of the king's temporary residence. The words of the oath read: "All of us will support the king's household and will inflict no injury upon one another. If anyone

---

Chou received spoils of war from Marquis Wen of Chin. The ritual is described in the section of the *Book of Documents* entitled *Wen-hou chih ming.*

28 The ceremonial carriage was gilded and of a type ordinarily used only by the king and members of his clan. The millet wine was for use in sacrifices to the spirits. *Hu-fen* or "tiger-fleet" warriors were members of the king's personal bodyguard. Through these gifts and the accompanying proclamation, Duke Wen of Chin is granted recognition as a *pa* or hegemon of the feudal lords.

29 The Chou king and the ruling house of Chin belonged to the same Chi family.

30 In a section of the narrative for this year not translated here, the *Tso* states that Duke Wen of Chin in fact summoned the Chou king to the meeting of the feudal lords described here, and after the meeting arranged for the king to hunt. According to the *Tso,* when Confucius came to compile the *Spring and Autumn Annals,* he considered that this example of a subject summoning his liege lord would not constitute a suitable precedent and he therefore stated simply that "The heavenly king went hunting at Ho-yang." That Confucius had a poor opinion of Duke Wen of Chin is suggested by *Analects* XIV, 15, which quotes Confucius as saying, "Duke Wen of Chin was crafty and not upright," though just what aspect of the duke's conduct elicited this criticism is not clear.

31 The Wei ruler, Duke Ch'eng, it will be recalled, had been driven out of his capital because he favored an alliance with Ch'u and had taken up residence in Hsiang-niu in Wei. Shu-wu was his younger brother, who was acting as ruler in his place.

should deviate from this alliance, may the bright spirits strike him dead and cause him to lose his army; may he enjoy no good fortune in his state, and may this extend to his grandsons and great-grandsons, whether young or old."

The gentleman remarks: This alliance accorded with good faith. In the military campaign, the ruler of Chin was able to attack through the power of virtue.[32]

The final section of the narrative describes the fate of the man who precipitated the battle and brought about Ch'u's defeat, the headstrong and luckless minister Te-ch'en.

Earlier, the Ch'u prime minister Te-ch'en had fashioned carnelian-ornamented caps and jade-studded martingales for his horses, but had not yet used them. Before the battle at Ch'eng-p'u, he dreamt that the god of the Yellow River said to him, "Give them to me and I'll present you with the marshes of Meng-chu."[33] Te-ch'en refused to hand them over.

Te-ch'en's son Ta-hsin and his kinsman Tzu-hsi enlisted the Ch'u minister Yung Huang to remonstrate with Te-ch'en, but he refused to listen. Yung Huang said, "If a man could benefit his country by giving up his life, he might well do so, to say nothing of giving up a few bits of carnelian and jade! These things are mere dirt and dung! If you can save your army by handing them over, why be so covetous?"

But still Te-ch'en refused. When Yung Huang emerged from the interview, he said to Ta-hsin and Tzu-hsi, "It will not be the gods who defeat the prime minister. He takes no care for the people of the country. In truth the prime minister will defeat himself!"

Later, when Te-ch'en had in fact met with defeat, the king of Ch'u sent

32 Because he had given his subjects proper moral instruction before leading them into battle.

33 A region in Sung, a nearby state that Te-ch'en was planning to attack. As we have seen earlier, offerings and gifts were made to the god of the Yellow River by throwing them in the river.

word to him, saying, "If you return to the state, how will you face the elders of Shen and Hsi?"[34]

Ta-hsin and Tzu-hsi said to the king's messenger, "Te-ch'en intended to kill himself but we persuaded him not to, telling him that the ruler would pass sentence on him in due time."

When Te-ch'en reached Lien-ku in Ch'u he committed suicide. The ruler of Chin, hearing of this, could not disguise his delight. "Now I have no more foes!" he exclaimed. "Wei Lü-ch'en will undoubtedly become the new prime minister of Ch'u, but he will think only of his own well-being. He will never consider the people!"

34 Small states allied with Ch'u whose young men had been killed in the battle. The king is hinting that Te-ch'en should not return alive.

F O U R T E E N

Duke Wen of Chin's Attack on Cheng

IN 630 DUKE WEN OF CHIN, ASSISTED BY HIS ALLY, DUKE Mu of Ch'in, launched an attack on the small state of Cheng. The purpose was to punish the ruler of Cheng, Duke Wen, for the rudeness he had shown to Duke Wen of Chin during the latter's period of wandering, and for deserting Chin and Ch'in and siding with Ch'u in the battle of Ch'eng-p'u. Cheng was situated southeast of Chin, in the Yellow River valley that served as a corridor for east-west traffic.

DUKE HSI 30TH YEAR (630 B.C.)

In the ninth month, the day *chia-wu,* the ruler of Chin and the ruler of Ch'in surrounded the capital of Cheng. They did this because earlier the ruler of Cheng had been discourteous to the ruler of Chin and had played false to Chin and favored Ch'u.[1] The Chin forces encamped at Han-ling and the Ch'in forces south of the Fan River.

Yi Chih-hu said to the ruler of Cheng, "The state is in danger! But if you will send Chu Chih-wu to meet with the Ch'in ruler, the attackers will surely withdraw."

The Cheng ruler attempted to implement this advice, but Chu Chih-wu declined to undertake the mission, saying, "Even in my young days I was no match for others. Now that I'm old, I'm quite incapable of accomplishing anything!"

1 See pp. 42 and 61 above.

The Cheng ruler said, "I was unwilling to make use of your services earlier, and to request you to act now that danger threatens is surely a fault on my part. But if Cheng is destroyed, you will have nothing to gain thereby!"

Chu Chih-wu agreed, and at night had himself let down by rope from the city wall and set off. Appearing before the Ch'in ruler, he said, "Ch'in and Chin are besieging Cheng, and Cheng realizes it is doomed. If by destroying Cheng you can bring benefit to yourself, then I beg your officers to get on with the task. But in such a case, you will be annexing a state that lies far off on the other side of your neighbor, Chin, and you know the difficulties that will entail. What reason could you have for overthrowing Cheng and thereby increasing the territory of your neighbor [which is what you will in effect be doing]? The fatter your neighbors grow, the thinner you will be. But if you will spare Cheng, so that it can act as your host on the eastern road, supplying the needs and deficiencies of your envoys when they pass, you will do yourself no harm, will you?

"Moreover, on an earlier occasion, you received a gift from the ruler of Chin, who promised you his cities of Chiao and Hsia.[2] But he had no sooner crossed the Yellow River in the morning to enter his state than in the evening he was building walls to wall you out, as you no doubt remember! Chin's greed knows no bounds. Once it has acquired Cheng on its eastern border, it will want to expand its western border as well. And if it does not slice off a piece of Ch'in, how can it do so? I leave it to you to decide if you wish to slice up Ch'in in order to benefit Chin!"

The Ch'in ruler, pleased with this advice, concluded an alliance with the men of Cheng, dispatching his officials Ch'i Tzu, Feng Sun, and Yang Sun to garrison Cheng and protect it from further attack. Then he returned to his own state.

Duke Wen's adviser Hu Yen wanted to attack the forces of the Ch'in ruler, but the duke said, "That will not do! If it were not for the assistance of that gentleman, I could never have gotten where I am! To profit from someone's assistance and then do him injury shows a lack of benevolence. To alienate one's allies shows a lack of wisdom. And to replace harmony with discord goes against the code of warfare. Let us return to our own state!"

Thereupon the Chin forces also withdrew.

2 I-wu or Duke Hui of Chin had earlier promised several of Chin's cities to Duke Mu of Ch'in in recognition of the help Duke Mu gave him in his efforts to return to Chin and become its ruler.

F I F T E E N

The Battle of Yao

THE BATTLE OF YAO, THE SECOND OF THE FIVE GREAT Battles, was a brief clash that took place in 627 between the two northwestern powers of Ch'in and Chin, who earlier had been allies in the Battle of Ch'eng-p'u. As we have seen, in 630 the ruler of Ch'in left three of his officials, Ch'i Tzu, Feng Sun, and Yang Sun, to garrison the capital of the state of Cheng and prevent the state from being overthrown by Chin. With the death of Duke Wen of Chin in 628, Duke Mu of Ch'in was persuaded to undertake an ill-advised attempt to make a surprise attack on Cheng. The Ch'in officials in Cheng were to aid the attack from within the city. But Ch'in's intentions soon became obvious to the other states, and in the summer of 627 Chin stepped in to confront the Ch'in invaders in a narrow defile in the Yao Mountains south of the Yellow River. The result was a disastrous defeat for the Ch'in army.

As is often the case, the *Tso chuan* shows itself to be more interested in describing motives and predictions regarding the battle than in depicting the action itself, and the engagement is disposed of in a single sentence. The narrative opens with an eerie scene at the preliminary interment of Duke Wen of Chin, and then shifts to focus upon the Ch'in garrison in Cheng and the court of Duke Mu of Ch'in, where we see an elder statesman whose wise counsel goes unheeded.

DUKE HSI 32D YEAR (628 B.C.)

In the winter Duke Wen of Chin died. On the day *keng-ch'en* preparations were made to inter the body at Ch'ü-wo. As it was being carried out of the capital at Chiang, a sound issued from the coffin like the lowing of an ox. The diviner Yen instructed the high officials to bow down, saying, "Our lord commands us to undertake an important affair. An army from the west will pass through and strike at us. If we attack it, we are certain to win a great victory!"

Ch'i Tzu [commander of the Ch'in troops stationed in Cheng] sent a report from Cheng back to his sovereign in Ch'in, saying, "The men of Cheng have given me custody of the keys to their northern gate. If you send an army in secret, you can capture the city!"

Duke Mu of Ch'in questioned his minister Chien Shu about this, and the latter replied, "I have never heard of wearing out the army attempting to make a surprise attack on a distant state. If our army is worn out and its strength exhausted, while the ruler of the distant state has meanwhile prepared for our attack, will the outcome not be disaster? If our army knows what it is doing, Cheng will certainly find out as well, and if in spite of our precautions we fail to win success, we will surely be faced with discontent. Anyway, if we must travel a thousand *li,* who could fail to guess our intentions?"

The duke ignored this advice and, summoning Po-li Meng-ming, Hsi Ch'i, and Po Yi, ordered them to lead the army out of the eastern gate.

Chien Shu wept and said, "Meng-ming, I see the army setting out, but I will not see it return!"

The duke sent word to him, saying, "What do you know about this? If you had died at a decent age, the trees on your grave mound would be an arm's length around by now!"

Chien Shu's son was with the army. Chien Shu wept and, taking leave of him, said, "If the men of Chin move to block our army, it will surely be at Yao. There are two ridges at Yao. That on the south bears the grave of Emperor Kao of the Hsia dynasty. That on the north is where King Wen of the Chou fled to escape the wind and rain. You will no doubt die between these two. I will go to gather up your bones there!"

The Ch'in army then proceeded east.

In the following scene we see a type of prophecy common in the *Tso chuan,* one based upon observation of the behavior and attitude of the actors, particularly as it pertains to principles of ritual and propriety. In the scene that follows this, a merchant from Cheng, traveling west to the royal capital of Chou, encounters the Ch'in invading army and, sizing up the situation, cleverly pretends that he has been sent by the ruler of Cheng to present gifts to the invaders, meanwhile sending a fast rider back to alert the Cheng ruler to the danger.

DUKE HSI 33D YEAR (627 B.C.)

Spring. The Ch'in army passed by the northern gate of the king's capital at Chou. The men on the left and right of the carriage drivers doffed their armor and dismounted [out of respect for the king]. But when remounting, the men of some three hundred carriages leaped up into their vehicles without waiting for them to stop.

The royal grandson Man, though still a boy, watched them and said to the king, "The army of Ch'in is overconfident and has no sense of propriety. It will surely meet defeat. He who is overconfident lays few plans; he who lacks propriety easily slips up. If one enters a perilous situation and slips up, and on top of that he doesn't know how to plan, can he escape defeat?"

The Ch'in army had reached the state of Hua [on the Cheng border] when Hsien Kao, a merchant of Cheng who was on his way to market in Chou, chanced to meet it. He first presented four tanned hides as a gift to the army, followed by twelve oxen, saying, "My sovereign, the ruler of Cheng, hearing that you were about to lead your army through his humble territory, takes the liberty of presenting these gifts to your troops. Poor as are the resources of his humble territory, he has made preparations to provide your troops, who have been so long away from home, with a full day's supply of grain and fodder should you decide to make camp, and an escort throughout the night should you proceed straight through without halting."

At the same time he sent a fast rider to report the advance of the Ch'in army to the ruler of Cheng.

Duke Mu of Cheng sent men to keep watch on the guest lodge where the Ch'in officials were staying. They found the Ch'in officials assembling their baggage, sharpening their weapons, and foddering their horses.

The duke sent Huang Wu-tzu to say to the Ch'in officials, "Gentlemen, you have resided a long time in my humble city, and I suppose the supplies of dried meat, grain, fresh meat, and animals provided for you are used up. That is perhaps why you are preparing to leave. However, Cheng has its

Yüan Gardens, like the Chü Park of your state of Ch'in. How would it be if you were to help yourselves to the deer in the Yüan Gardens and remain at leisure in our humble city a while longer?"[1]

[Their plot discovered,] Ch'i Tzu fled to the state of Ch'i and Feng Sun and Yang Sun fled to Sung.

Po-li Meng-ming said to the other commanders of the Ch'in army, "Cheng has made preparations for our attack. We can hope for nothing! If we attack, we cannot win; if we surround the city, we cannot maintain a siege. We had better go home!"

With this they wiped out the state of Hua and began the trip back to Ch'in.

At the Chin court, Yüan Chen said, "Ch'in ignored Chien Shu's advice and has worn out its people on a mission of greed. Heaven presents us with this opportunity, and an opportunity thus presented must not be lost! One must not allow an enemy to escape, for to do so means trouble in the future, while to reject the offer of Heaven is unlucky. We must attack the Ch'in army."

Luan Chih said, "We have not yet repaid the kindness shown by Ch'in to our late sovereign, Duke Wen. If we attack Ch'in's army, how could we justify it to our dead lord?"

But Yüan Chen said, "Ch'in, showing no pity for the fact that we are in mourning, has attacked Hua, a state of our own clansmen.[2] Ch'in has no sense of propriety! Why worry about obligations to such a state? I have heard that he who acts leniently towards an enemy for a single day brings on himself generations of trouble. If we lay plans to benefit the sons and grandsons of the ruling family, that will be something worth reporting to our dead lord!"

So the order was finally issued to attack the Ch'in army and a fast rider dispatched to enlist aid from the Chiang Jung people.[3] The late duke's heir dyed his mourning garments black and put on a white hemp sash. Liang Hung drove his chariot and Lai Chü was his right-hand attendant. In the summer, the fourth month, the day *hsin-ssu,* he defeated the Ch'in army at

1 Or perhaps the meaning is "help yourselves to the deer in the Yüan Gardens and give our humble city a rest!" The *Tso*'s famed economy of words is bought at a price, and there are many places such as this where we will probably never know which of two or more possible interpretations was intended by the compilers. The tone of the entire utterance here appears to be heavily ironic.

2 The ruling family of the small state of Hua belonged to the same Chi clan as that of Chin.

3 A branch of the Western Jung people who had been driven out of their territory by Ch'in and had sought protection in Chin.

Yao and took Po-li Meng-ming, Hsi Ch'i, and Po Yi prisoner. Then he returned to Chin and, still wearing his black garments, buried his father, Duke Wen. This was the beginning of the Chin custom of wearing black mourning garments.[4]

Under ordinary circumstances, the Ch'in commanders who were taken prisoner in the battle would probably have been executed. But in the following scene Lady Wen of the Ying family, a daughter of Duke Mu of Ch'in and widow of Duke Wen of Chin, intervenes and persuades her stepson, the new ruler of Chin, Duke Hsiang (r. 627–621), to return the prisoners to Ch'in so that her father can punish them himself. Though the narrative does not state it in so many words, it would appear that in doing so she was covertly acting in the interests of her father, who in fact did not punish the commanders, and against the interests of her late husband and his heir.

Lady Wen of the Ying family asked the new ruler about the fate of the three Ch'in commanders. "It was they who actually brought about the trouble between the rulers of the two states!" she declared. "If my former lord, the ruler of Ch'in, could only lay hands on them, his wrath would scarcely be appeased even by eating their flesh! Therefore, my lord, why demean yourself by executing them here? Send them back to Ch'in to be punished and you will make it possible for the ruler of Ch'in to accomplish his wish for vengeance."

The ruler of Chin consented to this.

When Yüan Chen appeared at court, he asked what had happened to the Ch'in captives.

"At the urging of my father's widow, I released them," replied the ruler.

Yüan Chen, enraged, said, "Prizes won by the warriors at great labor on the field of battle—and through a woman's trickery they are allowed to leave the state! He who deliberately discards the fruits of battle and nour-

4 Ordinarily, white was the color of mourning.

ishes the strength of his enemy need not wait long for the day of destruction!" And without turning his head, he spat.

The ruler dispatched Yang Ch'u-fu to pursue the Ch'in commanders, but when he reached the Yellow River he found they had already embarked in a boat. Unharnassing the outside left horse from his team of four, he indicated to Po-li Meng-ming that the Chin ruler wished to present the horse to him. Po-li Meng-ming bowed his head from the boat and said, "Through your lord's kindness I have been spared the fate of having my blood smeared on the war drums.[5] Instead I have been sent back to be punished by Ch'in. Though my sovereign may execute me, even in death I will not forget the gratitude I owe your lord. And if out of pity my sovereign should pardon me, I will be back within three years to accept your lord's gift!"[6]

The ruler of Ch'in, wearing white mourning garments, camped in the suburbs of his capital to await the army. He greeted the commanders with tears, saying, "I failed to heed the advice of Chien Shu and brought this shame upon you. The fault is mine!"

He did not deprive Po-li Meng-ming of his command, but said, "I was in error. What fault have you committed? How could I allow one blunder to overshadow your great merits?"

5 Drums and bells were smeared with blood to consecrate them. In the case of war drums, the blood of captured prisoners was sometimes used.

6 That is, to attack Chin again and wipe out the disgrace of his defeat. He carried out the threat, and over the following years Chin and Ch'in attacked each other almost annually.

SIXTEEN

An Inglorious Defeat for Sung

IN THE *TSO CHUAN*'S BATTLE DESCRIPTIONS, ONE SEEMS TO glimpse two quite different conceptions of warfare. The first treats war as a kind of game, an opportunity to display heroic behavior, often in the form of rather foolhardy acts of bravado. Associated with this is a chivalrous approach to one's enemy which entails not taking unfair advantage of him and even extending help when he is down. There are hints in the *Tso* that this is an older view of warfare, one that belongs to an age that is passing or has passed.

In contrast to this view of warfare as a sort of sport of gentlemen is a much more cynical and businesslike approach which emphasizes self-interest over any romantic ideas of chivalry, stressing the coordinated strategy of groups of fighting men rather than individual exploits.

In the following description of an attack carried out by Cheng upon the state of Sung, we see an example of a man who treated his enemy according to the presumably older more chivalrous code, and suffered for it. In addition, the man is roundly condemned by the ubiquitous *chün-tzu* or "gentleman" who appears so often in the *Tso* narrative to deliver judgment upon its events.

DUKE HSUAN 2D YEAR (607 B.C.)

In the spring of the second year the ducal son Kuei-sheng of Cheng received orders from Ch'u to attack Sung. The Sung leaders Hua Yüan and Yüeh Lü prepared to meet the attack.

On the day *jen-tzu* of the second month the two sides engaged in combat at Ta-chi in Sung. The Sung army suffered a crushing defeat. Hua Yüan was taken prisoner and Yüeh Lü was captured and killed. Four hundred and sixty chariots drawn by armored horses were seized, along with two hundred and fifty prisoners and the ears of a hundred slain soldiers.

The Sung official K'uang Chiao fought against the Cheng invaders. But when one of the men of Cheng fell into a well, he turned his halberd around and pulled the man out. The man then killed K'uang Chiao.

The gentleman remarks: K'uang departed from propriety and disobeyed orders. It is right that he should have been overpowered. In warfare, propriety decrees that leaders display resolution and valor and those under them heed orders. To kill the enemy is an act of resolution, and to do acts of resolution is to be valorous. He who departs from this deserves to die.

On the eve of the battle, Hua Yüan slaughtered a sheep and fed the meat to his men, but his carriage driver Yang Chen did not receive a portion. When the battle began, Yang Chen announced, "Yesterday's sheep was at your disposing. But today's affairs will be disposed by me!" Then he drove the chariot into the midst of the Cheng army, thus bringing about Sung's defeat.

The gentleman remarks: Yang Chen does not deserve to be called a human being! Because of a private grievance he brought defeat upon his state and devastation to its people. Can there be any offense greater than this? What the *Odes* says about "A man who has no goodness" must refer to someone like Yang Chen.[1] He destroyed his own people in order to satisfy himself.

The men of Sung presented a hundred war chariots and a hundred four-horse teams of piebald horses to Cheng as ransom for Hua Yüan. When half of the ransom had been paid, Hua Yüan escaped and returned to Sung.

He stood outside the gate of the capital and announced his name, after which he entered.[2] When he saw Yang Chen, he said,[3] "It was the horses that made you act that way."

Yang Chen replied, "It was not the horses—I did it!" Then he fled to the state of Lu.

Sung was repairing the walls of its capital and Hua Yüan acted as

1 The quotation is from "Airs of Yung," *Ch'un chih pen-pen,* Mao no. 49.

2 To show that he was not attempting to return in stealth.

3 The text actually says, "When he saw Shu-tsang, he said. . ." Commentators from early times have surmised that Shu-tsang must be another name for the carriage driver Yang Chen, and I have followed this interpretation since it seems to fit the text best. But other interpretations have been offered, among them that Shu-tsang is the name of a gatekeeper of the Sung city gate. One can see the perils involved in the *Tso*'s practice of using multiple names to refer to a single individual.

supervisor. As he went around inspecting the progress of the work, the workmen sang this song:

> Bulging of eye,
> belly like a sack,
> left his armor and came home,
> bushy-beard bushy-beard
> left his armor and came back![4]

Hua Yüan had one of the men accompanying him in his carriage say to the workers:

> Oxen still have hides,
> plenty of rhinos remain.
> Armor left—but why complain?

The workmen said,

> Hides he may have,
> but what of the red to lacquer 'em?[5]

Hua Yüan said, "I'd better be off! They have many mouths, I have only one!"

4 The workmen are jeering at Hua Yüan for his defeat and capture in battle.

5 The Chinese armor of this time was made of ox or rhinoceros hide and finished with red lacquer. The kind of flyting or bantering back and forth in rhyme displayed here appears in later historical works as well. See for example the biography of the Han dynasty wit Tung-fang Shuo in my *Courtier and Commoner in Ancient China* (New York: Columbia University Press, 1974), p. 82.

SEVENTEEN

The Responsibilities of Rulership

CONFUCIUS, IN A FAMOUS PRONOUNCEMENT IN *ANALECTS* XII, 11, declared that good government prevailed when "the ruler is a ruler, the minister a minister, the father a father, the son a son." The implication of course is that if a person ceases to fulfill the duties required of his particular position in society, he can no longer expect others to treat him as though he occupied that position.

The following episode, dated 607 like that above, begins with the stark declaration that "Duke Ling of Chin did not *chün,*" employing the word *chün* or "ruler" in a verbal sense; that is, did not conduct himself as a proper ruler should. The remainder of the passage describes the dire results that followed from this fact. Duke Ling, a son of Duke Hsiang and grandson of Duke Wen, came to power as a young man in 620 following the death of his father in the previous year. His accession was made possible through the backing of two of the chief ministers of Chin at the time, Chao Tun and his second cousin Chao Ch'uan.

DUKE HSUAN 2D YEAR (607 B.C.)

Duke Ling of Chin was no true ruler. He exacted heavy taxes and used the means to ornament his walls. From his terrace he shot at people with a crossbow and watched them flee the pellets. When his cook prepared a dish of bear's paws that was not thoroughly done, he killed him, stuffed the body in a basket, and had his women carry it through the audience chamber.

Chao Tun and Shih Chi, spying the dead man's hand, inquired what had happened.[1] Greatly distressed, they were about to remonstrate with the ruler, but Shih Chi said, "If we both remonstrate and he fails to listen, there will be no one to carry on. Let me go first. If he fails to heed me, you come after and continue to remonstrate."

Shih Chi advanced two stages into the hall and on his third advance reached the eaves of the inner court when the duke finally acknowledged his presence. "I know I am at fault," said the ruler, "I will change my ways."

Shih Chi bowed his head to the ground and said, "What man is without faults? But to have faults and correct them—nothing is finer that that! The *Odes* says:

> None who have not a beginning,
> but few can make a proper ending.[2]

This means that there are few who are able to mend their faults.

"If you are truly willing to make a proper ending, you will insure the safety of the state's altars of the soil and grain. And that will be a boon to more than your officials only.

"The *Odes* also says:

> When the embroidered robe has a hole,
> Chung Shan-fu will mend it.[3]

So faults can be mended. If you are willing to mend your faults, then the robe need not be discarded."

But the duke did not change his ways. Chao Tun frequently remonstrated with him, until the duke, annoyed at this, sent Ch'u Mei to do away with him.

Ch'u Mei went to Chao Tun's home at dawn but found the bed chamber already open. Chao Tun was dressed in his court robes, prepared for the morning audience with the ruler, but because it was still early, he was sitting in his seat dozing.

Ch'u Mei withdrew and said with a sigh, "A man who does not forget to be reverent and respectful in his duties deserves to be called a leader of the people. To inflict injury upon a leader of the people would be disloyalty.

1 Chao Tun was the son of Chao Ts'ui, the follower of Duke Wen of Chin who has appeared earlier; see p. 48 above. He and Shih Chi were leading statesmen in Chin at this time.

2 "Greater Odes," *Tang*, Mao no. 255.

3 "Greater Odes," *Cheng-min*, Mao no. 260. The hole in the embroidered robe of the ruler here stands for some fault in government. Chung Shan-fu was a model official of early times who is praised in the poem.

But to disobey the ruler's command would be bad faith. If I must commit one or another of these faults, it would be better to die!"

He dashed his head against a cassia tree and died.

In autumn, the ninth month, the ruler of Chin invited Chao Tun to drink with him. He concealed soldiers in the hall, intending to ambush Chao Tun.

The right-hand attendant in Chao Tun's carriage, Shih Mi-ming, learned of the plot and, hurrying up into the upper part of the duke's hall, said, "When a minister attends his lord at a banquet, it is a breach of etiquette for him to drink more than three cups!"

He then helped Chao Tun descend to the lower part of the hall.[4]

The duke set his fierce dog on the pair, but Shih Mi-ming struck the dog with his fist and killed it.

Chao Tun said, "Throw men away and use dogs if you will, but no matter how ferocious, what can they do?"

The two men fought their way out of the hall. Shih Mi-ming was killed in the fighting.

Once in the past, Chao Tun had been hunting at Mount Shou and had stopped for the night at a place called Shady Mulberry. There he encountered a starving man named Ling Ch'e. When he asked what ailed him, Ling Ch'e said, "I have not eaten in three days."

Chao Tun gave him food, but Ling Ch'e put half of it aside. When Chao Tun asked the reason, he said, "I have been abroad on official business for three years and I do not know if my mother is still alive or not. Now that I'm nearing home, I'd like to take this food to her."

Chao Tun urged him to finish the food and, filling a box with rice and meat and placing it in a sack, gave it to the man.

This same man was now acting as one of the duke's armed guards. But he turned his halberd against the other attendants of the duke and so made it possible for Chao Tun to escape. When Chao Tun asked him the reason, he replied, "I was the starving man at Shady Mulberry."

Chao Tun asked him his polite name and where he lived, but the man slipped away without answering, and in the end disappeared completely.

On the day *i-ch'ou,* Chao Ch'uan attacked and killed Duke Ling in the peach orchard.

4 Or, according to another version of the text, "Chao Tun descended to the lower part of the hall without taking time to put on his shoes." The Chinese at this time removed their shoes when they ascended to the upper part of the hall to eat or drink.

Chao Tun, who had not yet crossed the mountains [on the border of the state], returned to the capital.

The grand historian [Tung Hu] wrote: "Chao Tun assassinated his ruler" and showed the document to the court.

Chao Tun said, "That is not true!"

The historian replied, "You are the chief minister. When you fled you did not cross the border. Now you have returned you do not punish the culprit. If you are not responsible, who is?"

Chao Tun said, "Alas! The words:

> These longings of mine,
> they've brought this grief on me![5]

apply to me."

Confucius said: "Tung Hu was a good historian of ancient times. In recording principles he did not conceal anything. Chao Tun was a good official of ancient times. For the sake of the principle he was willing to receive a bad name. What a pity! If he had crossed the border he might have escaped the charge."

Chao Tun dispatched Chao Ch'uan to go to Chou and escort the ducal son Hei-t'un back to Chin, where he was set up as the new ruler.[6] On the day *jen-shen* he presented himself in the temple of his ancestor Duke Wu.

The passage dealing with the grand historian Tung Hu of Chin and Confucius' comment on the grand historian that occurs just before the end of this section is one of the most vexing and controversial in all the *Tso chuan.* In earlier episodes we have seen the *shih* or historians acting as diviners, and they also had charge of affairs pertaining to the calendar and the observation of heavenly bodies and portentous

5 Presumably the words of a poem. No such lines are found in the present text of the *Odes,* though they bear a close resemblance to lines in "Airs of Pei," *Hsiung-chih,* Mao no. 33, and "Lesser Odes," *Hsiao-ming,* Mao no. 207.

6 A son of Duke Wen of Chin, he had been living in the royal domain of Chou for some years. He reigned from 606 to 600 and is known posthumously as Duke Ch'eng of Chin.

occurrences in nature. Here we see the historian in his role as recorder of events at court, compiler of the type of records that presumably formed the basis for such chronicles as the *Spring and Autumn Annals* of the state of Lu and for the *Tso* itself. It is therefore highly disquieting to discover that the *t'ai-shih* or grand historian of Chin, rather than recording the facts as they occurred, is actually shown falsifying the record in order to make a moral point concerning the ultimate responsibilities of government. And it is further disturbing to find that Confucius, if the remarks attributed to him here are to be credited, fully approved of this type of falsification.

As stated earlier, the *Tso chuan* in its present form is arranged as a commentary upon the year-by-year entries of the *Spring and Autumn Annals.* The entry in the *Annals* for autumn of this year states: "Chao Tun of Chin assassinated his ruler I-kao." The whole passage in the *Tso chuan* (and the similar passage in the *Ku-liang Commentary*) may therefore merely be an attempt to explain why the *Annals* states that Chao Tun was the assassin, when in fact it was Chao Ch'uan. Since Confucius was traditionally supposed to have compiled or edited the *Spring and Autumn Annals* and to have taken responsibility for its contents, it would naturally be difficult for the commentators to state flatly that the entry in the *Annals* is in error. But one cannot help wishing they had not adopted the present tortuous method of explaining the discrepancy in the facts.

It may be noted that later historians in China fortunately did not attempt to imitate the practice of the grand historian of Chin. It was evidently felt that such distortions of truth for didactic purposes were justified only when there was a sage such as Confucius on hand to sanction them, and that historians of subsequent periods could best instruct posterity by adhering as closely as possible to the actual facts.

Another point in the *Tso chuan* narrative under discussion that has greatly troubled later critics is the suggestion, in both the words of the historian Tung Hu and those of Confucius, that Chao Tun could have absolved himself of any responsibility for the murder of his sovereign if he had only crossed the border of the state. In the historian's rebuke, the chief emphasis is surely upon the fact that Chao Tun has failed to punish the murderer, with the first part of the utterance, one feels, inserted mainly to balance the sentence and fill out the parallelism. But Confucius in his comment specifically reverts to the question of the crossing of the border, as though to imply that by simply stepping outside the territory of one's state one could thereby dissolve the ties of duty that bind a subject to his prince. Some commentators, in order to get around the dilemma, have attempted to interpret the passage to mean that if Chao Tun had only been outside the state when the murder took place, he might have escaped responsibility for it, or to mean that if he had left the state forever and never returned, he might have done so. But such interpretations strike me as intolerably forced. If the Gospels have their dark sayings, we must perhaps admit that this remark of Confucius represents one of the dark sayings of the *Tso chuan,* an utterance that will never be completely comprehensible to the modern reader.

EIGHTEEN

King Chuang of Ch'u Asks About the Cauldrons

ACCORDING TO THE LEGEND RELATED IN THE SELECTION THAT follows and in other early texts, Emperor Yü, the sage founder of the Hsia dynasty, collected metal from the nine provinces of ancient China and cast nine *ting* or three-legged cauldrons for use in the sacrifices of the ruling house. (Some accounts assert that there were not nine cauldrons, but only one, made from metal from all the nine provinces.)

In time the virtue of the Hsia dynasty declined until its last ruler Chieh was overthrown because of his unrighteous ways and a new dynasty, the Shang, set up. The cauldrons passed into the hands of this new dynasty. The Shang likewise declined and its last ruler, the evil tyrant Chou, was overthrown by the founders of the Chou dynasty (the name of the dynasty is written with a different character from that used for the name of the last Shang ruler).

When the new dynasty had taken custody of the cauldrons, its second ruler, King Ch'eng, divined to determine how long his own dynasty would last and received the answers recorded below. It is said that the cauldrons remained in the possession of the Chou rulers until 336 B.C. (or, according to another version, 327 B.C.), when they sank into the Ssu River at P'eng-ch'eng and were lost forever.

From the episode presented here, the phrase *wen-ting,* "to ask about the cauldrons," has come to mean to aspire to, or plot to seize, imperial power.

DUKE HSUAN 3D YEAR (606 B.C.)

The ruler of Ch'u attacked the Jung tribes of the Lu-hun region and then advanced as far as the Lo River, where he reviewed his troops on the border of the Chou royal domain.[1]

King Ting of the Chou sent the royal grandson Man to thank the Ch'u ruler for his trouble.[2]

The Ch'u ruler asked whether the cauldrons were large or small, light or heavy.

Prince Man replied, "The crux of the matter lies in virtue, not in the cauldrons. Long ago, when the Hsia dynasty was still possessed of virtue, the distant regions sent pictures of various objects and tribute of metal was submitted from the governors of the nine provinces. This was used to cast cauldrons with various objects depicted on them. All the hundreds of kinds of objects were to be found on them, so that the people could learn about the gods and the malevolent spirits. As a result, when the people entered the river or lake regions, the mountains or forests, they did not encounter such evil beings, and the mountain and water goblins could not confront them. Thus superior and inferior were brought into harmony and they enjoyed the providence of Heaven.

"Chieh [the last ruler of the Hsia] was dark in the ways of virtue and the cauldrons were transferred to the Shang dynasty, whose years numbered six hundred. But Emperor Chou of the Shang was violent and tyrannical, and the cauldrons thereupon passed to the Chou dynasty. When virtue is bright and comely, then the cauldrons, though small, are heavy. But when there is depravity and disorder, then although they are large, they are light.

"The bright virtue bestowed by Heaven has its limit and end. When King Ch'eng of the Chou dynasty fixed the cauldrons in place at his capital in Chia-ju, he divined by the tortoiseshell to determine the number of generations of the dynasty and was given the answer "thirty," and he divined to determine the number of years and was told "seven hundred." This was mandated by Heaven. Thus, although the virtue of the Chou dynasty may have declined, the mandate of Heaven is not yet ready to be

1 The Ch'u ruler is King Chuang (r. 613–591).
2 Prince Man has already appeared on p. 69 above.

transferred to another dynasty. It is too soon to ask if the cauldrons are heavy or light!"[3]

3 King Ch'eng, the third nominal ruler and second actual ruler of the Chou dynasty, came to the throne in 1115 B.C. according to traditional dating (or in 1020 according to another way of dating). Chia-ju is west of the present-day city of Lo-yang. The section of the *Book of Documents* known as the *Shao kao* or "Announcement to the Duke of Chou" describes the founding of the Chou capital at this site. Though it is difficult to make exact calculations, it would appear that just about seven hundred years did in fact elapse from the time when King Ch'eng was supposed to have conducted his divination and when the cauldrons were lost, and that about thirty Chou sovereigns reigned in succession. We may perhaps surmise, therefore, that either this passage was written after the fall of the dynasty, or that the figures were adjusted at a later date.

N I N E T E E N

The Battle of Pi

IN EARLIER NARRATIVES WE HAVE SEEN HOW THE SMALL STATE of Cheng in Honan just south of the Yellow River was pressed by its powerful neighbors, Chin to the north and Ch'u to the south, to enter into alliance with one or the other of them, and threatened with invasion if it refused to comply. Thus, for example, in 606 Chin troops invaded Cheng and forced it to conclude an alliance with Chin. In the same year, and again in 605, Ch'u invaded Cheng in retaliation for the latter's having gone over to the side of Chin. Ch'u invaded Cheng again in 604 and 603, and finally forced Cheng to conclude an alliance with Ch'u, the so-called "peace of Man." In 602, however, Cheng once more went over to the side of Chin, and in 600 Ch'u attacked Cheng to punish it for this violation of the "peace of Man." Chin came to Cheng's rescue on this occasion, and again in 599, when Ch'u repeated its attack on Cheng, at which time Cheng made peace with Ch'u. But Ch'u was not satisfied with Cheng's conduct, and early in 598 King Chuang of Ch'u once more mustered his forces for an attack on Cheng. This action, as we shall see in the following narrative, led in time to the Battle of Pi between Ch'u and Chin, the third of the Five Great Battles.

DUKE HSUAN 12TH YEAR (597 B.C.)

In the twelfth year, the spring, the ruler of Ch'u surrounded the Cheng capital. When the siege had continued for seventeen days, the people of Cheng divined by the tortoiseshell to determine if they should make peace with Ch'u, but the response was inauspicious. They then divined to see if they should carry out lamentations in the ancestral temple and range their chariots in the streets of the city.[1] This time the response was favorable. The people of the state accordingly conducted a great lamentation, and the guards manning the ramparts all wept.

The ruler of Ch'u withdrew his army, but when the men of Cheng took this opportunity to repair their walls, he advanced and surrounded the city once more.

After three months the Ch'u forces succeeded in capturing the city. They entered it through the Huang Gate and had proceeded as far as the main thoroughfare when the Cheng ruler, his torso bared and leading a sheep, came out to meet them.[2]

"Truly I am unfavored of Heaven!" he said. "Incapable of serving my lord, I have caused my lord to harbor anger and hence to trouble himself to come here to my humble city. Such is my offense—what could I hope for but to heed my lord's command?

"Perhaps I will be taken prisoner and led away south of the Yangtze to dwell by the shores of the sea—my lord has only to command it! Or perhaps my domain will be stripped from me and given to another of the feudal lords, and I and mine will serve him as man- and maidservant—my lord has only to command it!

"But perhaps my lord, graciously recalling the ties of friendship that formerly bound us, and hopeful of blessings from kings Li and Hsüan and dukes Huan and Wu, will refrain from destroying Cheng's altars of the soil and grain and will allow me once more to serve my lord and take my place alongside the nine prefectures.[3] If so, it will be truly a kindness on my lord's part and a fulfillment of my desires. And yet it is more than I dare hope for. I venture merely to reveal what is in my heart, and leave it to my lord to ponder."

The attendants of the king of Ch'u said, "Do not listen to him! Once you have conquered a state, there is no such thing as forgiveness!"

But the king said, "This prince knows how to humble himself before others, and he must therefore know how to employ his own people in good faith. What can we hope to gain by denying his request?"

1 One interpretation is that the chariots were to show that the population expected to be ordered out of the city. A quite different interpretation is that the chariots—in this view, war chariots—were intended to show that the people were prepared to fight to the death. The latter view seems to me more reasonable.

2 The Cheng ruler at this time was Duke Hsiang (r. 604–587). The bared torso and sheep were tokens of submission.

3 Kings Li and Hsüan were Chou rulers who reigned 878–828 and 827–781 respectively. Dukes Huan and Wu were Cheng rulers of the same period; Duke Huan was a son of King Li and younger brother of King Hsüan. "Nine prefectures" appears to refer to territories appropriated by Ch'u, though just what territories are meant, and whether "nine" is to be taken in a literal sense, is uncertain.

The king withdrew his troops to a distance of thirty *li* and consented to a peaceful settlement. The Ch'u official P'an Wang entered the Cheng capital to conclude the alliance, and Tzu-liang [the younger brother of the Cheng ruler] was sent to Ch'u to act as a hostage.

In summer, the sixth month, the Chin army set out to rescue Cheng. Hsün Lin-fu led the central army, with Hsien Ku to assist him.[4] Shih Hui led the upper army, with Hsi K'o assisting him, and Chao Shuo led the lower army, with Luan Shu as his assistant.[5] Chao K'uo and Chao Ying-ch'i served as supervising officials of the central army, Kung Shuo and Han Ch'uan as officials of the upper army, and Hsün Shou and Chao T'ung as officials of the lower army. Han Chüeh was appointed as marshal.

When the Chin forces reached the Yellow River, they received word that Cheng had already made peace with Ch'u. Hsün Lin-fu wanted to go back, saying, "We are too late to help Cheng and will only exhaust our own people—what use is that? If Ch'u, after returning home, should make another move, it will not be too late to attack!"

"Good counsel!" said Shih Hui. "I have heard that when employing military force, one looks for some opening before moving. When a state is unswerving in its attention to virtue, punishments, government, undertakings, regulations, and propriety, it cannot be opposed. There's no going to war with a state like that!

"When the lord of Ch'u attacked Cheng, he did so because he was angered by its duplicity, and later he pitied it because of its abject submission. While Cheng was rebellious, he attacked; when it was submissive, he forgave it. Thus the demands of virtue and punishment were fulfilled. To attack the rebellious is an act of punishment; to be gentle with the submissive, an act of virtue.[6] Ch'u carried out both.

"Last year Ch'u marched against Ch'en, this year it marches against Cheng, yet its people are not weary or worn out and there is no resentment or backbiting directed against its ruler—because its government is well-ordered.

"Again, when Ch'u uses its special battle formations,[7] its traveling mer-

4 Hsün Lin-fu took part earlier in the Battle of Ch'eng-p'u; see p. 52 above.

5 Chao Shuo was a son of Chao Tun, the prominent Chin statesman. Luan Shu was a son of Luan Chih, for whom see p. 52 above.

6 The word *te* here has the somewhat special meaning of a favor or good deed done to someone, and it might be more natural to translate it as "kindness." I have, however, stuck to the translation "virtue" in order to bring out the numerous word plays involved. This whole speech of Shih Hui is an example of the *Tso chuan* style at its most studiedly rhetorical.

7 *Ching-shih* or the "formations of Ching (Ch'u)," first put into effect by King Wu of Ch'u in 690; details are unknown.

chants, farmers, artisans, and shopkeepers are not prevented from going about their occupations, and its foot soldiers and chariot men are on close and friendly terms—special undertakings are planned so as not to interrupt normal tasks.[8]

"Since Sun-shu Ao became prime minister of Ch'u, he has selected the ordinances and regulations that are proper for the state of Ch'u.[9] Thus when the army is on the move, the men on the right advance in the direction pointed by the carriage shafts, while those on the left go in search of fodder, and the forward scouts with their cogon grass pennants make certain there are no enemy forces ahead. The central army does the planning, the army behind it uses its crack troops to guard the rear, and the various officers move in accordance with the objects displayed on the flags.[10] Thus the army functions smoothly and efficiently and there is no need to apply punishments, proof that the men of Ch'u know how to employ regulations.

"When the ruler promotes a man to office, if it is from among his own clan, he selects a person who is close to him, and if from among those of another surname, a person long known to him. In promotion he does not overlook virtue, in rewards he does not overlook merit, to the elderly he is particularly beneficent, and for strangers to his state he provides lodging. Gentlemen and persons of humble birth are clearly distinguished by differences in badge and clothing. The noble enjoy constant honor, the lowly have their various degrees of dignity, and thus the demands of propriety are not slighted.

"Where virtue is honored, punishments applied, government well ordered, undertakings timely, regulations obeyed, and propriety duly observed, how can one hope to make a successful attack? To advance when one can see possibilities and withdraw when one becomes aware of difficulties is the secret of wise military planning. To annex the weak and attack the benighted is the basis of the wise use of arms. I would ask that you, our commander, for the moment apply such methods of planning and use your arms in such a way. While there are still weak and benighted states, why need we concern ourselves with Ch'u?

8 Foot soldiers were conscripted from the peasantry, while members of the upper class rode in the chariots. The meaning presumably is that if special undertakings such as military expeditions are scheduled at times when they will not interfere with agricultural tasks, the peasants will not resent them.

9 According to legend, Sun-shu Ao was three times appointed prime minister of Ch'u and three times dismissed from that office. He is mentioned in *Mencius,* VI B, 15.

10 The *Ping-fa* or "Military Rules" chapter of the *Kuan Tzu* (section 17) states that a flag with a sun on it is raised to indicate daytime advance, one with a moon to indicate nighttime advance, one with a dragon to indicate a water route, one with a tiger to indicate a forest route, etc.

"Chung-hui has said, 'Attack disorder, overwhelm the doomed,' which means to annex the weak.[11] The *Cho* ode says:

> Glorious is the king's army;
> he reared it up out of darkness.[12]

which means to move against the benighted. And the *Wu* ode says:

> Was it not strong, his ardor?[13]

To succor the weak and move against the benighted was the duty he pursued with ardor. Was that not the correct course?"

But Hsien Ku said, "Not at all! Chin was able to become leader of the feudal lords because its army was valorous and its officials put forth effort. But if we let this feudal lord, Cheng, slip away from us, we cannot be said to be putting forth effort. And if we have an enemy, Ch'u, before our very eyes and fail to engage him, we cannot be called valorous. If I thought that any action of mine would cause Chin to lose its position as leader, I would rather die! After the army has been formed and sent on its way, if we withdraw because we hear that the enemy is powerful, that would be no manly act. To be appointed to the post of commander of the army and then end by behaving in an unmanly way—well, perhaps you other gentlemen can do it, but I cannot!"

In his capacity as assistant of the central army he proceeded to cross the river with the troops under him.

"This army is in danger!" said Hsün Shou. "This is what the *Book of Changes* describes in the shift from the hexagram *shih* or "the army" to *lin* or "the verge" when it says: 'The army proceeds by means of regulations. If they are not well observed, there is disaster.'[14]

"In conducting affairs, obedience in action will bring good results, but the opposite will not. When the multitude scatter, weakness results. When the river is clogged, a swamp is formed. Though regulations exist, each man does as he pleases. Hence the warning against regulations that are 'not well observed.' The regulations will dry up, like a pond that overflows and then dries up. It is blocked and not cleared out, and that brings disaster.

11 Jen Chung-hui was a chief minister in the time of the Shang dynasty. The "Announcement of Chung-hui" in the *Book of Documents* purports to be his words, though the present text was put together in Han times.

12 "Hymns of Chou," *Cho,* Mao no. 293. The poem is said to praise the founders of the Chou dynasty, who overthrew the "darkness" of the preceding Shang dynasty.

13 "Hymns of Chou," *Wu,* Mao no. 285. The ardor was that of King Wu, one of the founders of the Chou dynasty.

14 The quotation is from the description of the hexagram *shih.*

To fail to pass over is to be perpetually on "the verge." If there is a commanding general but he is not obeyed, how could one ever be other than on "the verge"? This is what the *Changes* is saying.[15] The result of an encounter now would be certain defeat! And Hsien Ku will be the cause of it. Though he may escape for the moment, when we return to Chin he is certain to face great blame!"

Han Chüeh, who was acting as marshal, addressed Hsün Lin-fu, the commander of the central army, saying, "Now that Hsien Ku has taken a portion of the army and plunged into the fray, you will be severely blamed. You are supreme commander, and if any of the others fail to obey orders, who is to blame but you? You have let an ally, Cheng, slip away, and lost part of your army, so your blame is already weighty. You had best go forward. If the expedition is not successful, a part of the onus can be apportioned to others. Rather than take all the blame yourself, better let six men share it!"

The Chin army thereupon crossed the river.

The rash action of Hsien Ku in crossing the Yellow River with the troops under his command in defiance of the orders of the supreme commander of the expedition, as we have just seen, brought about the crossing of the remainder of the Chin troops and in time precipitated the costly battle of Pi. In the following section, the narrative shifts to the opposing Ch'u army, led by King Chuang.

The Ch'u ruler led his army north and camped for the night at Yen in Cheng. Shen Yin commanded the central army, Tzu-chung was commander of the left, and Tzu-fan commander of the right.

The Ch'u ruler intended merely to water his horses at the Yellow River and then return to Ch'u, but then he received word that the Chin forces had

15 The hexagram *shih* is made up of the trigrams symbolizing water and earth respectively. In the hexagram *lin,* the trigram for water is replaced by that for pond or marsh, which also signifies weakness. The passage here plays on those various connotations of the two hexagrams.

already crossed the river. He favored returning to Ch'u, but his favorite, Wu Ts'an, wanted to engage the enemy.

The prime minister Sun-shu Ao was not in favor of this. "Last year we invaded Ch'en, this year we invaded Cheng," he said. "It is not as though we have not been busy! If we fight now and fail to win victory, will our anger be appeased merely by eating the flesh of Wu Ts'an?"

But Wu Ts'an retorted, "If we win victory, Sun-shu Ao will be criticized for having opposed the battle. And if we lose, my flesh will be in the hands of the Chin army, so how could you hope to eat it?"

Sun-shu Ao turned his carriage shafts toward the south and reversed the direction of his pennants [in preparation for withdrawal]. But Wu Ts'an said to the king, "Chin's leaders have just recently taken command and they do not know how to enforce orders. The assistant commander Hsien Ku is stubborn and perverse, a heartless man, and he is unwilling to heed commands. Each of the leaders of Chin's three armies wants to have his own way, and cannot. Subordinates would like to heed orders but have no competent officers to lead them, so that the men do not know who to follow. If things go this way, the Chin army is certain to be defeated. Moreover, you are a ruler—if you flee before men who are mere subjects, what will become of our altars of the soil and grain?" [16]

The king, disturbed by these arguments, ordered the prime minister Sun-shu Ao to turn his carriage shafts around again toward the north, and he encamped at Kuan to await the enemy.

The scene now shifts back to the side of Chin, where the Chin leaders continue to debate whether or not to engage the Ch'u forces in combat.

The Chin army was deployed between two mountains, Ao and Ch'iao. The state of Cheng dispatched Huang Hsü to go to the Chin army with this

16 A reference to the fact that, while the Ch'u army was commanded by the Ch'u ruler himself, that of Chin was commanded by officials of the Chin government.

message: "Cheng agreed to go along with Ch'u merely in order to preserve its altars of the soil and grain. It is not that we have played you false! The Ch'u army has won repeated victory and is puffed up with pride. Its army, in the field a long time, is on its last legs and does not take proper precautions. If you attack, and the Cheng army is there to second you, the Ch'u forces are bound to suffer defeat!"

Hsien Ku said, "Here is our chance to defeat Ch'u and win back Cheng. We must agree to this proposal!"

But Luan Shu of the lower army said, "Ever since Ch'u conquered Yung,[17] there is not a day when its ruler does not train his people and instruct them, saying, 'It is not easy to provide sustenance for the people! Disaster is upon you before you know it! Be cautious and fearful and never slacken!' And with regard to the army there is not a day when he does not train his troops and exhort them, saying, 'You cannot count on victory forever! Chou had his hundred conquests, but in the end he left no heirs!'[18] Or he instructs them with the example of Jo-ao and Fen-mao,[19] who set forth in crude carts and ragged clothing to open up and cultivate the hills and woodlands, or cautions them, saying, 'The sustenance of the people depends on diligence! Where there is diligence there will never be want!' How then can you say that Ch'u is puffed up with pride?

"Moreover, the former official of our state, Hu Yen, has said, 'If an army follows proper procedure, we say it is in its prime. If it bends the regulations, we say it is on its last legs.'[20] Now we have failed to act with virtue and have aroused the anger of Ch'u. It is we who have 'bent' things, while Ch'u took the 'proper' course, so you cannot say that its army is on its last legs.

"The personal troops of the Ch'u ruler are divided into two wings of fifteen war chariots each, with a hundred extra men to each wing. And accompanying each body of a hundred men are fifty supplementary troops and twenty-five auxiliary troops.[21] At dawn the men of the right wing mount their chariots first, and then when it is calculated that the sun has reached its height, the men of the left wing mount and continue in readiness until nightfall. The ruler's personal attendants take turns guarding him at

17 Ch'u conquered the small state of Yung in 611, fourteen years previous to this.

18 Chou is the evil last ruler of the Shang dynasty.

19 Ancestors of the Ch'u ruling family.

20 The *Tso* is quoting its own earlier account of Hu Yen's speech at the time of the Battle of Ch'eng-p'u; see p. 58 above.

21 As mentioned earlier, each war chariot carried three men and was accompanied by 72 foot soldiers, so the fifteen war chariots represent a force of 1,125 men. In the personal troops of the Ch'u ruler, these were in turn backed up by 175 additional men, giving a total of 1,300 men to each wing of the army.

night so as to be prepared for any eventuality. So you cannot say that the Ch'u army takes no proper precautions.

"Tzu-liang of Cheng is a man of honor, and P'an Wang is a highly respected official of Ch'u. P'an Wang has entered the Cheng capital and concluded an alliance between Ch'u and Cheng, and Tzu-liang has gone to take up residence in Ch'u. Hence Ch'u and Cheng are obviously on close terms. Now this envoy from Cheng comes urging us to engage Ch'u in battle. If we win, Cheng will come over to our side; if we do not win, it will go along with Ch'u. Cheng is using us to try to divine which course to follow! We must not heed this proposal of Cheng!"

Chao K'uo and Chao T'ung said, "We've led our troops this far—all that remains is to seek out the enemy! If we defeat the enemy and persuade Cheng to submit to us, what more is there to ask? By all means let us follow Hsien Ku's advice!"

Hsün Shou of the lower army said, "Chao T'ung and Chao K'uo are part of that crowd who will bring great blame!"[22]

Chao Shuo, commander of the lower army, said, "Luan Shu has spoken excellently! If he can put his words into effect, he is certain to become a leader in the state of Chin."

The junior chief minister of Ch'u paid a visit to the Chin army and said, "Our ruler in his youth met with a pitiful calamity and does not know how to express himself in seemly language.[23] But he has heard that when the two preceding rulers of Ch'u advanced into this present area, they did so in order to instruct the state of Cheng and settle it on its course.[24] How would he dare do anything to incur blame from Chin? We trust that you gentlemen will not linger for long in this region."

Shih Hui, the general of the Chin upper army, replied, "Long ago King P'ing commanded our former ruler, Marquis Wen, saying, 'Join with Cheng in assisting and supporting the royal house of Chou. Do not neglect the king's command!'[25] But now Cheng has failed to obey. Our ruler ordered us to question Cheng on this matter. He surely would not venture to do anything to trouble the envoys of your state! Nevertheless, we thank you for these kind words of command from your ruler."

Hsien Ku, however, regarded this as too fawning an answer, and he sent

22 Hsün Shou is referring to his earlier prediction that Hsien Ku is "certain to face great blame." See p. 89 above.

23 The "calamity" referred to is the death of his father King Mu in 614, when King Chuang came to the throne of Ch'u.

24 The preceding rulers are King Ch'eng (r. 671–626) and King Mu (r. 625–614).

25 King P'ing (r. 770–72) was the first ruler of the Eastern Chou period. Marquis Wen of Chin ruled 780–746.

Chao K'uo to go after the Ch'u envoy and give him a somewhat different reply, saying, "Our envoy did not speak correctly! Our ruler has ordered us here so we may make certain that your great nation removes all trace of itself from Cheng. He said to us, 'Do not flinch before the enemy!' And we have no intention of disobeying his orders!"

For a moment it appears as though there will be an amicable conclusion to the tense confrontation between the Chin and Ch'u forces. But then begins a series of challenges and taunts by members of both sides that continues until full-scale hostilities have been provoked.

The Ch'u ruler once more sent an envoy requesting a peaceful settlement with Chin. The men of Chin signified agreement, and a day was set for the concluding of the alliance.

Hsü Po of Ch'u was serving as carriage drive to Yüeh Po, with She Shu as right-hand attendant, and they set out to challenge the Chin army.

Hsü Po said, "I have heard that when you challenge an army, the driver drives so fast he sets the pennants streaming, swoops down on the enemy fortifications, and then returns to his own side."

"I have heard," said Yüeh Po, "that when you challenge an army, the man on the left discharges his finest arrows, then takes over the reins in place of the driver, who dismounts, straightens the horses' caparisons, adjusts their martingales, and then returns."

She Shu said, "I have heard that when you challenge an army, the man on the right dashes into the fortifications, kills one of the enemy and cuts off his ear, seizes a prisoner and then returns."

The three men then proceeded to carry out the actions that each had described and return to their places.

As they were doing so, the men of Chin set out after them, closing in on them from left and right. Yüeh Po discharged arrows at the horses on the left and at the men on the right, so that the Chin attackers could not advance. Then, when Yüeh Po had only one arrow left, a deer suddenly leaped up in front of his chariot. He shot the deer, the arrow sinking deep into its back.

Pao Kuei, one of the Chin attackers, bore down upon Yüeh Po's chariot from behind, whereupon Yüeh Po ordered She Shu to present the deer to him, saying, "Since the hunting season has not yet come around this year, I think you must be short of game. I make so bold as to present this for the table of your henchmen!"

Pao Kuei thereupon called off his attackers, saying, "The one on the left is an excellent shot and the one on the right knows how to speak. They are gentlemen!" With this he gave up the chase.

Wei Yi of Chin had earlier wanted to enter the service of the ducal family of Chin but had been unable to do so and, disgruntled over this, he now hoped to bring about a defeat for the Chin army. He therefore asked to be allowed to challenge the Ch'u army, but was refused permission. He then asked to be allowed to go as a peace envoy, and permission was granted. When he went, however, he proceeded to invite the enemy to engage in battle. Then he started back toward his own side.

P'an Tang of the Ch'u forces set out in pursuit. Wei Yi had gone as far as the swamp of Ying when he saw six deer. He shot one of the deer and, turning to look behind him, offered it to P'an Tang, saying, "Now while you're busy with military affairs, your cooks no doubt have trouble obtaining a supply of fresh fare. I venture to present this for your followers!" P'an Tang thereupon called off his attackers.

Chao Chan of Chin had earlier tried to obtain a ministerial post and failed, and moreover he was angry that Yüeh Po and the others who had come from the Ch'u side to challenge the Chin army had been allowed to escape. He therefore asked permission to incite the Ch'u forces to battle, but was refused. He then asked to be allowed to invite Ch'u to enter into an alliance, and was granted permission. He set off on his mission in company with Wei Yi.

Hsi K'o, assistant commander of the Chin upper army, said, "Now that these two malcontents have set off, we had best take precautions or we will surely suffer defeat."[26]

But Hsien Ku said, "When the men of Cheng urged us to fight, we couldn't make up our mind to do so. Then when the Ch'u men came

26 It is interesting to note that the "two malcontents" Chao Chan and Wei Yi represent two of the three great ministerial families that eventually overthrew the ruling house of Chin and divided its territory up into the three states of Wei, Chao, and Han, a move that took place shortly before 400 B.C.

seeking peace, we were unwilling to go along with that. This army can't seem to settle on a course of action! What good are a lot of precautions?"

Shih Hui, commander of the upper army, replied, "It would be well to take precautions anyway. If those two gentlemen who set off succeed in angering Ch'u, the Ch'u men will come swooping down upon us, and then our forces will be wiped out in no time. It's better to be prepared for them. If Ch'u has no hostile intent, then we can do away with the precautions and conclude an alliance. What harm will that do to amicable relations? And if Ch'u should come with hostile designs, the precautions will prevent our defeat. Even when the feudal lords come together at a meeting, they take care not to dismiss their personal bodyguards."

Hsien Ku, however, would have none of this.

Shih Hui ordered his officials Kung Shuo and Han Ch'uan to take command of seven ambush forces that were stationed in front of Mount Ao. As a result of this precaution, the upper army escaped defeat in the hostilities that ensued.

Chao Ying-ch'i of the central army meanwhile ordered his men to prepare boats ahead of time and range them along the banks of the Yellow River. As a result, when the defeat came, his forces were the first to get across the river.

P'an Tang, as mentioned earlier, went in pursuit of Wei Yi. Chao Chan for his part arrived at the Ch'u army after nightfall. He spread a mat for himself outside the gate of the army encampment and sent his followers into the camp.[27]

The Ch'u ruler had a personal force of thirty chariots, divided into left and right wings. At cockcrow the men of the right wing would mount their chariots and remain in readiness until noon, when they would go off duty. The left wing would then take over and continue until sundown, when they went off duty. Hsü Yen was carriage driver for the lead carriage of the right wing, with Yang Yu-chi as his attendant on the right. P'eng Ming was carriage driver for the left wing, with Ch'ü T'ang as his right-hand attendant.

On the day *i-mao,* King Chuang of Ch'u mounted the lead carriage of the left wing and set off in pursuit of Chao Chan. Chao Chan abandoned his chariot and dashed into a grove of trees. Ch'ü T'ang struck him down and snatched the tassets from his armor.

The men of Chin, fearful that these two officers Wei Yi and Chao Chan

27 Seating himself at the gate was no doubt a gesture designed to demonstrate his fearlessness.

would anger the Ch'u forces, moved their heavy wagons forward in an effort to provide shelter for them.

When P'an Tang, observing from a distance, saw the dust raised by the wagons, he sent a fast rider back to the Ch'u forces to report that the Chin army was advancing. The men of Ch'u for their part were fearful that their king would plunge in among the Chin forces, and so in the end they took to the field.

Sun-shu Ao, the Ch'u prime minister, said, "Let us go forward! Better to bear down on others than to let them bear down on us! The *Odes* says:

> The great war chariots, ten of them,
> press ahead to open the way.[28]

So shall we press ahead of others. And The Maxims for the Army says, 'When you press ahead of others you snatch their courage away.'[29] So shall we bear down on them!"

Thus in the end the Ch'u army advanced at full speed, its chariots racing, its foot soldiers dashing ahead, swooping down on the Chin army.

The Chin overall commander Hsün Lin-fu, hardly knowing what to do, sounded the drums and circulated an order throughout the army saying, "The first to cross the river wins a reward!" The central army and the lower army struggled with one another over the boats, until there were so many fingers in the bottoms of the boats that one could scoop them up by the handful.[30]

Most of the Chin army by this time had fled to the right in the direction of the river, but the upper army had not shifted its position. Meanwhile Ch'i, the Ch'u minister of works, led the foot soldiers of the right flank in pursuit of Chin's lower army.

The Ch'u ruler dispatched T'ang Chiao and Ts'ai Chiu-chü to deliver this message to Marquis Hui of T'ang:[31] "I, a greedy man of no virtue, have succeeded in confronting myself with a powerful enemy. This is entirely my own fault. However, if Ch'u fails to win victory, you will suffer shame as well. I therefore make bold to ask that you lend your skilled assistance in order to rescue the Ch'u forces."

At the same time he ordered P'an Tang to lead a division of forty auxiliary

28 "Lesser Odes," *Liu-yüeh*, Mao no. 177.
29 This text has been cited earlier; see "The Battle of Ch'eng-p'u," p. 56 above.
30 An example of the *Tso*'s style at its most condensed. The meaning is that the latecomers, attempting to board the boats, clung to the gunwales until those already in the boats, fearful of being capsized, chopped off their fingers.
31 T'ang was a small state that was allied with Ch'u at this time.

chariots and place them under the command of Marquis Hui of T'ang to act as a left flank of the Ch'u forces and go in pursuit of the Chin upper army.

Hsi K'o, assistant commander of the Chin upper army, said, "Shall we wait for their attack?"

Shih Hui, the commander, replied, "The Ch'u army is now at the peak of its vigor. If they make a concerted attack on us, our army is bound to be wiped out! Better to gather up our forces and quit the field. If we share disgrace with the other divisions of the army and spare the lives of our men, will that not be best?"

Using his troops to guard the rear, he accordingly carried out a retreat and avoided defeat.

The king of Ch'u caught sight of the chariots in his right wing and was about to change over and ride in them, but Ch'ü T'ang dissuaded him, saying, "You started out with these chariots in the left wing. You must stay with them to the end!"

From this time on, when the men of Ch'u rode in chariots, the left wing took precedence.

In the following example of "fair play" on the battlefield, the Ch'u pursuers hold off their attack and give instructions to one of their opponents who has encountered difficulties. Their reward for this gallantry is a stinging sarcasm.

Meanwhile, one of the chariots among the Chin forces fell into a hole and would not go forward. The men of Ch'u instructed its driver to remove the horizontal board in the front of the carriage. When this was done, the carriage moved forward a little, but the horses kept shying to the side. The men of Ch'u then instructed the driver to remove the pennant staff and place it on the crosspiece of the yoke. This done, the carriage finally got out of the hole.

The driver turned around and said, "We haven't had as much experience in running away as the men of your great country!"

[Fleeing from his Ch'u pursuers,] Chao Chan gave the two best horses from his team of four to his older brother and uncle so they could escape, while he made his own way back with the two that remained. But he encountered the enemy and, unable to proceed, abandoned his chariot and fled on foot into the woods.

Feng, a high official of Chin, came riding by in his chariot with his two sons. "Don't look back!" he said to his sons. But the boys, looking back, exclaimed, "Old Sir Chao is there behind us!"

Angrily the father ordered the boys to get down from the carriage and, pointing to a tree, said, "I will look for your bodies here!" Then he handed the mounting cord to Chao Chan so he could climb up, and escaped with him.

The next day when he looked for the bodies of his sons at the designated spot, he found the two corpses piled one on top of the other at the foot of the tree.

Hsiung Fu-chi of Ch'u took Chih-ying prisoner. Chih-ying's father Hsün Shou, an officer of the Chin lower army, set out with the men of his clan to recover his son. Wei Yi served as carriage driver, and many of the fighting men of the lower army accompanied them.

Each time Hsün Shou made ready to shoot, if he saw that the arrow was an especially good one, he set it aside in the quiver strapped to Wei Yi's back. Wei Yi remarked to him angrily, "You are more interested in saving arrows than in getting your son back! When we return home you can get all the arrows you'll ever need from the swamp of Tung!"[32]

Hsün Shou replied, "If I do not succeed in capturing the son of one of the enemy, how can I hope to get my own son back? That's the reason I don't want to waste any good arrows!"

He then shot the Ch'u official Hsiang Lao, killed him, and proceeded to load the corpse onto his carriage. He also shot the ducal son Ku-ch'en, took him prisoner, and then returned with these two prizes.

When evening came, the Ch'u army encamped at Pi. The remnants of the Chin army were unable to make camp but crossed the Yellow River during the night, the din of their crossing continuing all night long.

On the day *ping-ch'en* the Ch'u baggage wagons arrived at Pi. The Ch'u army accordingly advanced and took up a position at Heng-yung.

P'an Tang said to the king of Ch'u, "My lord, why not set up a military

32 The arrows were made from a kind of swamp willow called *p'u-liu*.

encampment and collect the bodies of the Chin dead and pile them up to make an imposing monument? I have heard that when you defeat an enemy, you must leave some mark of it for your sons and grandsons so they will not forget your act of military prowess!"

The Ch'u ruler said, "You would not understand such things! The character for *wu* or 'military' is made up of the characters for 'stop' and 'halberd.' When King Wu, the Military King, defeated the Shang ruler, he composed a hymn that went:

> We put aside shields and halberds,
> encase our bows and arrows.
> We seek illustrious virtue
> to spread among the states of Hsia—
> truly the king will guard it.[33]

And he also composed the *Wu* hymn, the last line of which says,

> Thus have you established your prowess.[34]

And the third hymn says,

> We spread the undertaking, carry it on;
> we go seeking to establish it.[35]

And the sixth says,

> He brought tranquillity to ten thousand states,
> repeated years of rich harvest.[36]

"Now the purpose of military action is to prohibit violence, put aside arms, guard the great cause of rulership, establish prowess, give peace to the people, bring harmony to the multitude, and enrich resources. Therefore, when one has accomplished these aims, he may be certain that his sons and grandsons will not forget his glorious achievements.

"But now I have caused the men of these two states Ch'u and Chin to bleach their bones upon the field, an act of violence. I have displayed my weapons in order to awe the other feudal lords, so I have not put aside arms. And since I have acted violently and not laid aside arms, how can I guard

33 "Hymns of Chou," *Shih-mai,* Mao no. 273.
34 "Hymns of Chou," *Wu,* Mao no. 285.
35 "Hymns of Chou," *Lai,* Mao no. 295. It is not clear why the text calls this the "third" hymn, unless the hymns were arranged in a different order in early texts of the *Odes* from their present arrangement.
36 "Hymns of Chou," *Huan,* Mao no. 294. All these poems praise the accomplishments of King Wu of the Chou dynasty.

the great cause? And while Chin continues to exist, how can I establish my prowess? When I have so signally gone against the desires of the people, how can the people be at peace? Since I am without virtue and instead approach the other feudal lords with force and coercion, how can I bring harmony to the multitude? And if I profit from the peril of others, relish their disorders, and seek only my own glory, how can I hope to enrich resources?

"Of these seven virtues that pertain to military action, I cannot claim a single one. What then do I have to show to my sons and grandsons? Let us build a temple to the former lords of the state, and I will simply announce to them the completion of the affair. I can claim no prowess in the use of military might!

"In ancient times when enlightened kings attacked those who had failed to show reverence, they seized their leaders and heaped up their corpses in an act of great punishment. The kind of 'imposing monument' that resulted was meant to serve as a warning to transgressors and evildoers. But now Chin is not guilty of any fault. Its people to a man have shown their utmost loyalty in dying to carry out their lord's commands. How could we think of erecting such a 'monument'?"

He proceeded to sacrifice to the Yellow River and then, erecting a temple to the former lords of the state, announced the completion of the affair and returned home.

In this campaign, the Cheng minister Shih Chih in fact invited the Ch'u army to enter the state, thinking to divide up the territory of Cheng between Ch'u and himself and set up the ducal son Yü-ch'en of Cheng as the new ruler. On the day *hsin-wei,* Cheng executed the ducal son Yü-ch'en and Shih Chih.

The gentleman remarks: What the historian Yin Yi said about "never exploiting disorder" refers to this kind of situation.[37] The *Odes* says:

> Disorder and sorrow sicken us—
> where in the end lies the blame?[38]

It lies with him who attempts to exploit disorder!

The rulers of Cheng and Hsü paid a visit to Ch'u.

37 The words of the historian Yin Yi have already been quoted, in "The Battle of Han," p. 34 above.
38 "Lesser Odes," *Ssu-yüeh,* Mao no. 204.

In the fall the Chin army returned home. The Chin commander Hsün Lin-fu asked to be put to death because of his defeat. The Chin ruler, Duke Ching, favored granting his request, but Shih Chen-tzu remonstrated with him, saying, "That will not do! At the Battle of Ch'eng-p'u the Chin army occupied the Ch'u encampment and lived off the enemy's rations for three days, and yet Duke Wen of Chin still had a worried look. Those attending him said, "If you look so worried when there is occasion for delight, would you look delighted if there were occasion for worry?' But Duke Wen replied, 'The Ch'u commander Te-ch'en is still alive, so my worries cannot cease. Even an animal, when cornered, will fight, and how much more so the minister of a state!' Later, however, when the ruler of Ch'u forced Te-ch'en to commit suicide, Duke Wen was indeed delighted, as we well know, and exclaimed, 'Now I have no more foes!'[39] It was as though Chin had won a double victory and Ch'u had been doubly defeated. Thus for two reigns the rulers of Ch'u were unable to contend for supremacy.[40]

"But now, through this defeat, Heaven is perhaps giving a grave warning to the state of Chin. If on top of that we put Hsün Lin-fu to death, this will constitute a double victory for Ch'u. And then will it not be a long while before we ourselves can again contend for supremacy?

"In serving his lord, Hsün Lin-fu in moments of advance has thought only how to demonstrate his loyalty to the fullest, and in moments of retreat has pondered how he might mend his errors. He is a true guardian of the nation's altars of the soil and grain. How could you think of putting him to death?

"This defeat of his is like an eclipse of the sun or the moon—it does no harm to their ordinary brightness!"

The Chin ruler thereupon restored Hsün Lin-fu to his position as commander.

39 See "The Battle of Ch'eng-p'u," p. 64 above.

40 The remainder of the reign of King Ch'eng (r. 671–626) and the reign of King Mu (r. 625–614). King Mu was succeeded by King Chuang (r. 613–591), the ruler of Ch'u at the time of the narrative.

The following year, 596, Hsien Ku, the impetuous assistant commander of the Chin central army whose rash crossing of the Yellow River precipitated the Battle of Pi, invited the Red Ti tribes to invade the state. For this meddlesome act of treachery and for his part in the defeat at Pi, he was put to death along with the members of his family.

DUKE HSUAN 13TH YEAR (596 B.C.)

In the autumn the Red Ti tribes attacked Chin, advancing as far as Ch'ing, invited into the state by Hsien Ku.

In the winter the men of Chin conducted an investigation to determine the responsibility for the defeat at Pi the previous year and for the clash with the Red Ti at Ch'ing. The blame was placed on Hsien Ku and he was put to death. All the members of his family were wiped out.

The gentleman remarks: The evil that comes to a person he calls down upon himself. This applies to men like Hsien Ku.

T W E N T Y

King Chuang of Ch'u Lays Siege to Sung

THE CH'U ARMIES HAD SCARCELY RETURNED FROM THEIR victory over Chin at the Battle of Pi than King Chuang of Ch'u began taking steps to bring about new hostilities. When envoys traveling from the court of one feudal state to another had to proceed through the territory of a third party, it was customary to request permission to do so from the ruler of that state. In the narrative that follows, King Chuang instructs two of his envoys to deliberately flout this custom when passing through the states of Sung and Cheng. Cheng was friendly with Ch'u at this time and could be counted on to overlook this breach of etiquette. But Sung was allied with Ch'u's rival Chin, and King Chuang no doubt hoped in this way to provoke Sung into some action that would give him an excuse for attacking it.

DUKE HSUAN 14TH YEAR (595 B.C.)

The Ch'u ruler dispatched his minister Shen Chou to go on a friendly mission to Ch'i, saying, "Do not request permission from Sung to pass through its territory." He also dispatched the ducal son P'ing of Ch'u to go on a friendly mission to Chin, telling him not to request permission from Cheng to pass through its territory.

Shen Chou knew that he was hated in Sung because of the part he had played at Meng-chu,[1] and he said, "Cheng is sensible in such matters, but Sung is deaf to reason. The envoy to Chin will suffer no harm, but I am certain to be killed!"

King Chuang said, "If they kill you, I'll attack them!"

Shen Chou thereupon entrusted his son Shen Hsi to the king's care and set off.

When Shen Chou arrived in Sung, the men of Sung detained him. Hua Yüan of Sung said, "To pass through our territory without requesting permission is to treat us like a borderland of Ch'u. If we are to be treated as a borderland of Ch'u, we are doomed! On the other hand, if we kill Ch'u's envoy, Ch'u is bound to attack us. And if it attacks us, we are likewise doomed! Doom waits us either way!" They put Shen Chou to death.

When the Ch'u ruler heard of this, he pushed back his sleeves and sprang to his feet. He had reached the raised walkway in front of the hall before his attendants could catch up with him with his shoes, he was out the main gate before his sword could be brought to him, and he had gone as far as the marketplace of P'u-hsü before his carriage arrived.[2]

In autumn, the ninth month, the Ch'u ruler surrounded the capital of Sung.

DUKE HSUAN 15TH YEAR (594 B.C.)

The men of Sung dispatched Yüeh Ying-ch'i to report this crisis to the state of Chin.

The ruler of Chin wanted to go to the rescue, but Po Tsung said, "That will not do! The men of old times had a saying, 'No matter how long the whip, it won't reach to the horse's belly.' Heaven is now bestowing favor on Ch'u, and we cannot contend against that. Powerful as Chin may be, can it contravene Heaven?

1 In 617, when the rulers of Ch'u, Cheng, and Sung met at the swamp of Meng-chu in Sung to hunt, Shen Chou, who was a member of the party, had the carriage driver of the Sung ruler flogged because of an alleged offense committed by the lord of Sung.

2 The Chinese at this time, as we have seen earlier, removed their shoes when seating themselves in the raised part of the hall. Here King Chuang is so incensed that he dashes from the hall without waiting for his attendants to bring him his shoes and sword and to summon his carriage.

"The proverb says: 'Lofty or lowly lie in the mind.' Rivers and lakes accept their share of filth, mountain groves shelter venemous creatures, the loveliest gems have their hidden flaws, and the ruler of a state must at times swallow dishonor. Such is the way of Heaven. You had best wait a while."

The Chin ruler thereupon desisted. He did, however, dispatch Hsieh Yang to go to Sung and urge the men of Sung not to surrender to Ch'u, telling them that Chin had called out all its armies and they would soon be arriving in Sung.

While Hsieh Yang was enroute to Sung, the men of Cheng took him prisoner and handed him over to Ch'u. The Ch'u ruler pressed lavish bribes on him to make him betray his mission. At first he refused, but after being urged three times he finally agreed.

He was ordered to climb up in a towered carriage and address the people of Sung. But when he did so, he proceeded to relay the message that had been entrusted to him by the ruler of Chin.

The Ch'u ruler was about to have him put to death, sending a messenger to berate him in these words: "You gave me your promise and now you have gone back on it! Why? I have not broken faith with you—it was you who betrayed me! Now hurry and take your punishment!"

Hsieh Yang replied, "I have heard that it is the duty of the ruler to issue orders properly, and the mark of good faith in a minister to carry them out properly. When good faith joins with duty in action, there is benefit to the nation. And when one calculates so as not to miss an opportunity for benefit and thus guards the altars of the soil and grain, he is a true sovereign of the people.

"Duty cannot keep faith with two rulers, and good faith cannot obey two sets of orders. Your attempt to bribe me shows you do not understand the true nature of orders. When I received my orders and set out, I was determined to fulfill them even though it meant death. How could I be bribed? I gave my promise merely so that I might carry out my orders. A minister counts it a blessing to die carrying out his orders. My lord, the ruler of Chin, has ministers who act in good faith, and I, who am one of them, have succeeded in fulfilling my mission. Though I die, what more could I ask?"

The Ch'u ruler pardoned him and sent him back to Chin.

Summer, the fifth month: the Ch'u army prepared to abandon the siege against the Sung capital.

Shen Hsi bowed his head before the horses of the king of Ch'u and said,

"My father knew he was going to his death, yet he did not dare to disobey Your Majesty's order. And now Your Majesty would betray your word!"[3]

The king did not know how to reply. But the carriage driver of the Ch'u official Shen Shu-shih said, "Set up some barracks here and call the farmers back. Then Sung is bound to come to terms."[4]

The king followed this advice.

The people of Sung grew fearful and dispatched Hua Yüan to go in secret at night to the Ch'u encampment. He succeeded in making his way to the bedside of the Ch'u commander Tzu-fan,[5] whom he roused from sleep. "My ruler has sent me to inform you of our distress," he said. "He instructs me to tell you that within the city we are reduced to eating one another's children and cracking their bones to use for fuel. Nevertheless, if you insist upon an alliance while encamped at our walls, we will never consent, though it means the annihilation of our state. Withdraw from us for a distance of thirty *li*—then we will heed whatever demands you make."[6]

Tzu-fan, frightened, agreed to these terms and reported to the king. The king withdrew a distance of thirty *li.*

Sung concluded peace with Ch'u and Hua Yüan went over to the Ch'u side to act as a hostage. The words of the alliance read: "We will not deceive you, and you will not play false with us."

3 King Chuang's promise that if harm came to Shen Chou, he would attack Sung in retaliation.

4 That is, make it clear that the Ch'u army intends to encamp in the area until the city capitulates. The Sung farmers who worked the fields surrounding the city walls had fled when the Ch'u forces appeared on the scene.

5 He was commander of the right at the Battle of Pi; see p. 89 above.

6 While enemy troops remained encamped before the city walls, the men of Sung could not pretend that they were entering upon an alliance freely and as equals. Hence their request that the enemy withdraw to a distance of thirty *li.* On this and other types of alliances in the *Tso chuan,* see W. A. C. H. Dobson, "Some Legal Instruments of Ancient China: The *Ming* and the *Meng,*" in Tse-tsung Chow, ed., *Wen-lin: Studies in the Chinese Humanities,* pp. 269–282 (Madison: University of Wisconsin Press, 1968).

T W E N T Y - O N E

An Old Man Repays a Debt of Gratitude

DUKE HSUAN 15TH YEAR (594 B.C.)

Autumn, seventh month: Duke Huan of Ch'in attacked Chin, encamping his forces at Fu-shih in Chin.

On the day *jen-wu* the Chin ruler assembled his troops at Chi. . . . By the time he reached Lo, his commander Wei K'o had defeated the Ch'in army at Fu-shih and captured Tu Hui, a man of Ch'in noted for his unusual strength.

Earlier, Wei K'o's father Wei Wu-tzu had had a favorite concubine who had borne him no children. Falling ill, he gave orders to his son, saying, "See that she is provided with a husband." When his illness grew more severe, however, he said, "See that she is put to death and buried with me!"

At length, when he died, his son Wei K'o arranged for the concubine to be married, saying, "When the illness was severe, my father's mind became deranged. I abide by the orders he gave when his mind was clear." [1]

Later, when Wei K'o engaged the Ch'in forces in battle at Fu-shih, he saw an old man tying grasses together in such a manner as to block Tu Hui's way. Tu Hui stumbled over the grasses and fell to the ground, making it possible for Wei K'o to capture him.

1 Concubines, servants, and even government officials were on occasion put to death so they could "follow" a deceased master in death. Wei K'o's action here is often cited to support the contention that a parent's commands are to be obeyed not blindly but with discretion.

That night the old man appeared to Wei K'o in a dream and said, "I am the father of the woman you gave away in marriage. You followed the orders that your late father gave when he was still in his right mind. I have done this to repay you."

T W E N T Y - T W O

The Battle of An

THE BATTLE OF AN, THE FOURTH OF THE FIVE GREAT BATTLES, began with an attack by Duke Ch'ing (r. 598–582) of Ch'i on the nearby state of Lu. In the opening passage that follows, the area of Lu attacked is referred to as "our border" because the *Tso chuan,* at least after it was arranged so as to function as a commentary on the *Spring and Autumn Annals,* the chronicle of the state of Lu, speaks as though it were written from the standpoint of Lu.

DUKE CH'ENG 2D YEAR (589 B.C.)

Second year, spring: Duke Ch'ing of Ch'i attacked our northern border and surrounded the city of Lung. Lu-p'u Chiu-k'uei, a favorite of Duke Ch'ing, led the assault on the gate and was captured by the men of Lung. The Ch'i ruler said, "Don't kill him! I will swear an alliance with you and will not enter your boundaries!"

The men of Lung refused to listen but killed the man and exposed his corpse on the city wall.

Duke Ch'ing in person beat the war drum, his fighting men scaled the walls, and in three days they had siezed the city of Lung. The Ch'i forces then continued their invasion, pushing south as far as Ch'ao-ch'iu.

Duke Mu (r. 599–589), ruler of the small nearby state of Wei, thereupon dispatches some of his officials to lead a force and invade Ch'i. They encounter the Ch'i army as it is returning from the invasion of Lu.

The Wei ruler dispatched Sun Liang-fu, Shih Chi, Ning Hsiang, and Hsiang Ch'in to invade Ch'i. Along the way they encountered the Ch'i army.

Shih Chi wanted to turn back, but Sun Liang-fu said, "That will not do! If you set out with an army to attack someone and then turn around when you meet up with the opposing army, what will you say to your ruler? If you know the expedition is hopeless, you should not start out in the first place! But now that we have already met up with the enemy, it is best to fight!"

At this point in the text there appear two character reading *hsia yu,* "In summer there was . . . ," apparently the beginning of an entry of which the remainder has dropped out of the text. It presumably paralleled the entry in the *Spring and Autumn Annals* for this year, which reads, "In summer, the fourth month, the day *ping-hsü,* Sun Liang-fu of Wei led an army and fought with the Ch'i army at Hsin-chu. The Wei army suffered a severe defeat." The *Tso chuan* narrative then continues.

Shih Chi said, "Our army has been defeated. If you do not wait a while but try to attack again, I am afraid our forces will be completely wiped out. And if you lose all your men, how will you report back to the ruler?"

No one was able to reply to these objections. Shih Chi then continued addressing Sun Liang-fu: "You are the chief minister of the state. If you were to be captured, it would be a disgrace. You take your forces and withdraw! For myself, I will stay here!"

At the same time he spread word among his men that large numbers of war chariots were on the way to relieve them. At this, the Ch'i army likewise halted and set up camp at Chü-chü in Wei.

At this time Chung-shu Yü-hsi, the commandant of Hsin-chu, came to Sun Liang-fu's rescue, and so he was able to escape. Later, the men of Wei tried to reward Chung-shu Yü-hsi by enfeoffing him with a city, but he declined. Instead he requested that he be allowed to have a set of hanging musical instruments and to use silk trappings on the girths of his horses when he appeared at court.[1] His request was granted.

Confucius, hearing of this, remarked:[2] "What a pity! Better he had been given any number of cities! Tokens and titles—these alone must not be lightly handed out. It is the duty of the ruler to see to that. Titles create trust, and trust insures the proper use of tokens. Tokens are the embodiment of ritual, ritual makes it possible to carry out righteousness, righteousness is the source of benefit, and benefit insures peace to the people. These are vital concerns of the government. If tokens and titles are lightly handed out to others, this permits such persons to participate in the government, and the government will be doomed. And the state will soon follow in its wake—there will be no way to prevent it!"

Sun Liang-fu returned from Hsin-chu but, without entering the Wei capital, proceeded directly to the state of Chin to beg for troops. Tsang Hsüan-shu, an official of the state of Lu, also went to Chin to beg for troops. Both men addressed their requests to Hsi K'o.[3]

The Chin ruler granted Hsi K'o a force of seven hundred chariots.[4] But Hsi K'o said, "That is the number used at the Battle of Ch'eng-p'u. At that time the wisdom of our former ruler Duke Wen and the alacrity of his commanders insured a victory for Chin. But I am incapable even of acting as a lackey to such commanders of former times!" He accordingly asked for eight hundred chariots, and was granted them.

Hsi K'o acted as commander of the central army, Shih Hsieh (Fan Wen-tzu) as commander of the upper army, Luan Shu as commander of the lower

1 These were privileges reserved to feudal rulers and were inappropriate to a person of Chung-shu Yü-hsi's rank. Hence the objections in the next paragraph voiced by Confucius.

2 Confucius, referred to here by his polite name Chung-ni, was born in 552 or 551 and died in 479. Hence he was not alive at the time of the events described here.

3 The Chin commander Hsi K'o has appeared earlier in the account of the Battle of Pi. See p. 86 above. As Sun Liang-fu and Tsang Hsüan-shu no doubt knew, Hsi K'o had a particular reason for hating Duke Ch'ing of Ch'i and wishing to see military action taken against him. Under Duke Hsüan 17th year (592 B.C.), the *Tso chuan* states that Chin sent Hsi K'o as an envoy to meet with Duke Ch'ing of Ch'i in the latter's capital. Duke Ch'ing stationed his mother behind a curtain so she could watch the arrival of the envoy. As Hsi K'o mounted the steps, she burst out laughing. Hsi K'o was so incensed that he swore to have vengeance on the state of Ch'i. The *Tso chuan* does not make clear why the duke's mother laughed, but the account in the *Kung-yang Commentary,* Duke Ch'eng 1st year, suggests that it was because Hsi K'o was lame. At that time Hsi K'o requested permission to launch an attack on Ch'i in order to vent his anger, but he was refused by the ruler of Chin.

4 The Chin ruler at this time was Duke Ching (r. 599–581).

army, and Han Chüeh as marshal, and with these forces they went to the rescue of the states of Lu and Wei. Tsang Hsüan-shu [who had returned to Lu] came to Chin to meet them and guide them along the way, and Chi Wen-tzu of Lu led his own troops to join them.

When they reached the territory of Wei, the marshal Han Chüeh was about to put to death one of the soldiers under his command. Hsi K'o raced to the scene, hoping to spare the man's life, but by the time he got there the man had already been executed. Hsi K'o immediately had the body circulated among the troops as a warning, and at the same time announced to his carriage driver, "I will share the blame for this!"

The Chin forces then proceeded in the wake of the Ch'i army until they reached Hsin in Wei.

The two hostile forces are now ready to confront one another: the combined armies of Chin, Lu, and Wei on the one hand, whose ruling houses all belong to the same Chi family, and the Ch'i army opposing them. Employing elaborately polite and self-deprecating language, they state their grievances and challenge one another to combat.

Sixth month, the day *jen-shen:* the Chin armies arrived at the foot of Mount Mi-chi in Ch'i.

The Ch'i ruler issued an invitation to battle, saying, "You have troubled yourself to come with your ruler's troops to my humble territory. With the few paltry forces at my command, I beg to meet with you on the morrow."

The Chin commander replied, "Lu and Wei are the brothers of Chin. They have come to us complaining that morning and evening your great nation of Ch'i vents its malice upon their humble territories. Our ruler, moved to pity, has dispatched his officers to request you to desist, cautioning us that we are not to tarry for long in your territory with our legions. We are prepared to advance, but not to retreat. You need not trouble to incite us further!"

The Ch'i ruler replied, "What your officers suggest accords with my own wishes. Had you not suggested it, I would have met with you all the same!"

A man of Ch'i named Kao Ku dashed into the ranks of the Chin army and, hurling a stone he was carrying, struck one of the enemy. He took the man captive, and mounting the man's chariot, tied the trunk of a mulberry tree to it [as a token of the feat] and paraded his captive back and forth in front of the Ch'i fortifications, saying, "You who would do valorous things —shall I sell you some of my spare valor?"

On the day *kuei-yu* the armies drew up their ranks at An in Ch'i. Ping Hsia acted as carriage driver for Duke Ch'ing, the ruler of Ch'i, with Feng Ch'ou-fu as the duke's attendant on the right. Hsieh Chang was the carriage driver for the Chin commander Hsi K'o, with Cheng Ch'iu-huan as right-hand attendant.

The Ch'i ruler said, "I will mow down these forces and wipe them out first before I have breakfast!" He galloped into the field without waiting for his horses to be decked in armor.

Hsi K'o was wounded by an arrow and the blood flowed to his shoes, but he never stopped sounding the war drum.

"I've been wounded!" he said. But his carriage driver Hsieh Chang said, "When we first entered the fray, an arrow went right through my hand and reached as far as my elbow! But I broke it off and went on driving. The left wheel is crimson with the blood, but did I dare say anything about being wounded? You must bear the pain!"

Cheng Ch'iu-huan, Hsi K'o's attendant on the right, said, "Since we first entered the field, whenever we came to a difficult spot, I have always dismounted and pushed the carriage. You wouldn't have noticed, though, being wounded."

Hsieh Chang said, "The eyes of the whole army are on our pennant and their ears listen for our drum. Advancing or retreating, the troops follow us. From this chariot one man can control the entire enterprise. Just because you are wounded, would you ruin this great undertaking for your sovereign? When you don armor and take up weapons, you should be resolved to die! While your wound has not yet killed you, you must go on!"

Then he gathered the reins into his left hand and used his right hand to help Hsi K'o wield the drumstick and sound the drum. The horses raced forward so that no one could stop them, and the troops followed after. The Ch'i army was soundly defeated and its remnants chased three times around the hill of Hua-pu-chu.

Having described the final outcome of the battle—a resounding defeat for the Ch'i army on its own home ground—the narrative now goes back to focus on events that took place on the eve of the battle or on other parts of the battlefield, including an encounter in which Duke Ch'ing of Ch'i barely escaped being taken prisoner.

Before the battle, the Chin marshal Han Chüeh dreamt that his father, Han Tzu-yü, said to him, "Tomorrow avoid standing on the left or the right!"

For this reason Han Chüeh stood in the center of his carriage and acted as driver when he pursued Duke Ch'ing of Ch'i on the battlefield.

Ping Hsia, Duke Ch'ing's carriage driver, [observing Han Chüeh's approach,] said, "Shoot the carriage driver—he is a gentleman!"

Duke Ch'ing replied, "If you say he's a gentleman, it would not be proper etiquette to shoot him!" He therefore shot the man on Han Chüeh's left, who pitched forward and fell from the carriage. Then he shot the man on the right, who fell backward into the carriage dead.

Just then Ch'i-wu Chang, a Chin officer who had lost his chariot, approached and begged Han Chüeh to take him into his own chariot. Ch'i-wu Chang, mounting the chariot, tried to stand first to the left of Han Chüeh and then to the right, but Han Chüeh elbowed him aside in both cases and instead stationed him in the rear.

Han Chüeh then bent down in order to lay out the body of his slain right-hand attendant in a more suitable posture, and while he was doing so, Feng Ch'ou-fu, Duke Ch'ing's attendant on the right, changed places with the duke.

When the duke's chariot reached the spring at the foot of Mount Hua-pu-chu, the outside horse in the team of four became entangled in a tree and the chariot came to a halt. The previous evening, when Feng Ch'ou-fu was sleeping in one of the troop wagons, a snake had crawled out from under the wagon and bitten him in the forearm, but he had concealed the wound [so as to be able to attend the duke in battle]. Because of his injury, however, he could not push the chariot free, and thus Han Chüeh caught up with them.

Han Chüeh seized the horse trappings, stationed himself in front of the horses, bowed his head twice in polite greeting, and held up a wine cup with a gift stone attached to it as an offering.

"My sovereign has dispatched his officers to plead on behalf of Lu and Wei, but has warned us not to allow our legions to stray by mistake into your territory," he said. "Your humble servant, finding himself engaged in these military actions, has unfortunately been unable to avoid doing so, for he feared that to flee from the scene altogether might bring disgrace upon both rulers. Now that I find myself in the company of your honored warriors, I make bold to offer my unworthy services, undertaking to fulfill whatever office may happen to be vacant."[5]

Feng Ch'ou-fu ordered Duke Ch'ing to get down from the carriage and go to the spring to fetch water to drink.[6] Meanwhile the Ch'i official Cheng Chou-fu appeared on the scene with one of the duke's attendant chariots, which he himself was driving with Yüan Fei as his right-hand attendant. They took the duke into their carriage, and in this way he was able to escape capture.

Han Chüeh presented his prisoner, Feng Ch'ou-fu, to the Chin commander Hsi K'o. Hsi K'o was about to have him put to death when Feng Ch'ou-fu cried, "From now on no one will be willing to endure hardship in his lord's place! Here is a man who does so, and you are going to execute him!"

Hsi K'o said, "This man thinks nothing of facing death so his lord may escape. If I execute him it will be an ill-omened act. Better to pardon him and thereby encourage others to serve their lord." He accordingly spared the man's life.

After Duke Ch'ing of Ch'i had escaped capture, he set about searching for Feng Ch'ou-fu. Three times he left his own forces and entered among the enemy troops, and each time he left the Ch'i ranks, he did his best to encourage those who held back. Then he made his way in among the Ti tribe soldiers.[7] The Ti soldiers all bared their halberds as though to attack

5 Though conducting himself with utmost courtesy, Han Chüeh in effect is announcing that he is taking Duke Ch'ing—or rather Feng Ch'ou-fu, the man whom he mistakenly believes to be Duke Ch'ing—prisoner.

6 Since Feng Ch'ou-fu is impersonating the duke, he orders the real duke to fetch water in order to divert suspicion from him and get him out of the way.

7 Soldiers of the Ti tribes who were accompanying the Chin army. As will be seen, they were apparently fearful of the Ch'i ruler and unwilling to attack him, as were the soldiers of the state of Wei.

but in fact concealed him with their shields so that he was able to pass into the ranks of the Wei army. The Wei troops likewise allowed him to escape. Eventually he made his way back to the Ch'i capital by way of Hsü Pass.

When the duke encountered the men guarding the cities along his route, he said, "Look sharp! The Ch'i army has been defeated!"

There was a woman who failed to make way for the duke. "Has the ruler escaped?" she asked.

"He has escaped," the duke replied.

"Has the leader of the crack troops escaped?"

"He has escaped."

"If the ruler and my father have escaped, that's all I ask!" she said and hurried away.

"The duke admired her sense of propriety,[8] and later inquiring who she was, found she was the wife of the supervisor of fortifications. He presented her with the city of Shih-chiao.

The Chin forces pursued the Ch'i army, entering the state by way of Ch'iu-yü and attacking the city of Ma-ching.[9]

The Ch'i ruler dispatched Pin Mei-jen to offer as gifts the steamer vessel and jade chiming stones from the states of Chi and certain territories.[10] If these gifts were not acceptable, he was to agree to Chin's request to fight it out.

Pin Fei-jen offered his gifts, but the Chin commander Hsi K'o refused them, saying, "We must have the daughter of T'ung-shu of Hsiao as our hostage, and Ch'i must make certain that all the divisions between the fields within its domain run east and west."[11]

Pin Fei-jen replied, "The daughter of T'ung-shu of Hsiao is none other than the mother of our ruler! If our two states are equals, then she ranks the same as the mother of the ruler of Chin. You have undertaken to relay commands to the other feudal lords, but if you insist that we make hostages of our mothers in order to ensure good faith in our agreements, how can

8 Because she asked first about the ruler and then about her father. Note that she does not ask about her husband.

9 Since the battle was fought at An in Ch'i, it is not clear why the text speaks here of the Chin forces "entering the state."

10 The steamer, presumably a ceremonial vessel of considerable worth, and the chiming stones had no doubt been seized by Ch'i when it overthrew the small state of Chi in 690 B.C. The territories offered were probably those taken earlier from Lu and Wei.

11 The daughter of T'ung-shu, ruler of the state of Hsiao, was the mother of Duke Ch'ing of Ch'i, the woman whose scornful laughter had so enraged Hsi K'o. Commentators opine that Chin requested the roads between the fields be made to run east and west so that Chin, situated to the west of Ch'i, could more easily invade Ch'i if it gave trouble in the future.

this possibly accord with the commands of the Chou king? In fact it is a most unfilial order!

"The *Odes* says:

> While filial sons are unslacking,
> forever shall be given you good things.[12]

But if you issue such an unfilial order as this to the other feudal lords, is that not at variance with virtue and goodness?

"When the kings of former times divided up the world and established boundaries, they considered what was right for the crops and land and proceeded in a way that would be advantageous. Therefore the *Odes* says:

> We draw boundaries, we divide,
> making field paths run south, run east.[13]

But now when you decree boundaries and divisions for the feudal lords, you say that 'the divisions between the fields must all run east and west.' This will be to the advantage of none but your war chariots, for it ignores what is right for the land. Is it not, in fact, at variance with the commands of the former kings?

"To controvert the former kings is to act unrighteously, and if you do that, how can you serve as leader of alliances?[14] It would appear that in fact Chin lacks the qualifications for that role!

"When the four kings of former times ruled, they implanted virtue and fulfilled the shared desires of the empire.[15] When the five hegemons held sway, they were diligent and worked to win over the other feudal lords, encouraging them to obey the king's commands.[16] But you seem to believe that you can unite the feudal lords behind you by seeking to satisfy boundless desires.

"The *Odes* says:

12 "Greater Odes," *Chi tsui,* Mao no. 247.

13 "Lesser Odes," *Hsin-nan-shan,* Mao no. 210.

14 *Meng-chu* or "alliance leader," the leader or most powerful state among a group of feudal lords entering into an alliance. The ruler's name appears first among the signers and he takes the lead in punishing violaters of the alliance. Legge translates the term as "lord of covenants," but this strikes me as somewhat too Biblical sounding.

15 "Four kings" is not a common term in early Chinese texts, but Tu Yü identifies them as Yü, the founder of the Hsia dynasty; T'ang, the founder of the Shang; and Wen and Wu, the founders of the Chou.

16 The term "five hegemons" is troublesome here, since the usual lists of the feudal leaders who were numbered among the "five hegemons" includes persons who lived after the time dealt with in this passage. In an attempt to get around this difficulty, Tu Yü cites an alternative list of "five hegemons" that appears to date from Han times and consists of K'un-wu of the Hsia dynasty, Ta-p'eng and Shih-wei of the Shang, and Duke Huan of Ch'i and Duke Wen of Chin of the Spring and Autumn period. The first three are very hazy figures and may be the names of feudal states rather than of individuals.

> Conducting government in a mild and gentle manner,
> a hundred blessings gathering round.[17]

But you in truth are not mild and gentle, you cast away the hundred blessings, though you harm only yourself and not the other feudal lords!

"If, despite all this, you will not give ear to our request, our ruler has ordered us to relay these words: 'You have troubled yourself to come with your ruler's troops to my humble territory, and with the few paltry forces at my command, I undertook to "entertain" your followers. But my forces, quailing before your ruler's might, suffered a crushing defeat. Perhaps, however, you will be kind enough to take thought for the fortunes of this land of Ch'i and will spare our altars of the soil and grain, allowing us to carry on the old ties of friendship that bound us in the past. If so, then our only thought will be to offer you these insignificant articles that belonged to our former rulers and these lands and territories, not daring to begrudge them.

"But if you will not heed our request, then we beg permission to gather up the scattered ashes of our army, turn our backs to the city wall, and meet with you one more time. If our humble city should prove lucky in battle, we will still abide by your wishes, to say nothing of if we should prove unlucky. How would we dare do otherwise than obey?"

Lu and Wei cautioned Hsi K'o to heed these words, saying, "The ruler of Ch'i hates us! The men he has lost in this battle are all close kin or intimates. If you do not agree to his terms, he is bound to look on us with severe enmity!

"And you—what more can you hope for? You will gain the treasures of the nation, and we will recover our territory. If we escape from our present difficulties, that will be glory enough! Remember that the fate of both Ch'i and Chin rests in the hands of Heaven. It is not Chin alone that enjoys favor from above!"

Hsi K'o replied to Ch'i's proposal by giving his consent. "We, the officers of Chin, led our forces here so that we might plead on behalf of Lu and Wei," he said. "If now we may report back to our ruler with this proposal from your sovereign, we would be greatly obliged to him. We are prepared to abide by your command in all things."

The Lu official Ch'i Cheng then led his forces back to the capital of Lu to escort Duke Ch'eng of Lu to the peace proceedings.

In the seventh month the Chin army and the representative of Ch'i, Pin

17 "Hymns of Shang," *Ch'ang fa,* Mao no. 304.

Fei-jen, concluded an alliance at Yüan-lou. The alliance stipulated that Ch'i should return to Lu the fields in Wen-yang that belonged to Lu.

Duke Ch'eng of Lu met with the Chin amy at Shang-ming. He presented to each of the three Chin commanders a ceremonial carriage and robes and accoutrements appropriate to an official of the three highest grades. In addition the marshal, the minister of works, the leader of chariots, the commander of scouts, and the junior officers of the Chin army each received a set of robes appropriate to a lesser official.

When the Chin army returned home, the commander Shih Hsieh entered the capital after the others. His father Shih Hui said, "Surely you knew how anxiously I was waiting for your return, didn't you!"

Shih Hsieh replied, "The army had won victory and the people of the state were greeting it with joy. If I had entered ahead of the rest, I would necessarily have cut a very conspicuous figure. It would have looked as though I were trying to steal renown from the other commanders. Therefore I did not dare go first."

His father said, "Now I know you will come to no harm." [18]

When the commander Hsi K'o had an interview with Duke Ching of Chin, the duke said, "Your efforts won the day!"

But Hsi K'o replied, "Rather it was Your Lordship's instructions, and the efforts of my colleagues. What part did my own efforts play in it?"

When Shih Hsieh appeared before the duke, the latter thanked him for his troubles and spoke in the same way as he had to Hsi K'o.

Shih Hsieh replied, "It was all due to the commands issued by Hsün Keng and the execution of them by Hsi K'o.[19] What part did my efforts play in it?"

When Luan Shu appeared for an interview, the duke spoke to him in the same way he had to the others.

Luan Shu replied, "It was due to Shih Hsieh's direction and the fact that our officers followed their orders. What part did my efforts play in it?"

18 Because Shih Hsieh has the proper attitude of humility.

19 Hsün Keng, son of Hsün Lin-fu, was commander of the Chin upper army but did not take actual part in the present battle.

T W E N T Y - T H R E E

The Death of Duke Ching of Chin

DUKE CHING OF CHIN, A GRANDSON OF THE ILLUSTRIOUS Ch'ung-erh or Duke Wen of Chin, headed the state from 599 until his death in 581. During this time Chin won a noteworthy victory over the state of Ch'i, as we have seen in the account of the Battle of An. But, as in the reigns of Duke Ching's two predecessors, awesome power continued to be wielded by members of the Chao family, relatives of Ch'ung-erh's faithful follower Chao Ts'ui, and in fact Duke Ching came to power because one of the family, Chao Ch'uan, murdered the previous ruler, Duke Ling, in 600, as we have seen on p. 78 above. The most memorable thing about Duke Ching, an otherwise somewhat colorless figure, is perhaps his macabre death, which is described in the passage below.

DUKE CH'ENG 10TH YEAR (581 B.C.)

Duke Ching dreamt that he saw a huge ogre with disheveled hair that hung down to the ground, beating his chest and leaping around, saying, "You killed my grandsons, an evil deed![1] God has promised me revenge!" The ogre broke down the main gate of the palace, and then the door to the inner apartments, and came in. The duke fled in terror to his chamber, but the

1 In 583 Duke Ching put to death the high officials Chao T'ung and his brother Chao K'uo on charges that they were plotting rebellion. The charges, which were probably slanderous, were brought by a woman who had had an adulterous affair with their youngest brother Chao Ying-ch'i, who had been banished from the state. All three brothers were sons of Chao Ts'ui by Duke Wen's daughter; see p. 48 above. At this point, the Chao family was very nearly wiped out. According to the traditional interpretation of this passage, as represented in Tu Yü's commentary, the ogre was the spirit of one of the Chao family ancestors who was seeking revenge for the death of the Chao brothers, though it should be noted that the *Tso* narrative itself does not state this.

ogre broke down that door as well. At that moment the duke awoke and sent for the shaman of Mulberry Field. The shaman described the duke's dream just as it had been.

"What will become of me?" asked the duke.

"You will not live to eat the new grain!" replied the shaman.

The duke fell gravely ill and sent for a doctor from the state of Ch'in. The ruler of Ch'in dispatched a physician named Huan to treat the duke. Before the physician arrived, the duke dreamt that his illness appeared to him in the form of two little boys. One boy said, "He is a skilled physician and I am afraid he will do us injury. Where can we flee?" The other replied, "If we reside in the region above the diaphram and below the heart, what can he do to us?"

When the physician arrived, he told the duke, "I can do nothing for your illness. It is situated above the diaphram and below the heart, where treatment cannot affect it, acupuncture will not penetrate, and medicine will not reach. There is nothing I can do."

"You are a good doctor," said the duke and, entertaining him with all courtesy, he sent him back home.

In the sixth month, the day *ping-wu,* the duke decided he wanted to taste the new grain and ordered the steward of his private domain to present some. When his butler had prepared it, he summoned the shaman of Mulberry Field and, pointing out the error of his prophecy, had him executed. Then he started to eat the grain, but his stomach swelled up and, hurrying to the privy, he fell down the hole and died.

One of the duke's servants had dreamt in the early morning hours that he was carrying the duke on his back up to Heaven, and consequently he was delegated that day to bear the duke's body on his back out of the privy, after which he was executed so that he could attend the duke in death.

T W E N T Y - F O U R

Lü Hsiang Severs Relations with Ch'in

LATE IN 580, CH'IN AND CHIN AGREED TO MEET AT LING-HU in Chin to conclude an alliance of friendship. But although the Chin ruler Duke Li (r. 580–573), who had just come to power, arrived at the appointed spot, his counterpart, Duke Huan (r. 603–577) of Ch'in, changed his mind and declined to cross the Yellow River, sending a delegate to Ling-hu in his place. Despite this fact, an alliance of sorts was concluded, but almost immediately violated by Ch'in. In 578, less than two years later, Duke Li of Chin sent his high official Lü Hsiang, a son of Wei Ch'i, to rebuke Ch'in for its violation of the pact and break off relations. The *Tso chuan* narrative implies that Lü Hsiang's speech on the occasion was delivered orally, though if it was, he almost certainly read from a prepared text, since the speech is so lengthy and complex in content. It is considered one of the literary high points of the *Tso chuan* and, like many of the formal speeches in the *Tso,* makes heavy use of parallelism and other rhetorical devices. To bolster its argument, it cites historical events that are mentioned elsewhere in the *Tso,* as will be pointed out in the notes, but its interpretation of such events is frequently distorted in order to favor Chin's position.

DUKE CH'ENG 13TH YEAR (578 B.C.)

Summer, fourth month, the day *mou-wu:* The ruler of Chin dispatched Lü Hsiang to sever relations with the state of Ch'in by speaking thus:

"In past times, when our Duke Hsien and your Duke Mu maintained friendly relations, they joined efforts and shared a single mind, confirming their agreement with oaths of alliance and strengthening it with marriage bonds.[1]

"Later, when Heaven inflicted misfortune on the state of Chin, the future Duke Wen made his way to Ch'i, and the future Duke Hui made his way to Ch'in. But when further misfortune fell and Duke Hsien passed away, Duke Mu did not forget the old ties of gratitude, and instead made it possible for Duke Hui to become ruler of Chin and to carry on the sacrifices of the state. Duke Hui was unable to display any appreciable merit, however, and brought on the Battle of Han.[2] But Ch'in repented of the action it took at that time and opened the way for our Duke Wen to achieve success. This was made possible by Duke Mu.

"Duke Wen in person buckled on armor and headpiece, tramped the mountains, marched by the rivers, crossed the narrow and perilous places, chastising the feudal lords of the east, forcing the descendants of Yü, Hsia, Shang, and Chou to pay respects to the court of Ch'in.[3] In this way he repaid the old debt of gratitude he owed to Duke Mu.

"Later, when the men of Cheng violated your lord's borderlands, our Duke Wen led the feudal lords to join with Ch'in in besieging Cheng.[4] But the high officials of Ch'in, without consulting our ruler's wishes, selfishly concluded an alliance with Cheng. The other feudal lords were outraged by this action and wanted to attack Ch'in at any cost.[5] But Duke Wen, fearful and apprehensive, succeeded in appeasing them. Thus the fact that the Ch'in armies were able to return home unscathed was in truth due to the great assistance which we lent to our neighbor to the west!

"When misfortune fell and Duke Wen passed away, Duke Mu offered no condolences, but contemptuously treated our ruler like one long dead. He likewise belittled our Duke Hsiang because of his youth, trespassing upon our territory of Yao, betraying and shattering the bonds of friendship between our two states and attacking our fortified towns. He devastated and laid waste the city of Pi in Hua, scattering and driving away our own brothers, bringing strife and chaos to our allies and threatening the overturn of our own land.[6]

1 Duke Mu's wife was a daughter of Duke Hsien of Chin.

2 When the Ch'in armies invaded Chin and took Duke Hui prisoner. See pp. 30–37 above.

3 Yü refers to Emperor Shun, whose rule preceded that of the Hsia dynasty.

4 Chin and Ch'in did in fact besiege the Cheng capital in 630, though not, it seems, because of any previous violation of Ch'in's borders by Cheng, but because of the rude treatment Cheng earlier accorded Duke Wen of Chin. See "Duke Wen of Chin's Attack on Cheng," p. 65 above.

5 The alliance with Cheng was actually concluded by Duke Mu of Ch'in, but the speaker for the sake of diplomacy imputes the action to Ch'in's officials. Clearly Chin disapproved of the alliance, but there is no evidence to suggest that the other feudal leaders did so.

6 The small state of Hua, with its capital at Pi, was an ally of Chin, and its rulers belonged to the

"Duke Hsiang had not forgotten the old accomplishments performed by your ruler, yet he feared the destruction of his own altars of the soil and grain, and so he took part in the Battle of Yao. But still he hoped that Duke Mu would forgive his offenses. Duke Mu, however, refused to heed his words and instead began plotting against us with the state of Ch'u. But Heaven was moved by our sincerity of heart, and King Ch'eng's life was brought to an end.[7] Thus Duke Mu was unable to carry out the designs he had nurtured against us.

"Then Duke Mu of Ch'in and Duke Hsiang of Chin passed away and were replaced by Duke K'ang and Duke Ling.[8] Duke K'ang was of our lineage, yet he sought to destroy and cut off our ducal family and to overturn our altars of the soil and grain, leading a band of noxious pests against us and bringing turmoil to our borders. As a result, we were obliged to engage in the campaign at Ling-hu.[9] But Duke K'ang did not reform his ways, instead invading our territory at Ho-chü, attacking our Su River area, plundering our Wang-kuan, laying waste our Chi-ma. So we had to do battle at Ho-ch'ü.[10] Thus it was Duke K'ang who disrupted the friendly relations that had existed between our two states and blocked the road that runs east from Ch'in to Chin

"When Your Lordship succeeded to power, our ruler Duke Ching stretched his neck and gazed west in anticipation, saying, 'Perhaps he will look kindly on us!' But Your Lordship would not favor our call for an alliance. Instead you took advantage of our troubles with the Ti people to invade our river districts, set fire to our cities of Chi and Kao, disrupt and lay waste our agricultural enterprises, and wreak havoc on our border territories. So we were obliged to mass our troops at Fu-shih.[11]

"Then Your Lordship, repenting of these prolonged misfortunes and hoping to elicit blessings from the former rulers Duke Hsien and Duke Mu,

---

same clan as the rulers of Chin. On Ch'in's destruction of Hua at the time of the Battle of Yao, see p. 70 above.

7 King Ch'eng (r. 671–626) of Ch'u was murdered by his own heir, who succeeded him as King Mu.

8 Both rulers died in 621, Duke Mu to be succeeded by his son Duke K'ang (r. 620–609), Duke Hsiang by his son Duke Ling (r. 620–607). Duke K'ang was Duke Mu's son by the daughter of Duke Hsien of Chin.

9 When Duke Hsiang of Chin died in 621, one group of officials in Chin favored passing over his young son, the future Duke Ling, and setting up the ducal son Yung, a son of Duke Wen who was residing in Ch'in. Ch'in dispatched armed forces to escort Yung to Chin, and these were attacked by forces supporting Duke Ling at Ling-hu in Chin in 620 and defeated.

10 An indecisive clash that took place between the Ch'in and Chin armies in 615.

11 In 594 the Chin forces attacked the Lu, a branch of the non-Chinese people known as the Red Ti, whose ruler was married to an elder sister of Duke Ching of Chin, and wiped them out. Shortly after, Duke Huan of Ch'in invaded Chin but was defeated by the Chin forces at Fu-shih.

sent Po-chü[12] to deliver your commands to our Duke Ching, saying, 'Let us, you and I, set aside our dislikes and share the same likings, renewing old ties of gratitude in memory of the accomplishment of former ties.'

"Before any oaths could be concluded, however, Duke Ching passed away. And so our present ruler went to meet with you at Ling-hu. But Your Lordship failed to act properly and turned your back on the oaths of alliance that were concluded there.

"The White Ti occupy the same province as Your Lordship. They are enemies to you, though to us they are relatives by marriage.[13] Yet Your Lordship came to us with a command, saying, 'You and I together will attack the Ti!' Our ruler did not dare to consider the marriage ties that bind him to the Ti but, fearful of Your Lordship's might, received the command from your officials. But then you played us false, going to the Ti and saying, 'Chin intends to attack you!' The Ti, while acknowledging the information, in their anger sent a report of the matter to us.

"The men of Ch'u, disgusted at the way you favor now one party and then another, likewise came and reported to us, saying, 'Ch'in, having turned its back on the alliance concluded at Ling-hu, comes seeking an alliance with us. Calling upon God on high in the bright heavens, on the three former dukes of Ch'in and the three former kings of Ch'u to be its witnesses,[14] it declares that although it maintains relations with Chin, it does so only with a view to the profits it can gain thereby. I, the ruler of Ch'u, am repelled by such want of gratitude and therefore reveal these things to you so that Ch'in may be punished for its insincerity!'

"When the other feudal leaders learned of all this, they were pained in heart, troubled in mind, and indicated that they would rally around and side with me, the ruler of Chin.[15] I will lead them to a meeting so that we may hear your commands, hopeful always that we may establish friendly ties. If Your Lordship will deign to heed the other feudal lords and to take pity upon me and favor me with an alliance, that will fulfill my wishes. If you indicate your willingness to do so, I will then take steps to placate the

12 A son of Duke Huan of Ch'in.

13 The tribes called the White Ti lived in the area known in ancient times as Yung Province, roughly the present-day provinces of Shensi and Kansu where the state of Ch'in was located. Though, as seen in note 11 above, there were marriage ties between the Chin ducal family and the Red Ti, there is no evidence of such ties between Chin and the White Ti and it is uncertain just what Lü Hsiang is alluding to here. The terms White Ti and Red Ti are said to derive from the color of the clothing worn by members of the respective tribes.

14 Dukes Mu, K'ang, and Kung of Ch'in and kings Ch'eng, Mu, and Chuang of Ch'u.

15 In this closing section of the oration, Duke Li speaks in his own voice rather than through the voice of his envoy Lü Hsiang.

other feudal lords and we will withdraw, for surely we would never venture to incite disturbance! But if Your Lordship does not grant us this great favor, then inept person that I am, I am afraid I cannot persuade the other feudal lords to withdraw of their own accord!

"I have ventured to lay this matter fully before the authorities, hoping they will carefully consider where their best interests lie."

Duke Huan of Ch'in, having already concluded the alliance of Ling-hu with Duke Li of Chin, had then proceeded to make overtures to the Ti people and the state of Ch'u, hoping to lead their forces in an attack upon Chin. That is why the other feudal lords sided with Chin in this fashion.

Luan Shu led the Chin central army, with Hsün Keng as his assistant. Shih Hsieh commanded the upper army, with Hsi Ch'i to assist him, and Han Chüeh led the lower army, with Hsün Ying assisting. Chao Chan acted as commander of the new army, with Hsi Chih as his assistant.[16] Hsi Yi was the carriage driver for the Chin ruler, with Luan Chen as the duke's attendant on the right.

The Lu official Meng Hsien-tzu said, "The Chin commanders and the carriage men are in harmony—this army is certain to achieve great things!"

In the fifth month, the day *ting-hai,* the Chin army led the armies of the other feudal lords to a battle with the Ch'in army at Ma-sui in Ch'in. The Ch'in army was severely defeated.

16 The new army, made up of three parts like the older army, was created in 588 to provide command posts for leaders who had distinguished themselves in the Battle of An in the previous year.

TWENTY-FIVE

The Battle of Yen-ling

THE BATTLE OF YEN-LING, THE LAST OF THE *TSO CHUAN'S* Five Great Battles, was brought about when the small, centrally located state of Cheng, formerly allied with Chin to the north of it, decided to transfer its alliance to the state of Ch'u in the south. This precipitated a clash between the youthful Duke Li (r. 580–573) of Chin and King Kung (r. 590–560) of Ch'u that took place in 575 at Yen-ling in Cheng. The description of the encounter, though choppy and made up largely of brief vignettes that shift back and forth in locale from one side of the conflict to the other, is among the most vivid passages of narrative in the *Tso chuan*. The encounter resulted in a disastrous defeat for Ch'u.

DUKE CH'ENG 16TH YEAR (575 B.C.)

Sixteenth year, spring: the ruler of Ch'u dispatched the ducal son Ch'eng from Wu-ch'eng to offer the state of Cheng the fields south of the Ju River if it would ally itself with Ch'u. Cheng thereupon turned against Chin, its former ally, and sent Tzu-ssu to conclude an alliance with the Ch'u ruler at Wu-ch'eng.

The Chin ruler prepared to attack Cheng. His military commander Shih Hsieh said, "If we try to satisfy our wishes now, and all the other feudal leaders turn against us, then Chin may in the end achieve satisfaction.[1] But

1 The utterance is deliberately paradoxical. Shih Hsieh means that if Duke Li and the other leaders of Chin face massive opposition from the other states, they may wake to the folly of their ways and mend them, which will lead to an eventual improvement in Chin's situation. But if only Cheng opposes the state, they will never realize their errors. Shih Hsieh's utterance sounds a note of irony that pervades the whole narrative that follows by predicting that Chin can only profit in the long run if it suffers defeat.

if Cheng is the only state that turns against us, then grief will not be long in coming to Chin!" But the military commander Luan Shu said, "I cannot bear to see Chin loose its allies among the feudal lords in my time. We must attack Cheng!"

The Chin ruler thereupon mobilized his armies. Luan Shu acted as commander of the central army, with Shih Hsieh assisting him. Hsi Ch'i commanded the upper army, with Hsün Yen to assist him. Han Chüeh commanded the lower army, Hsi Chih was assistant commander of the new army, while Hsün Ying remained behind to guard the state. Hsi Ch'ou went first to the state of Wei and then to Ch'i, in both places requesting troops to assist Chin. Luan Yen came to Lu requesting troops.[2] The Lu official Meng Hsien-tzu said, "Chin will be victorious!"[3] On the day *mou-yin* the Chin forces set out.

When the men of Cheng received word of the Chin army, they sent envoys to inform Ch'u. The Cheng official Yao Kou-erh was among those who went. The Ch'u ruler set out to relieve Cheng, assigning his marshal Tzu-fan to lead the central army, the prime minister Tzu-ch'ung to lead the left wing, and the minister of the right, the ducal son Jen-fu, to lead the right wing.

When they passed the city of Shen, Tzu-fan entered the city and called on Shen-shu Shih.[4] "What do you think of our army?" he asked.

Shen-shu Shih replied, "Virtue, penalties, circumspection, righteousness, propriety, good faith—these are the implements of battle. Virtue serves to impart blessing, penalties to correct error, circumspection to deal properly with the gods, righteousness to bring about what is profitable, propriety to assure timeliness, and good faith to protect one's possessions. [When these are correctly applied,] the people will enjoy a plentiful livelihood and virtue will be properly observed, enterprises will be profitable and religious observances well regulated, undertakings will be timely and will result in material gain. Superiors and inferiors will be harmonious and amicable, affairs will go forward without clash. No demands will be unfilled, and each person will understand the standards to be observed:

"Therefore the *Odes* says:

> You have established our multitudes of people;
> none who do not observe your standards.[5]

2 On the reason for the use of the verb "came" here, see "The Battle of An," p. 109.

3 Tu Yü opines that Meng Hsien-tzu based his prediction on the fact that the Chin envoy Luan Yen behaved in a ritually correct manner.

4 A high official of Ch'u noted for his wise counsel, at this time living in retirement at his fief in Shen.

5 "Hymns of Chou," *Ssu-wen*, Mao no. 275. The "you" of the poem is Hou Chi, ancestor of the Chou

When this is done, the gods send down good fortune and the seasons pass without hurt or calamity. The people's livelihood is rich and abundant, they are harmonious and compliant in their obedience. There are none who do not exhaust their strength in carrying out the commands of superiors, risking death to mend their shortcomings. This is the source from which comes victory in battle.

"But now the state of Ch'u casts aside its own people at home and abroad breaks with its allies. It profanes the sacred bonds of alliance and betrays its solemnly given word. Its undertakings are unseasonable and it exhausts its people in selfish pursuits. The people have lost faith in their rulers, for whether they advance or retire, they are held guilty. When men fear what lies behind, who will be willing to risk death? You had better look to your safety! I will not be seeing you again!"

Yao Kou-erh returned to Cheng ahead of the Ch'u forces. Tzu-ssu asked him about the Ch'u army, and he replied, "They advance too rapidly, and when they pass through a narrow place, they do not maintain proper order! Going too fast gives one no time to plan, and failing to maintain order destroys the ranks. If you make no plans and let your ranks get out of order, how can you fight a battle? I'm afraid Ch'u will be no use to us!"

In the fifth month the Chin army crossed the Yellow River. When word came that the Ch'u forces were about to appear on the scene, the Chin commander Shih Hsieh wanted to turn back. "If we make as though we are fleeing from the Ch'u army, we can perhaps relieve some of the ills of the state.[6] The task of uniting the feudal leaders is not something we are capable of accomplishing, and we should leave it to those who are! If our own officials can learn to cooperate in an amicable manner in serving their ruler, that will be enough!" he said.

But the overall commander Luan Shu said, "That will not do!"

In the sixth month the Chin and Ch'u forces met at Yen-ling in Cheng. Shih Hsieh wished to avoid a battle, but Hsi Chih said, "At the Battle of Han, Duke Hui's forces made a poor showing. In the campaign at Chi, Hsien Chen was unable to report back on the success of his mission. And in the military action at Pi, Hsün Lin-fu could not engage a second time with

royal family. The translation is intended to represent the way the compilers of the *Tso chuan* probably understood the lines of the poem and not necessarily the original meaning.

6 As in the utterance above, Shih Hsieh hopes that Duke Li and the other leaders of Chin will be shocked into a reconsideration of their policies and the state saved from further trouble and misrule.

the enemy.[7] These all reflect disgrace on Chin! You yourself are aware of what befell these earlier rulers. If now we run away from Ch'u, we will be adding to the disgrace!"

But Shih Hsieh said, "When the former rulers of Chin engaged in such frequent battles, they had their reasons. At that time Ch'in, the Ti people, Ch'i, and Ch'u were all powerful opponents. If the Chin rulers had not put forth their utmost efforts, their sons and grandsons would have been left in a weak position. But now three of these powerful opponents have been tamed. The sole enemy left to us is Ch'u. Only a sage ruler can free himself from troubles both abroad and at home. And since we are not sages, if we have peace abroad, we are certain to suffer from internal ills. Would it not be better to let Ch'u alone so it may continue to inspire us with fear on the foreign front?"

On the day *chia-wu,* the last day of the month, the Ch'u forces at dawn pressed forward toward the Chin army and began forming their ranks. The officers of the Chin army were greatly alarmed, but Shih Hsieh's son Fan Kai dashed forward and said, "Fill in the wells, smash the fireplaces, form the ranks here in the encampment and make way for the heads of the columns to advance![8] Heaven will decide whether the day goes to Chin or Ch'u—what have we to fear?"

But his father Shih Hsieh seized a halberd and chased after him, saying, "The life and death of the nation hangs upon Heaven! What does a boy like you know about this?"

Luan Shu said, "The Ch'u forces are in a frivolous and halfhearted mood. If we strengthen our fortifications and wait three days, they are sure to withdraw. When they do, we can swoop down on them and be certain of gaining victory!"

Hsi Chih said, "Ch'u has six flaws that we must not fail to exploit. The two great ministers who command it are at loggerheads.[9] The king's personal troops have been in the field a long time. The Cheng ranks are in disorder. The Man troops are not drawn up in proper ranks.[10] The army

7 At the Battle of Han the forces of Duke Hui of Chin not only did not fare well, but the duke, as we have seen in "The Battle of Han," p. 33 above, was actually taken prisoner by his Ch'in opponents. In the clash between the Ti tribes and the Chin forces at Chi in 627, the Chin commander Hsien Chen plunged in among the enemy and was killed. The Ti, who were defeated in the encounter, later handed back his head. On the defeat of the Chin forces under Hsün Lin-fu by the Ch'u army at Pi, see p. 96 above.

8 The Ch'u forces had pressed so closely that the Chin army had no room to move forward, so Fan Kai is urging that it form its ranks on the site of the encampment.

9 Tzu-fan and Tzu-ch'ung.

10 Reinforcements from the Man tribes living in the area around Ch'u.

does not scruple to draw up its ranks on the last day of the month.[11] Drawn up in ranks, the men are noisy enough, and now that they press forward for the engagement, they are even noisier. Every man looks behind him and none have a heart to fight. Troops that have been in the field a long time are likely to make a poor showing. And in addition they violate the prohibitions of Heaven by fighting on the last day of the month. We are certain to overpower them!"

The ruler of Ch'u climbed up in a towered carriage and gazed far off at the Chin army. Tzu-ch'ung ordered the minister Po Chou-li to attend the king and stand behind him.[12]

"Why are those people rushing around to left and right?" asked the king.

"They are calling together the army officers."

"They're all gathering in the center of the camp!"

"They are plotting their strategy."

"They're putting up a tent!"

"So they may respectfully consult the former rulers by divination with the tortoiseshell."

"They're taking down the tent!"

"They are going to issue the orders."

"Such commotion, and all that dust rising!"

"They are filling in their wells and smashing their fireplaces in preparation for the advance."

"They're all mounting their carriages! Now those on the left and right are holding their weapons and dismounting!"

"They will take the oath of battle."

"Will they fight now?"

"I cannot tell yet."

"They've mounted, but now those on the left and right are getting down again!"

"The prayer of battle."

Thus Po Chou-li explained the movements of the duke of Chin's troops to the king of Ch'u.

Meanwhile, Miao Fen-huang was at the side of Duke Li of Chin, explaining to him the troops of the king of Ch'u.[13] The duke's advisors all said, "He

11 The last day of the month, when the yin force "runs out," was considered inauspicious for military actions.

12 Po Chou-li was an official of Chin who had deserted to the Ch'u side the previous year because his father had been put to death. Note the highly dramatic form of the passage that follows.

13 Miao Fen-huang was a man of Ch'u who had fled to Chin in 605.

has the best men in the state in his service![14] And his troops are numerous! We can never match them!"

But Miao Fen-huang said to the Chin ruler, "Ch'u's best fighters are all among the king's personal troops in the central army. If you will just divide up your best fighters and have them attack his left and right wings, and when that is done, concentrate all your three armies on an attack on the king's troops, the king is certain to suffer a severe defeat."

The Chin ruler divined by the milfoil stalks regarding this plan. The historian performing the divination announced, "The reply is auspicious. The hexagram obtained is *fu* or 'return.' 'A southern country cringes. One shoots its prime king, hits him in the eye.'[15] If the country cringes and the king is wounded, how can that be anything but defeat?" The duke of Chin decided to follow the advice.

There was a swamp in front of the Chin encampment and the carriages therefore all went to the left or right to avoid it. Pu Yi drove the carriage for Duke Li of Chin, with Luan Chen acting as the duke's attendant on the right. P'eng Ming was the carriage driver for King Kung of Ch'u, with P'an Tang as right-hand attendant. Shih Shou was driver for Duke Ch'eng of Cheng with T'ang Kou the right-hand attendant.

The Chin commanders Luan Shu and Shih Hsieh led the men under them and flanked the duke's troops on either side. The duke's carriage sank into the swamp, whereupon Luan Shu was about to take the duke into his own carriage. But Luan Chen, Luan Shu's son and the duke's right-hand attendant, said, "Go on your way, Shu! You have your own great task to do for the state—how can you presume to take on this as well? To take on someone else's task is infringement, to neglect your own task is dereliction, and to abandon your post is criminal! That makes three offenses, and you must not be guilty of them!"[16] Then he dragged the duke of Chin's carriage up out of the swamp.

14 Or, according to the older interpretation put forward by Tu Yü, "He has one of our best men (i.e., Po Chou-li) to advise him!"

15 These are the words of the prognostication. Though *fu* is the twenty-fourth hexagram in the *Book of Changes*, no such words are found in the present text of that work.

16 Ordinarily a son would never use his father's personal name or speak to him in such a manner. That Luan Chen does so here is explained by the fact that both father and son are in the presence of their sovereign, Duke Li of Chin.

At this point the narrative backtracks slightly to the day *kuei-ssu,* the twenty-eighth day of the sixth month, the day before the day *chia-wu,* when the battle took place, in order to record two prophetic incidents that took place on the eve of the battle.

On the day *kuei-ssu,* Tang, the son of P'an Wang, and Yang Yu-chi, both of them men of Ch'u, were piling up suits of armor to see how many they could shoot their arrows through. They succeeded in penetrating seven plates of armor. They showed the results to the king of Ch'u, saying, "As long as Your Majesty has two subjects like us, why worry about the battle?"

But the king replied angrily, "You're a disgrace to the nation! Tomorrow morning your skill in the art of archery will prove to be the death of you!" [17]

Meanwhile, Wei Ch'i of Chin dreamt that he shot at the moon and hit it, but when he turned to go, he sank into a pool of mire. Consulting a diviner, he was told, "The sun symbolizes the Chou royal surname Chi. The moon symbolizes the other surnames. So this must refer to the king of Ch'u. You shot and hit the moon, but when you turned to go, you sank into the mire. This means you will surely die."

When the day of battle came, Wei Ch'i did in fact shoot King Kung and hit him in the eye. The king summoned Yang Yu-chi, handed him two arrows, and ordered him to shoot at Wei Ch'i. Yang Yu-chi hit Wei Ch'i in the neck, and the latter fell over dead on his bow case. Then Yang returned the other arrow to the king and reported on his mission.

The narrative now returns to the battle itself and we are shown an example of the elaborate courtesy which was observed, by some warriors at least, even in the case of encounters between enemies on the field of combat.

The Chin commander Hsi Chih three times encountered the personal troops of the king of Ch'u. Each time he caught sight of the Ch'u ruler he

17 The king evidently disapproved of this kind of reliance on feats of strength.

invariably dismounted from his carriage, removed his helmet, and scurried away like the wind.

The king of Ch'u dispatched his minister of works Hsiang to present Hsi Chih with a bow and deliver this message: "In the thick of battle I perceive someone wearing red-dyed leather gaiters who appears to be a gentleman. Whenever he recognizes me, he scurries away. I wonder if he has suffered some wound?"

When Hsi Chih saw the envoy approaching, he doffed his helmet and listened to the message. Then he said, "I, Chih, your lord's subject from a foreign state, have had occasion to follow my own lord into battle. Through the favor of your lord, I have been permitted to be among those who don helmet and breastplate. I do not venture to kneel before his command, but do make so bold as to tell him in response to his gracious inquiry that I am quite well, am I not? In view of the present circumstances, I make bold to salute his envoy with no more than a short bow." [18]

He thereupon made three short bows to the envoy and withdrew.

The narrative continues with a series of brief vignettes showing the conduct and prowess of various outstanding fighters on both sides of the combat.

The Chin commander Han Chüeh was pursuing Duke Ch'eng of Cheng in battle. Han Chüeh's carriage driver Tu Hun-lo said, "Let's race after him! His driver keeps looking around and doesn't have his mind on the horses. We can overtake them!"

But Han Chüeh said, "I couldn't bear to inflict disgrace upon the ruler of a state a second time!" and he gave up the chase. [19]

18 The *su* bow was a rather curt salutation made with the hands pressed together. Military etiquette directed that one who was wearing armor should not kneel, which is why Hsi Chih when he speaks to the envoy says he will not venture to kneel. Referring to himself as a "foreign subject" of the king of Ch'u and asserting that it was through the favor of the king that he was permitted to participate in the battle are examples of the elaborately polite courtly language of the period.

19 Han Chüeh is referring to the fact that some years earlier, in the Battle of An, he pursued Duke Ch'ing, ruler of the state of Ch'i, and took him prisoner. See "The Battle of An," p. 115 above.

Hsi Chih also pursued Duke Ch'eng of Cheng. His right-hand attendant Fu Han-hu said, "Send the foot soldiers around to cut him off in front. I'll climb into his carriage from behind, take him prisoner and drag him down!"

But Hsi Chih said, "Anyone who injures the ruler of a state will be punished!" and he too gave up the chase.

Duke Ch'eng's carriage driver Shih Shou said, "It was simply because Duke Yi of Wei failed to lower his banner that he was defeated at Ying!"[20] He proceeded to take down the duke's banner and put it away in his bow case.

The duke's right-hand attendant T'ang Kou said to Shih Shou, "You stay by the ruler's side. Today's defeat is disastrous! I'm not as good at such things as you are—you take the ruler and make your getaway. With your permission, I'll stay behind!" And there he died.

The Ch'u forces were driven into a narrow defile. Shu-shan Jan, one of the Ch'u warriors, said to Yang Yu-chi, "Despite our ruler's prediction,[21] you will have to shoot now, since it's for the sake of the nation!" Shu-shan Jan seized one of the enemy soldiers and hurled him so violently that the body struck a Chin chariot and broke its crossbar. With this the Chin army's advance was finally halted, though they succeeded in capturing the ducal son Fei of Ch'u.

Luan Chen, right-hand attendant to Duke Li of Chin, spotting the banner of the Ch'u commander Tzu-ch'ung, made this request of the duke. "The men of Ch'u say that that banner is the battle flag of Tzu-ch'ung, so that man must be Tzu-ch'ung. When I went as envoy to Ch'u some time ago, Tzu-ch'ung asked me about the brave men of the state of Chin. I replied, 'They like to keep their troops in order.' 'What else?' he asked. I replied, 'They like to be free of trouble.' Now that our two states are engaged in combat, if we do not send an envoy to their side, it will not seem as though we keep our men in very good order. And if, when a crisis comes, we can't keep our word and maintain good order among our troops, we can hardly claim to be free of trouble. With your permission, I would like to send an envoy to offer Tzu-ch'ung a drink."

The duke gave his consent. Luan Chen dispatched a man to bear a cask of

20 In 660 the state of Wei was attacked by the Ti tribes, and its ruler, Duke Yi, was pursued and killed in the swamp of Ying. Shih Shou is saying that Duke Yi might on that occasion have escaped if he had taken down the banner that marked his carriage as that of the ruler.

21 The prediction made by the king of Ch'u on the eve of battle that Yang Yu-chi's archery would be the death of him; see p. 133 above.

wine and offer a drink to Tzu-ch'ung with this message: "Our ruler, being short of envoys, has had to press me, Luan Chen, into service as his halberd bearer. Therefore I cannot have the pleasure of waiting on you in person, but I have sent my envoy So-and-so to offer you a drink."

Tzu-ch'ung said, "Luan Chen—when he and I talked together that time in Ch'u, it must have been in preparation for this occasion. How well I recall it!"

He took the wine and drank it. Then, after dismissing the envoy, he ordered the war drums to resume sounding.

The battle began at dawn, and was still going on when the stars came out. The Ch'u commander Tzu-fan gave orders to his officers to tend to the wounded, replace the lost men and carriages, put in order the armor and weapons, and inspect the carriages and horses. They were to eat at cockcrow and thereafter simply follow orders.

The men on the Chin side were alarmed by these preparations, but Miao Fen-huang circulated among the troops, saying, "Inspect your carriages, replace the men you've lost, fodder your horses, sharpen your weapons, range your chariots, and make sure your ranks are firm! Eat breakfast where you bedded down and repeat the battle prayer—tomorrow we will fight again!" He then released the Ch'u prisoners.[22]

When King Kung of Ch'u received word of these preparations, he sent for Tzu-fan so he could plot his strategy. But Tzu-fan's page Ku-yang had been serving wine to his master, and Tzu-fan was so drunk he could not appear for the interview.[23]

King Kung said, "Heaven is defeating Ch'u! I cannot wait any longer!" He fled with his troops under cover of night.

The Chin troops entered the Ch'u encampment and for three days ate the stores of grain there. The Chin commander Shih Hsieh, stationing himself in front of the ruler's war horses, said, "Our ruler so young, we his ministers so lacking in ability—how did we ever achieve this? Let the ruler take warning! The "Documents of Chou" says: 'There is no constant mandate.'[24] The mandate resides with the virtuous."

22 So they could report to the Ch'u army that the Chin troops were preparing to fight again the following day.

23 *Han Fei Tzu* section 10 gives a somewhat more detailed account of the incident, relating how Tzu-fan, thirsty from the battle, called for a drink of water. His page Ku-yang, with the best intentions, offered him wine, insisting it was water, and finally persuaded his master to drink. Tzu-fan, it is said, was so fond of wine that, once he had begun drinking, he could not stop till he was drunk. See my *Han Fei Tzu: Basic Writings* (New York: Columbia University Press, 1964), p. 50.

24 *Book of Documents,* "The Announcement to K'ang."

The Ch'u army returned home, and when it reached Hsia in Ch'u, King Kung sent a messenger to say to his commander Tzu-fan, "On an earlier occasion when a commander led his troops to defeat, the ruler was not a member of the expedition.[25] [But this time I was a member,] so I do not hold you responsible. I was the one at fault."

Tzu-fan bowed twice, touched his head to the ground and said, "If the ruler should grant me the favor of death, I would be eternally in his debt. My troops in fact fled the field—the fault was mine."

Tzu-ch'ung, the other Ch'u commander, sent word to Tzu-fan, saying, "That earlier commander who lost his troops—you've heard how he ended! Why aren't you preparing to do likewise?"[26]

Tzu-fan replied "Even if I did not have the example of that earlier commander before me, I would heed your words, my lord. Would I dare to act unrighteously? I have brought about the loss of my ruler's army. How could I forget that it is my duty to die!"

When the king learned what Tzu-fan had in mind, he sent a messenger to stop him, but before the messenger could reach him, Tzu-fan had taken his life.

The narrative of the Battle of Yen-ling began with Shih Hsieh's paradoxical statement that if Chin were to face serious difficulties abroad, that might prove to be the salvation of the state. Ironically, however, Chin emerged the victor in the conflict that ensued. In the following passage, which deals with events in the year after the battle, we see Shih Hsieh's reaction to the victory.

DUKE CH'ENG 17TH YEAR (574 B.C.)

When Shih Hsieh returned from the Battle of Yen-ling, he ordered the invocator of his clan to offer up prayers for his death. "Our ruler is arrogant

25 The king is referring to the Ch'u defeat by the Chin armies in 632 at the Battle of Ch'eng-p'u. At that time the Ch'u commander was Tzu-yü Te-ch'en. After the battle, he committed suicide to atone for his disgrace.

26 As may be seen, the two Ch'u commanders remained bitter enemies to the end.

and spendthrift, and now he has defeated his enemies," he said. "Heaven is worsening the sickness that besets him. Trouble will surely follow. Those who love me would do well to pray for my speedy death, so I may not live to see the troubles. That would be a blessing to our clan."

In the sixth month, the day *mou-ch'en,* Shih Hsieh died.

As Shih Hsieh predicted, troubles were not long in coming. In the close of 574, Duke Li, increasingly extravagant and willful in his ways, became impatient of the restraints of his power imposed by members of the Hsi family and had three of its leaders, Hsi Ch'i, Hsi Ch'ou, and Hsi Chih, executed. Luan Shu and another minister in turn seized the duke and in the first month of the following year had him put to death, thus bringing to an end his uneasy reign.

TWENTY-SIX

The Siege of Pi-yang

PI-YANG WAS A SMALL STATE IN SOUTHERN SHANTUNG that was traditionally allied with Ch'u. In the narrative that follows, the forces of Ch'u's enemy Chin, aided by troops from Lu and other of the feudal states, lay siege to the Pi-yang capital, proposing to conquer it and hand it over to Hsiang Shu, an official of Sung who had been useful to Chin in the past. The passage is noteworthy for the descriptions of the deeds of bravado performed by the attackers, particularly those in the party headed by Ch'in Chin-fu of Lu. These men include one Ho of Tsou, who demonstrated prodigious strength by hauling up the portcullis or sliding gate of the city so his comrades could escape entrapment, and who has traditionally been identified as the father of Confucius. The identification first appears in the biography of Confucius in chapter 47 of the *Shih chi* or *Records of the Historian,* a text that dates from the early part of the first century B.C., but is presumably based upon an earlier tradition.

DUKE HSIANG 10TH YEAR (563 B.C.)

Hsün Yen and Shih Kai of Chin asked permission to attack Pi-yang and present it to Hsiang Shu of Sung as a fief. Hsün Ying said, "The city is small but stoutly guarded. Even if you overcome it, it will be no great feat of arms, and if you don't, you'll be a laughingstock!"

They insisted they be given permission, however. On the day *ping-yin* they laid siege to the city but could not conquer it.

Ch'in Chin-fu, a retainer of the Meng family of Lu, dragging a heavy wagon, joined the assault. The men of Pi-yang opened the city gate, whereupon the fighting men from the various feudal states made a rush for it. Then the men of Pi-yang lowered the portcullis. But Ho, a man of Tsou, pushed the portcullis back up so that the men could get out.

Ti Ssu-mi took the wheel from a large wagon, covered it with armor, and used it as a shield. With this clasped in his left hand and a halberd brandished in his right, he headed his own squad of attackers. Meng Hsien-tzu remarked, "This is what the *Odes* means when it says, 'He has strength like a tiger!' "[1]

The defenders let down a strip of cloth from the city wall, whereupon Ch'in Chin-fu climbed up it. When he reached the parapet, they cut the cloth in two. He fell to the ground, but they hung out the cloth again, and after he had regained his senses, he climbed up once more. He climbed up three times, till the men on the wall said they had had enough, after which he finally withdrew. He carried off the pieces of cloth, and for three days went around the encampment showing them to people.

Since the forces of the various feudal states had been engaged in the siege for a long time, Hsün Yen and Shih Kai requested the Chin commander Hsün Ying to terminate the siege, saying, "The summer rains will be upon us and we're afraid we won't be able to get home. We request that the armies be allowed to return."

Hsün Ying was so furious he threw his armrest at them, though it passed between the two men. "*You* thought up this idea to capture Pi-yang and give it to Sung, and you came and told me afterward. I was afraid of disrupting your plans and so I did not oppose you. You have already enlisted the ruler's support, caused the other feudal lords to call out their troops, and even dragged an old man like myself into your scheme. And now that you have failed to win any military gain, you want to shift the blame to me by telling people I was the one who forced you to go home and if it hadn't been for that, you could have won. Well, I *am* a weary old man, and I will not take on such heavy responsibilities! If within seven days you have not conquered the city, I am going to hold *you* responsible!"

On the day *kuei-yin* of the fifth month, Hsün Yen and Shih Kai led their troops in an assault on Pi-yang, personally braving the shower of arrows and stones. On the day *chia-wu,* they wiped out all resistance.

1 "Airs of Pei," *Chien hsi,* Mao no. 38. Meng Hsien-tzu, an official of Lu, has appeared earlier in the role of commentator on the action; see pp. 126, 128 above.

TWENTY-SEVEN

The Death of Hsün Yen of Chin

IN 555 THE RULER OF CHIN, DUKE P'ING (R. 557–532), LED an attack on the state of Ch'i in retaliation for Ch'i's aggressions against Chin's ally, Lu. His chief commanders were Hsün Yen and Shih Kai, whom we have seen earlier in the account of the siege of Pi-yang. Though the Chin forces and those of their allies were highly successful in their attack, they had to abandon the campaign midway because of an invasion launched by Ch'u against another of Chin's allies, Cheng. The following passage describes the death of Hsün Yen, the chief Chin commander, as he was returning from the attack in the spring of 554.

DUKE HSIANG 19TH YEAR (554 B.C.)

Hsün Yen fell ill with boils, and a swelling appeared on his head. He had crossed the Yellow River into Chin and gone as far as Chu-yung when he became too sick to proceed and his eyes protruded from his head. The other high officials of Chin who had gone home ahead of him all returned to where he was. Shih Kai asked to be allowed to see him but was denied an interview. Then he asked who should be appointed to succeed Hsün Yen as commander, to which Hsün Yen replied "Wu, my son by the woman of Cheng, will do."

On the day *chia-yin* of the second month Hsün Yen died, but his eyes remained wide open and his jaws were clamped shut and could not be pried apart.[1]

1 It was customary to open the mouth of the corpse and place a piece of jade or other valuable substance in it before burial.

Shih Kai washed his hands and stroked the corpse, saying, "I will serve your son Wu just as faithfully as I would you!" But the eyes continued to stare.

Luan Ying said, "It must be because the business in Ch'i is not yet completed." He too stroked the corpse and said, "Your life may be over, but if I fail to carry on in your place in the undertaking in Ch'i, may the Yellow River punish me!"

With this the eyes finally closed and the stone could be placed in the mouth.

When Shih Kai emerged from the room, he said, "How shallow of me to have said what I did!"

T W E N T Y - E I G H T

The Assassination of Duke Chuang of Ch'i

THE CHIEF ACTORS IN THE EPISODE THAT FOLLOWS, DUKE Chuang of Ch'i (r. 553–548) and his high minister, Ts'ui Shu, are anything but attractive figures. Duke Chuang by his stupidity and immoral behavior clearly courts the fate that overtakes him, while Ts'ui Shu is simply another example of the scheming head of a powerful ministerial family who betrays his duty to the ruling house. But as so often in the *Tso chuan,* the interest in the passage lies not so much in the sordid actions of the principals as in the opportunities that the flow of events affords to lesser personages in the narrative to demonstrate their dedication to higher ideals. The episode is famous in particular for the example of the dauntless historians who choose to die rather than falsify the record, an example that no doubt served as a source of inspiration to later historians of China.

DUKE HSIANG 25TH YEAR (548 B.C.)

The wife of the lord of T'ang in Ch'i was an older sister of Tung-kuo Yen, a retainer of Ts'ui Shu. When the lord of T'ang died, Tung-kuo Yen drove Ts'ui Shu to the lord's residence so he could offer condolences. Ts'ui Shu observed the lord's wife, Lady Chiang, and admired her beauty. He instructed Tung-kuo Yen to arrange a marriage.

Tung-kuo Yen said, "Man and wife must be of different surnames. But you, my lord, are descended from Duke Ting of Ch'i, and I am descended from Duke Huan. It is out of the question.!"[1]

Ts'ui Shu divined by the milfoil stalks and arrived at the hexagram *k'un* or "adversity," which changed into the hexagram *ta-kuo* or "excess."

The historians who conducted the divination all declared the response to be auspicious. But when Ts'ui Shu showed the results to the Ch'i minister Ch'en Wen-tzu, he said, "Husband gives way to wind, wind blows the wife away. Such a match will never do![2] Moreover, the interpretation reads: 'Troubled by rocks, thorns and briers to rest on, the man enters his house but does not see his wife—misfortune!'[3] 'Troubled by rocks' means he cannot cross over. 'Thorns and briers to rest on' means that what he leans on injures him. 'He enters his house but does not see his wife—misfortune!' means he has no place to turn to."

Ts'ui Shu said, "She's a widow, so what does all that matter? Her former husband has already suffered the misfortune!" Thus in the end he married Lady Chiang.

Duke Chuang of Ch'i carried on an adulterous affair with Lady Chiang, paying frequent visits to Ts'ui Shu's house. At one time he took Ts'ui Shu's hat and presented it to someone else. His attendant said, "That will not do!" But the duke replied, "Is Ts'ui the only person who deserves a hat?"[4]

For these reasons, Ts'ui came to hate the duke. Also, when Duke Chuang took advantage of the trouble in Chin to launch an attack on that state, Ts'ui said, "Chin is certain to pay us back for this!"[5] He therefore resolved to assassinate the duke in order to ingratiate himself with Chin, but could find no opportunity to do so. However, the duke thrashed one of his attendants named Chia Chü and then later allowed the man to wait on him again. This man spied on the duke for Ts'ui Shu.

In the summer, the fifth month, the ruler of the state of Chü came to pay

1 Duke Ting was the son of T'ai-kung Wang, founder of the state of Ch'i. Duke Huan reigned 685–643. Both Ts'ui Shu and Tung-kuo Yen and his sister thus belonged to branches of the Chiang family, the ruling family of Ch'i. Ts'ui and Tung-kuo at this time were place-names and not surnames.

2 The lower trigram in the hexagram *k'un* is *k'an,* which stands for the middle son, i.e., a man. In the hexagram *ta-kuo, k'an* is replaced by the trigram *sun,* which symbolizes the wind, while the trigram in the upper part of both *k'un* and *ta-kuo* is *tui,* which stands for the youngest daughter, i.e., a woman. Hence Ch'en's remark about the husband giving way to wind and wind blowing away the wife. Presumably the historians who had declared the response to be auspicious were merely toadying to Ts'ui Shu.

3 Ch'en is quoting the explanation of the third line from the bottom of the hexagram *k'un* given in the *Book of Changes.*

4 Or, following the interpretation of Yü Yüeh, who punctuates after *pu,* "Not so! Does a man like Ts'ui have only one hat?" In either case, the manner in which the duke makes free with Ts'ui's hat is symbolic of his treatment of Ts'ui's wife.

5 Duke Chuang's attack on Chin took place in 550 B.C.

a court visit to Ch'i because of the military action carried out by Chü at Chü-yü.[6]

On the day *chia-hsü* a banquet was held for the ruler of Chü at the northern outer wall of the capital. Ts'ui Shu, pleading illness, played no part in the affair.

On the day *i-hai* Duke Chuang went to Ts'ui Shu's house to inquire how he was. While there, he sought out Ts'ui Shu's wife, Lady Chiang. She led him into a chamber, but then she and Ts'ui Shu slipped out by a side door. The duke began rapping on a pillar and singing.[7]

Meanwhile, the duke's attendant Chia Chü instructed the party of men who had accompanied the duke to remain outside while he went in the house. Then he shut the gate on them. At that point Ts'ui Shu's soldiers made their appearance.

The duke clambered up to the upper terrace, where he begged to be allowed to go free. His request was refused. He begged to be allowed to conclude an alliance with Ts'ui Shu, but his request was refused. He begged to be allowed to take his own life in the ancestral temple, but his request was refused.

The soldiers all said, "The ruler's minister Ts'ui Shu is sick and cannot inquire of the ruler's orders. Since this house is close to the ducal palace, we retainers of the Ts'ui family have been assigned to patrol the area at night. If there are trespassers, the only orders we have are to attack!"[8]

The duke tried to climb over the wall, whereupon someone shot at him with an arrow and hit him in the thigh. He fell backward from the wall, and in this way was finally assassinated.

Chia Chü, Chou Ch'o, Ping Shih, the ducal son Ao, Feng Chü, To Fu, Hsiang Yi, and Lü Yin all died in the fighting.[9]

The invocator T'o-fu had been conducting sacrifices at Kao-t'ang. When he returned to the capital to report on his mission, he was killed by the Ts'ui forces before he could even remove his hat.

Shen K'uai, who was serving as supervisor of fisheries, withdrew from

6 In 550, when Duke Chuang was on his way back from his attack on Chin, he attacked the state of Chü, situated just southeast of Ch'i. He was wounded in an attempt to storm the city gate at Chü-yü and his attack ended in failure. But because Chü was a small and relatively powerless state, it was obliged to sue for peace with Ch'i.

7 The duke was signaling to Ts'ui Shu's wife to join him.

8 The soldiers are pretending they do not know the identity of the man they are pursuing.

9 These eight men are said to be attendants of the duke who died fighting on his behalf at Ts'ui Shu's home. The Chia Chü mentioned here is apparently different from the duke's traitorous attendant of the same name.

court and said to his house steward, "You take your family and flee. I intend to die here!" The steward replied, "If I were to flee, I would be going against the righteousness of your decision!" So they all of them died together.

The Ts'ui family forces killed Tsung Mieh at P'ing-yin.[10]

The Ch'i official Yen P'ing-chung stood outside the gate of the Ts'ui family mansion.[11] His followers said, "Do you intend to die?"

"Was he my ruler only? Why should I die for him?"

"Will you go abroad?"

"What crime have I committed? Why should I flee?"

"Will you go home then?"

"My ruler is dead! How can I go home like this? Nevertheless, when one acts as ruler of the people, how is it right to abuse the people? He should conduct himself as master of the altars of the soil and grain. And one who acts as minister to a ruler, how can he think only of his emoluments? He should help to sustain the altars of the soil and grain. Therefore if a ruler dies for the sake of the altars of the soil and grain, then one should die with him. If he flees for the sake of the altars of the soil and grain, one should flee with him. But if he dies for personal reasons, or flees for personal reasons, then unless one is among his intimates or particular favorites, who would presume to share his fate?

"Moreover, just because a man has risen up against his ruler and assassinated him, why should that oblige me to die for the ruler, or why should it oblige me to flee for him? And yet how could I simply return home like this?"

When the gates were opened, Yen P'ing-chung entered the house, pillowed the body of the duke on his lap and wept over it. Then he stood up, performed three ritual leaps, and departed.[12]

Someone told Ts'ui Shu that Yen P'ing-chung should by all means be killed. But Ts'ui Shu said, "The people look up to him. By sparing him I can gain the support of the people."

Lu P'u-kuei fled to Chin and Wang Ho fled to Chü.[13]

10 Tsung Mieh, like the eight men mentioned above, was an intimate of Duke Chuang.

11 Yen P'ing-chung or Yen Ying served as a high official under dukes Ling, Chuang, and Ching of Ch'i. A philosophical work entitled *Yen Tzu ch'un-ch'iu* or *Spring and Autumn of Master Yen* contains anecdotes dealing with his life and government policies, in part drawn from the *Tso chuan*.

12 Yen performs the ritual of lamentation out of respect for his dead lord, though this act might well have cost him his life. But, as he has already made clear, he will take no steps to avenge the murder.

13 These men too were supporters of the murdered duke.

When Shu-sun Ch'iao-ju was in Ch'i, Shu-sun Huan arranged for Shu-sun Ch'iao-ju's daughter to enter the household of Duke Ling of Ch'i.[14] She gained favor with the duke and bore him a son who later became Duke Ching.

On the day *ting-ch'ou* Ts'ui Shu set up this son, Duke Ching, as ruler of Ch'i, with himself as prime minister. Ch'ing Feng was appointed prime minister of the left. They swore an oath with the people of the state in the ancestral temple of the founder. The words of the oath began, "Should anyone fail to ally himself with the Ts'ui and Ch'ing families . . ." Yen P'ing-chung raised his eyes to heaven and said with a sigh, "Should I fail to ally myself with those who are loyal to the ruler alone and who work to benefit the altars of the soil and grain, may the Lord on High witness it!" Only then would he smear his lips with the blood of the sacrifice.

On the day *hsin-ssu* the new duke and his high officers concluded an alliance with the ruler of Chü.

The grand historian wrote in his records: "Ts'ui Shu assassinated his ruler."[15] Ts'ui Shu had him killed. The historian's younger brother succeeded to the post and wrote the same thing. He too was killed, as was another brother. When a fourth brother came forward to write, Ts'ui Shu finally desisted.

Meanwhile, when the assistant historian living south of the city heard that the grand historians had been killed, he took up his bamboo tablets and set out for the court. Only when he learned that the fact had been recorded did he turn back.

In conclusion, we may note that the auguries of ill fortune that were revealed when Ts'ui Shu consulted the milfoil stalks in connection with his marriage to Lady Chiang did not prove to be mistaken. In 546, two years after the events described

14 Shu-sun Ch'iao-ju of the state of Lu fled to Ch'i in 575 B.C.

15 The entry in the *Spring and Autumn Annals* regarding this event reads: "Ts'ui Shu of Ch'i assassinated his ruler Kuang."

above, Ts'ui Shu and his entire family were wiped out by his fellow prime minister Ch'ing Feng.

TWENTY-NINE

Prince Chi-cha of Wu

KUNG-TZU (THE DUCAL SON) CHA, OR PRINCE CHI-CHA OF WU, was the youngest son of King Shou-meng of the southern state of Wu. On the death of King Shou-meng in 561, attempts were made to persuade him to take the throne, since that had been his father's wish, but he adamantly refused in order to make way for his older brothers. (See Duke Hsiang 14th year.) He was enfeoffed in a place called Yen-ling and is often referred to as Yen-ling Chi-tzu. In the following pages we see him carrying out a diplomatic mission to Lu and other feudal states, commenting upon a performance of ancient songs and dances that he witnessed in Lu, and offering astute advice to the men in power.

DUKE HSIANG 29TH YEAR (544 B.C.)

Prince Chi-cha of Wu came to Lu on a courtesy visit. He had an interview with the Lu official Shu-sun Mu-tzu and was pleased with him. But he said to Shu-sun Mu-tzu, "I am afraid you will not get to live out your natural life. You are fond of goodness but inept in selecting men for service. I have heard that a gentleman must exercise care in selecting men. You, sir, are a high official of Lu, a member of its ruling family, and are entrusted with major government responsibilities. If you are not more cautious in matters of promotion, how can you carry them out? Disaster will most certainly overtake you!"

Prince Chi-cha requested to be shown the music of Chou.[1] The musicians

1 Chou musical performances in many cases included dances and hence are spoken of as visual rather than merely aural experiences. The state of Lu was founded by the Duke of Chou, one of the great sages

were accordingly ordered to perform for him the *Chou nan* and *Shao nan* songs. "Splendid!" he said. "Here are the beginnings of greatness, though it has yet to be fully realized. But there is diligence and no feeling of rancor."

Then they performed for him the songs of Pei, Yung, and Wei. He said, "Splendid! Such depth! Persons who are concerned but not despairing. I have heard that the virtue of K'ang-shu and Duke Wu of Wei was like this.[2] These must be the 'Airs of Wei'!"

They performed for him the songs of the king's region. He said, "Splendid! There is thought but no fear. These must be when the Chou moved east."[3]

They performed for him the songs of Cheng. "Splendid!" he said. "But the sound is so fussy, more than the people can bear! Can such a state endure for long?"

They performed for him the songs of Ch'i. "Splendid!" he said. "Broad and majestic—the grand manner! The exemplar of the eastern sea—who else but T'ai-kung?[4] Such a state knows no limits!"

They performed for him the songs of Pin. He said, "Splendid! So relaxed! Joyful, but not excessively so. Perhaps from the time of the Duke of Chou's eastern campaign!"[5]

They performed for him the songs of Ch'in. "This is the ancient Hsia sound!" he said. "And because Ch'in has the Hsia sound, it is great—the height of greatness! This is the old home of Chou, is it not?"[6]

They performed for him the songs of Wey.[7] He said, "Splendid! So

---

of the early Chou period, and presumably took special care to preserve the ancient music and ritual of the Chou court. In the passage that follows, the musicians first perform songs from the various sections of the *Shih ching* or *Book of Odes*. In Chi-cha's impressionistic comments, many of which are prophetic in nature, it is not always clear whether he is referring to the verbal content of the songs or to their musical accompaniment. It should be noted that the music and dances of this early period were lost centuries before the first commentaries on the *Tso chuan* were written, so the commentators' notes on this passage represent little more than educated guesswork.

2 K'ang-shu was a younger brother of the Duke of Chou and the first ruler of the state of Wei. Duke Wu was a virtuous ruler of Wei in the early eighth century B.C.

3 The king's region is the Chou capital at Lo-yang. In the early eighth century the Chou court was forced by barbarian invasion to abandon its ancient capital in Shensi and move east to Lo-yang. This marked the beginning of the long decline of Chou power.

4 Lü Shang or T'ai-kung Wang, who acted as advisor to the founders of the Chou dynasty, was the first ruler of the state of Ch'i on the eastern seacoast in the Shantung Peninsula.

5 That is, from the time when the Duke of Chou marched east to put down a revolt, a period of the consolidation of Chou power. Pin was in the area of Shensi where the Chou people were said to have lived before their ascent to power.

6 Hsia, the name of the first of the Three Dynasties of antiquity, here stands for the west, the direction of the state of Ch'in. The word can also mean "great." Ch'in was the area where the Chou people originated and had their capital in the time of their glory.

7 Wey was a small state later swallowed up by the state of Chin. (I have romanized the name as Wey

moderate and mild! Great but with restraint, simple and easy to follow. If virtue came to the aid of this, we would see a model ruler."

They performed for him the songs of T'ang. "The thought is deep!" he said. "These people are the descendants of T'ao T'ang, are they not?[8] Otherwise, why would they be so troubled in thought about the distant future? Who would be like this unless he were descended from some outstandingly virtuous ancestor?"

When they performed for him the songs of Ch'en, he said, "A state with no true ruler—how can it survive for long?"

On the songs of Kuai and the other states, he made no comment.[9]

When they played for him the *Hsiao ya* or "Lesser Odes," he said, "Splendid! There is thought in them but no duplicity. There is rancor but it is not put into words. They must represent the period when the Chou virtue had declined. Yet one can tell those people are the descendants of the former kings!"

When they played for him the *Ta ya* or "Greater Odes," he said, "Such breadth! Such gentle harmony! Circuitous, yet there is a directness in them. They must represent the virtue of King Wen!"

When they played for him the *Sung* or "Hymns," he said, "This is the ultimate! Direct but not overbearing, distant but not perfidious, varied but not to excess, repetitive but not tiresomely so, plaintive but not downcast, joyous but not unbridled, employing but never depleting, expansive without being assertive, doling out, yet not to a prodigal degree, gathering in, yet not in a greedy manner, resting without stagnating, moving forward without becoming unduly facile. The five notes are harmonized, the eight airs well balanced.[10] Movements that are measured, restraints that are properly ordered—these are qualities shared by all who abound in virtue!"

When he watched the performance of the dance with the ivory flute and that with the southern pipes, he said, "Splendid! And yet there seems to be a feeling of regret."[11]

---

rather than Wei to distinguish it from the other state of Wei already mentioned above.) Chi-cha's remarks here are probably intended to apply to the state of Chin.

8 T'ao T'ang is another name for the ancient sage ruler Emperor Yao. T'ang is the old name for the state of Chin.

9 Chi-cha has in fact commented on all the *Kuo feng* or "Airs of the States" sections of the *Book of Odes* except those devoted to the songs of Kuai and Ts'ao, though not in the exact order in which they are presently found in the *Odes*.

10 The five notes are those of classical Chinese music. The "eight airs" are variously defined as the airs or modes typical of the eight directions, or as the tones of instruments made respectively of metal, stone, strings, bamboo, gourds, earth, grasses, and wood.

11 The ivory flute and southern pipes are objects held in the dancer's hand. These dances are said to

When he saw the dance of Great Wu, he said, "Splendid! Chou at its height must have been like this!"[12]

When he saw the *Shao hu* dance, he said, "The greatness of the sage! And yet he seems to feel some lack of virtue—so difficult is it to be a sage!"[13]

When he saw the Great Hsia dance, he said, "Splendid! He strives but considers it no virtue. Who but Yü could proceed in this fashion!"[14]

When he saw the *Shao hsiao* dance, he said, "The height of virtue![15] Superb! Like Heaven—nothing it does not shelter. Like earth—nothing it does not sustain. Whoever else may abound in virtue, he could add nothing to this! I will cease my viewing. If there are other kinds of music, I would not venture to request them."

Since Prince Chi-cha had come on his mission in order to announce the accession of a new ruler in Wu, he now proceeded to the state of Ch'i to make the same announcement there.[16] He was pleased when he met the Ch'i official Yen P'ing-chung but said to him, "You must quickly return the cities you have been enfeoffed with and the reins of government! If you have no cities and no governmental powers, you can escape difficulty. The power of government in the state of Ch'i will in time pass into certain hands. But until it does, the troubles will not cease!"

As a result of this advice Yen P'ing-chung, through the offices of Ch'en Huan-tzu, returned the powers of government and the cities he possessed to the authorities. Because he did so, he was able to escape the troubles brought on by the Luan and Kao families.[17]

Prince Chi-cha then paid a courtesy call to Cheng, where he had an interview with Tzu-ch'an.[18] He treated Tzu-ch'an as though he were an old

---

represent the virtue of King Wen of the Chou. King Wen was not fully able to realize his ideal of benevolent government, hence the feeling of regret in the music or the dance.

12 Great Wu was the dance of King Wen's son and successor, King Wu, who completed the task of founding the Chou dynasty.

13 The *Shao hu* dance is said to depict the virtue of King T'ang, the founder of the Shang dynasty which preceded the Chou. According to another interpretation, the "lack of virtue" is not a lack in T'ang himself but in the music's power to depict him, in which case the last phrase should read, "so difficult is it to depict a sage!"

14 The Great Hsia dance depicts the virtue of the sage ruler Yü, founder of the Hsia dynasty which preceded the Shang.

15 The *Shao hsiao* dance depicts the virtue of Shun, the sage who ruled before Yü. Note that the progression is backward in time, and that the more ancient the ruler, the greater his virtue.

16 According to the *Spring and Autumn Annals* entry for this year, King Yü-chai (r. 547–544) of Wu was assassinated by a gatekeeper in the early part of this year. So Prince Chi-cha was presumably visiting various states to announce the accession of Yü-chai's successor, I-mo (r. 543–527). Both Yü-chai and I-mo were elder brothers of Prince Chi-cha.

17 These troubles took place in 532. Prince Chi-cha's statement that power in the state of Ch'i will in time "pass into certain hands" is no doubt a veiled prediction of the rise of the T'ien family, who in 386 B.C. set themselves up as rulers of Ch'i.

18 A famous statesman of Cheng highly praised by Confucius in the *Analects*. He is the subject of the narrative that follows this. According to the *Tso chuan*, he died in 522.

acquaintance and gave him a belt of white silk. Tzu-ch'an in return presented him with a robe of fine hemp.

The prince said to Tzu-ch'an, "The governing powers in Cheng are too extravagant and trouble is on the way. The government is certain to come into your hands. When you exercise the power of government, be careful to observe ritual principles! If you do not, the state of Cheng will face ruin!"[19]

19 The passage continues with descriptions of the prince's visits to Wei and Chin, but these have been omitted in the translation. Prince Chi-cha is depicted here as a typical example of the *hsien,* the worthy man or seer, whose extreme sensitivity to principles of moral and ritual rectitude and ability to judge other men's characters allows him to see far into the future and discern the course that political events will take.

T H I R T Y

Tzu-ch'an's Government Policies

AS ALREADY STATED IN THE INTRODUCTION, IN MOST OF THE feudal states at this time, particularly those that had been in existence for some centuries, the ruling family had become increasingly weak and ineffectual. More and more, power became concentrated in the hands of the great ministerial families, whose members by custom filled the high government posts. Most of these ministerial families were descended from the rulers themselves, as indicated in part by the designations Kung-tzu, "ducal son," (i.e., ruler's son), and Kung-sun, "ducal grandson," that so often prefixed their names and in time came to be regular surnames. Many of the leaders of these ministerial families used their positions simply to amass wealth and conduct themselves in unlicensed fashion, but others proved to be able administrators who did much to further the fortunes of the state. The following anecdotes deal with a famous example of the latter type, the Cheng statesman Kung-sun Ch'iao or Tzu-ch'an, who has already appeared in the preceding episode. These anecdotes closely resemble the type of material found in late Chou philosophical works such as the *Kuan Tzu* and *Yen Tzu ch'un-ch'iu,* which purport to describe the government policies and principles of outstanding statesmen of the Spring and Autumn period.

DUKE HSIANG 30TH YEAR (543 B.C.)

Tzu-p'i of Cheng handed over the government to Tzu-ch'an.[1] The latter attempted to decline, saying, "The state is small and hemmed in by larger

1 Tzu-p'i was one of a group of high officials in Cheng who had been quarreling among themselves for power. Tzu-ch'an first became an official of Cheng in 554 and had played an important role in government affairs since that time. Now he is being given the post of *hsiang* or prime minister.

states, the members of the ruler's clan are numerous and many of them enjoy his favor—it is impossible to govern properly!"

But Tzu-p'i said, "I will lead the others in obeying your orders. Who will dare oppose you? If you govern well, what difference if the state is small? When a small state knows how to serve its larger neighbors, it will be treated with lenience."

After Tzu-ch'an had taken over the government, he wanted the ducal grandson Tuan to carry out a task for him and began by presenting Tuan with the gift of a city.

Tzu-t'ai-shu said, "This country belongs to all of us! Why should he alone be enfeoffed with a city?"

Tzu-ch'an replied, "It is hard to expect men to have no desires at all. In all cases, it is because they can satisfy their desires that they undertake a task and press it to completion. So the completion depends not on the man himself, but upon the one who provides the satisfaction—myself, in this instance. Why should I begrudge him the city? The city is not going to go away, is it?"

Tzu-t'ai-shu said, "What will the neighboring states think?"

Tzu-ch'an said, "It is not as though I were promoting disharmony. And if we go about our tasks in harmony, what fault can our neighbors find in us? The "Documents of Cheng" has it: 'To bring peace and stability to the state, attend first to the great families.'[2] So now I am first of all attempting to pacify the great, and then we will see what follows."

The ducal grandson Tuan, having received the fief, became fearful of the consequences and tried to return the city, but in the end Tzu-ch'an made him keep it.

After the death of Po-yu, Tzu-ch'an sent the grand historian with an order appointing the ducal grandson Tuan to the post of government minister.[3] Tuan declined to accept, whereupon the grand historian withdrew, but then Tuan asked to be given the appointment. When the appointment was once more presented, however, he again declined. This happened three times, until at last he accepted the document and went to court to express his thanks. Tzu-ch'an as a result came to despise him as a person, though he saw to it that Tuan's rank was second to his own.

Tzu-ch'an arranged for the capital and the outlying regions to have distinctive types of carriages and equipages, the upper and lower classes to

2 No such text is extant. The title suggests that the individual states kept collections of "documents" *(shu)* or historical texts of their own, similar to those preserved in the *Shu ching* or *Book of Documents*.

3 Po-yu was a high official who had been killed earlier in the year, along with many of his supporters, in the internal struggles in Cheng. Tuan is being given the post of *ch'ing*.

have different kinds of clothing, the fields to be marked off with boundary ridges and irrigation ditches, and the farmhouses and wells to be symmetrically arranged.[4] If there were persons among the great families who were steadfast and frugal in their ways, he acknowledged that fact by giving them rewards; if there were those who were overbearing and extravagant, he used that as a reason to demote them.

Feng Chüan was preparing to sacrifice to his ancestors and asked permission to go hunting for game, but Tzu-ch'an refused the request, saying, "Only the ruler uses fresh game in his sacrifices. The rest of us make do with what is at hand."[5]

Feng Chüan was enraged and, after leaving the interview, summoned his retainers in preparation for an attack. Tzu-ch'an was about to flee to Chin but Tzu-p'i stopped him and instead expelled Feng Chüan, who fled to Chin. Tzu-ch'an requested that he himself be given Feng Chüan's lands and villages. After three years he arranged for Feng Chüan to be recalled, at which time he returned his lands and villages to him, along with the revenues that had accrued from them.

After Tzu-ch'an had administered the government for one year, the people of the state sang a song that went:

> He took our robes and caps, then changed them;
> took our fields and acres, rearranged them—
> Who'll rid us of Tzu-ch'an? We'll acclaim him!

But after three years had passed, they sang this song:

> We have sons and brothers—
> Tzu-ch'an tutored them.
> We have fields and acres—
> Tzu-ch'an bettered them.
> Should Tzu-ch'an die,
> who could replace him?

4 The reference is perhaps to groups of five families that were mutually responsible for each other; or perhaps it refers to the well-field system in which eight families were grouped around a common well. Yang Po-chün takes the word translated as "clothing" to mean "duties," and interprets the end of the sentence as referring to a system of land taxation.

5 Feng Chüan was an official belonging to one of the powerful families of Cheng.

DUKE HSIANG 31ST YEAR (542 B.C.)

Diplomatic concerns and the demands of etiquette made it necessary for the feudal lords to pay frequent visits to one another, and the reception they received abroad did not always meet with their satisfaction. In the following anecdote we see how Tzu-ch'an expressed his disapproval at the treatment his lord, Duke Chien (r. 656–530) of Cheng, received on one occasion at the hands of the ruler of the powerful state of Chin, Duke P'ing (r. 557–532). Note the scrupulously polite language used by both parties in the dispute.

In the month when Duke Hsiang of Lu passed away, Tzu-ch'an was accompanying the ruler of Cheng on a visit to the state of Chin. The Chin ruler, using the plea that he was in mourning, had not yet granted the Cheng ruler an interview.[6] Tzu-ch'an thereupon ordered that the walls around the guest lodge where his party was quartered be broken down and his vehicles and horses be brought into the grounds.

The Chin official Shih Wen-po protested, saying, "Because the laws and regulations of our humble city are inadequately administered, robbers and thieves abound, and therefore when parties from the other feudal lords are gracious enough to visit our lord, we find it difficult to insure their safety. For this reason our ruler has ordered his officials to take full precautions with regard to the guest lodge, fitting it with tall gates and stout walls so that visitors will not be troubled. But now, sir, you have destroyed the walls! Though you may instruct your own attendants to take full precautions, what about the visitors from other states who come after?

"Our humble city acts as leader of the alliances, and therefore we have taken care to repair the thatch-roofed walls and put them in readiness for guests from abroad.[7] But if each guest who stays here knocks them down, then how can we render proper service? Hence our ruler has sent me to inquire of your intentions in this matter."

Tzu-ch'an replied, "Because our humble city of Cheng is narrow and small in size and squeezed in among powerful neighbors, we never know

6 Duke Hsiang of Lu died in the sixth month of 542, the thirty-first year of his reign. The ruling families of Lu, Chin, and Cheng all belonged to the Chi clan, so it was not unreasonable for the Chin ruler to claim he was in mourning for the ruler of Lu, though apparently Tzu-ch'an saw this as a mere excuse.

7 On the term "leader of the alliances," see "The Battle of An," p. 117*n*14.

when we may be faced with reprovals or demands. Therefore we have not dared to remain at ease but have gathered together all the articles that our humble territory has to offer and brought them so that we may present them with our seasonal greetings. But we have arrived at a time when those in charge of affairs are not at leisure, and have not yet been granted an interview. In addition, we have not yet received any communication from your ruler, so we do not know when an interview will be granted.

"We do not dare hand over the goods we have brought, but neither do we dare stack them where they will be exposed to the weather. If we hand them over, they will be stored away in your lord's warehouses and no one will know what they are. We must therefore be allowed to unpack and display them before we dare hand them over. But if we stack them where they will be exposed to the weather, we are afraid they will suffer from unseasonal heat or damp or become spoiled or infested with insects, and then our humble city will face double the usual blame for its inferior goods.

"I have heard that when Duke Wen of Chin was leader of the alliances, he lived in a mean and lowly palace and did without pleasure towers, terraces, and pavilions so he could provide a spacious lodging for the feudal lords who came to visit. His guest lodge was fashioned like the ruler's own quarters and equipped with storehouses and stables. The minister of works periodically saw to the repair and leveling of the roadways, and the plasterers at regular intervals replastered the rooms of the lodge. When any of the feudal lords appeared on a visit, those in charge of illumination set up torches in the courtyard, while watchmen patrolled the grounds of the lodge. Shelter was provided for vehicles and horses, local attendants replaced those who had come with the visitors, and those in charge of vehicles kept the linchpins properly greased. Thus the various servants, menials, and grooms each looked after his respective duties, and each of the hundred types of officials supplied the items he specialized in.

"The duke did not detain his visitors longer than necessary, yet none of their affairs was neglected. He shared the cares and delights of his guests, and if danger threatened he provided them with patrols. He taught them things they did not know, and took pity on their needs. Thus the guests felt as though they were at home—what need had they to fret about unforeseen disasters? They had no fears concerning brigands or thieves, nor did they have to be worried about heat or dampness.

"But now the T'ung-ti Palace[8] spreads over several miles, while the feudal lords are quartered like menials! The gate is not big enough to admit

8 A detached palace belonging to the rulers of Chin.

a carriage, and yet one cannot go over the walls. Thieves and bandits strut in broad daylight and precautions are not taken against natural disaster. No date has been set for the reception of guests, and we have no way of knowing the ruler's intentions. If we had not broken down the wall, there would have been no way to store the goods and we would have faced more blame than ever!

"May we venture to ask the authorities what they wish us to do? The ruler may be in mourning for Lu, but that event grieves our humble city as well. If we may be allowed to present the goods we have brought, we will then, with your lord's kind permission, repair the wall and be on our way. We certainly will not shrink from that small labor!"

Shih Wen-po reported to the ruler of Chin. The Chin official Chao Wen-tzu said, "Cheng's complaint is just. We have shown a lack of virtue. It was our fault for housing one of the feudal lords in a place walled like servants' quarters!" He ordered Shih Wen-po to apologize for this act of thoughtlessness.

When Duke P'ing of Chin received the Cheng ruler, he treated him with extra politeness, lavished entertainment and hospitality on him, and sent him on his way. Then he set about building a proper guest lodge for the feudal lords.

Yang-she Shu-hsiang said, "Truly, words cannot be dispensed with, as we see from this.[9] Because Tzu-ch'an knew how to use words, the feudal rulers relied on him. How could we ever do away with words? The *Odes* says:

> In the mildness of the words
> is the people's concord.
> In the geniality
> is the people's repose.[10]

Tzu-ch'an understood this."

In the twelfth month the Wei official Pei-kung Wen-tzu accompanied his ruler, Duke Hsiang (r. 543–535) of Wei, on a visit to Ch'u, which was

9 Yang-she Shu-hsiang was a wise official of Chin who, like Confucius and Tzu-ch'an, often appears in the *Tso chuan* as a kind of mouthpiece for virtue and sagacity. His remarks here in praise of "words" are in effect a defense of eloquence and artful speaking. It should be noted that Tzu-ch'an's long speech on the guest lodge is highly polished and makes generous use of the balanced phrases and parallelisms so much admired in early Chinese rhetoric, though whether it is representative of the style of Tzu-ch'an's own time is perhaps questionable.

10 "Greater Odes," *Pan*, Mao no. 254.

necessitated by the alliance in Sung.[11] When they passed through the state of Cheng, the Cheng official Yin Tuan went to meet them at Fei-lin and comfort them for their trouble. At that time he used the kind of language he would have used if he had been paying a courtesy call to the state. Pei-kung Wen-tzu then went to the Cheng capital to pay a call and express thanks for the visit. The ducal grandson Hui, an official of Cheng, acted as receiver of envoys, with P'eng Chien-tzu and Tzu-t'ai-shu delegated to greet the guest.

After the ceremony was over, Pei-kung Wen-tzu said to the ruler of Wei, "Cheng observes ritual principles. It will enjoy good fortune for several generations to come, and will most likely escape attack from any of the great powers. The *Odes* says:

> Who can take hold of something hot
> without first moistening his hand?[12]

Ritual in the conduct of government is like the moistening which cools the heat. If one uses the moistening to save oneself from the heat, then what injury can come about?"

In carrying out affairs of government, Tzu-ch'an selected men of ability and employed them. P'eng Chien-tzu was good at judging in matters of major importance, and Tzu-t'ai-shu was personable, talented, and eloquent. The ducal grandson Hui knew how to deal with the neighboring states, and he was very well informed concerning the clans and surnames of their various officials and their ranks, social standing, and degree of ability. He was also skilled at drawing up documents. P'i Ch'en was good at planning. If the planning was done in the countryside, he could hit on something successful, though not if it was done in the city.

If the state of Cheng was confronted with some affair involving the other feudal lords, Tzu-ch'an would accordingly ask the ducal grandson Hui how it affected the neighboring countries, and would have him draw up most of the documents needed. He would then go in a carriage with P'i Ch'en for a drive in the countryside and have P'i Ch'en consider the pros and cons of the plan. After that, he would report the results to P'eng Chien-tzu and get his judgment. When a course of action had been settled on, he would hand things over to Tzu-t'ai-shu and have him carry them out, delegating him to meet with the foreign guests. Because of this procedure, the affairs of Cheng

11 The feudal lords gathered in Sung in 546 to discuss the question of disarmament and enter into an alliance. In 543, when the Sung capital suffered a fire, they gathered there once more to offer assistance. It is not certain which occasion is referred to here.

12 "Greater Odes," *Sang jou*, Mao no. 257.

seldom went awry. This is what Pei-kung Wen-tzu meant when he said that Cheng "observes ritual principles."[13]

The people of Cheng used to discuss the administration of the state when they gathered at leisure in the village schools. The Cheng official Tsung Jan-ming said to Tzu-ch'an, "How would it do to abolish the village schools?"

Tzu-ch'an said, "Why do that? In the morning and evening when the people are at leisure or have finished their work, they gather to discuss the good and bad points of my administration. The points they approve of I encourage, and those they criticize I correct. They are my teachers. Why would I want to abolish them? I have heard of wiping out resentment by loyal service and good works, but I have never heard of stopping it by force. True, one can cut it off for a time. But it is like damming up a river. When there is a major break in the dikes many persons are bound to suffer. If the people's resentment were to break out in the same way, I would never be able to save the situation. It is better to leave a little break in the dikes for the water to drain off. It is better that I hear the people's complaints and make them my medicine."

Tsung Jan-ming said, "Now I understand that you are indeed capable of managing affairs, and that I am truly a person of no talent! If you will in fact proceed in this manner, then everyone in the state of Cheng will benefit, and not only a few officials like myself."

When Confucius heard of this incident, he remarked, "People say that Tzu-ch'an was not a good man, but judging from this I find it impossible to believe."[14]

The last anecdote in the series concerns the Cheng official Tzu-p'i, whom we have

13 Note how this passage parallels the statement in *Analects* XIV, 9: "The Master said, 'In preparing government orders, P'i Ch'en made the rough draft, Shih-chu (Tzu-t'ai-shu) checked and revised it, the receiver of envoys Tzu-yü (the ducal grandson Hui) polished it, and Tzu-ch'an of Tung-li gave it the proper elegance and tone.' "

14 Confucius was only nine years old at the time dealt with in the narrative, so presumably this judgment was delivered some years later. Compare the passage in *Analects* V, 15: "The Master said of Tzu-ch'an, 'He had four ways that characterize a gentleman. In his personal conduct he was courteous, in serving his superior he was respectful, in caring for the people he was kindhearted, and in employing the people he was just.' "

seen above handing over the government to Tzu-ch'an. It has been suggested that the "city" to which Tzu-p'i wishes to assign his protégé Yin Ho as administrator may be his own, that is, a city that he holds in fief from the ruler of Cheng, though this is not certain.

Tzu-p'i wished to place Yin Ho in charge of a city. Tzu-ch'an said, "He is too young. You don't know if he can do the job or not."

Tzu-p'i said, "He is honest. I am looking out for him—he would never turn against me. I want to assign him to this position so he can have a chance to learn. Then he will know better how to govern.

"That will not do!" said Tzu-ch'an. "If one is looking out for a person, he tries to benefit him. Now you are looking out for this man and you want to assign him to a government post. But this is like taking someone who doesn't even know how to handle a knife and employing him to cut things up. He is certain to inflict all kinds of injury on himself. You try to look out for the man, but all you do is injure him. In that case, who would ever dare let you look out for him?

"You are the veritable rooftree of the state of Cheng. If the rooftree cracks and the rafters collapse, then I and everyone else will be crushed! How can I help but speak out on this matter?

"If you had a beautiful piece of embroidery, you would not give it to someone who was just learning to cut things up, would you? Great government posts, great cities—these we depend upon for our protection and livelihood, yet you want to give them to someone who is just learning how to manage them! Don't they mean more to you than a piece of embroidery?

"I have heard that one learns first and then enters the government. I have never heard that one enters the government in order to learn. If you proceed in this fashion, there are bound to be those who suffer!

"Take the case of hunting. If one is accustomed to shooting with a bow and driving a carriage, he may bag plenty of birds. But if he has never even mounted a carriage, shot a bow, or driven, then he will be in constant fear of making a mistake or overturning. How will he have any time to think about the catch?"

Tzu-p'i said, "Excellent! Forgive my thoughtlessness. I have heard that the gentleman strives to understand what is great and far in the distance, while the petty man strives to understand what is small and close at hand. I am a petty man. Robes and garments I wear next to my own body—these I know and so I am careful about them. But great offices and great cities—though my livelihood depends on them, they seem far away and so I don't bother to think of them. If it had not been for your words, I would not have understood the matter. In the past I said to you, 'You take care of the state of Cheng. I will take care of my own family, and in that way insure my livelihood. That will be best.'[15] But now for the first time I realize that that is not enough. From now on, I hope I may look to you for advice even on how to run my family affairs."

Tzu-ch'an said, "People's minds differ, just as their faces do. I would not venture to insist that your face be the same as mine. It's just that in my mind I sensed a certain danger and so I mentioned the matter to you."

Tzu-p'i believed in Tzu-ch'an's loyalty and therefore delegated government affairs to him. As a result, Tzu-ch'an was able to bring order to the state of Cheng.

15 Tzu-p'i is perhaps referring to the time when he handed over the management of the government to Tzu-ch'an.

THIRTY-ONE

The Death of King Ling of Ch'u

KING LING OF CH'U BECAME RULER IN 541 BY MURDERING HIS nephew, King Chia-ao (r. 544–541), and seizing the throne from him. In the years that followed, as we see below, he carried out many other violent and willful acts that served to arouse opposition to his rule. The narrative describes the revolt headed by three of his younger brothers that brought about his death in 529, the twelfth year of his reign. It opens with a scene in which the king, encamped at a place called Kan-ch'i or Dry Gulch and engaged in besieging the small neighboring state of Hsü, boasts of how his military exploits have put fear into the Chou ruler and the other feudal lords and inspired them to have greater respect for Ch'u, a state they formerly looked upon with contempt. One of the king's officials attempts to warn him against such arrogance and persuade him to change his ways, but the king is incapable of heeding the advice.

DUKE CHAO 12TH YEAR (530 B.C.)

King Ling of Ch'u held a winter hunt at Chou-lai and then camped by the tail of the Ying River.[1] He dispatched his officials, the marquis of T'ang, the viscount of P'an, the marshal Tu, Wu, the overseer of Hsiao, and Hsi, the overseer of Ling, to lead the troops and lay siege to the capital of Hsü in order to put fear into Hsü's ally, the state of Wu. The ruler of Ch'u then moved his encampment to Kan-ch'i so he could lend support to the attack.

Snow was falling, and the king donned a feather cap, a feathered robe

1 The place where the Ying River flows into the Huai, in present day Anhui Province.

from the state of Ch'in, a cape of kingfisher feathers, and shoes of leopard skin, and with a whip in hand, ventured forth. The official Hsi-fu, who was acting as his carriage driver, attended him.

The overseer of the right Tzu-ko came to pay his evening respects.[2] When the king saw him, he removed his cap and cape, laid aside his whip, and conversed with him.

"Long ago," said the king, "my ancestor, King Hsiung-i, joined with Lü Chi, the royal grandson Mou, Hsieh-fu, and Ch'in-fu in serving King K'ang.[3] At that time the four states of Ch'i, Wei, Chin, and Lu all received a portion of the Chou ruler's wealth, but our state alone received nothing. Now I have dispatched an envoy to the Chou court to request that the cauldrons be given us as our portion. Do you think the king will grant my request?"[4]

"Surely he will give them to you, my king!" Tzu-ko replied. "In former times the Ch'u ruler, King Hsiung-i, hid himself in this far-off region of Ching-shan. Riding in a crude cart, dressed in ragged clothing, he dwelt among the grass and weeds, paced the mountain forests, and in this way served the Son of Heaven. He had only peachwood bows and thornwood arrows to present as his contribution to the king's business. Ch'i, on the other hand, was the native state of King K'ang's grandmother, while the founders of Chin, Lu, and Wei were all King K'ang's uncles or great uncles.[5] This is why Ch'u received no portion, while the others did. Now, however, the Chou ruler and the four states of Ch'i, Chin, Lu, and Wei bow before you and serve you. They will do whatever you command. How could they begrudge you the cauldrons?"

King Ling said, "Long ago K'un-wu, the uncle of one of my remote ancestors, made his home in the old area of Hsü.[6] But now the men of the state of Cheng in their greed have taken over the lands in that area and will not return them. If I ask for them, do you suppose Cheng will give them to me?"

2 Tzu-ko was an official of the state of Cheng who had sought refuge in Ch'u and was given the post of overseer of the right. As will be seen in the following sentence, King Ling treated him with deference.

3 Hsiung-i was the first ruler to be enfeoffed in the state of Ch'u. Lü Chi was the son of T'ai-kung Wang, first ruler of Ch'i. The royal grandson Mou was the son of K'ang-shu, first ruler of Wei. Hsieh-fu was the son of T'ang-shu, first ruler of Chin. Ch'in-fu was the son of the Duke of Chou, first ruler of Lu. King K'ang, who according to traditional dating reigned 1078–1053, was the son of King Ch'eng and grandson of King Wu, the founders of the Chou dynasty.

4 On the cauldrons of Chou, see p. 81 above.

5 The mother of King Ch'eng was a daughter of the founder of Ch'i. The founders of Chin and Lu were both brothers of King Ch'eng, while the founder of Wei was King Ch'eng's uncle.

6 According to the account in *Shih chi* 40, "The Hereditary House of Ch'u," K'un-wu was the eldest of six brothers, the youngest of whom became the ancestor of the Ch'u ruling family. This was in a remote age before the Hsia dynasty.

Tzu-ko replied, "Surely they'll give them to you, my king! If Chou does not begrudge you the cauldrons, how would Cheng dare begrudge you the lands?"

King Ling said, "Long ago, the other feudal lords regarded me as someone far away and feared the state of Chin. But now I have built huge walls around the capital cities of the states of Ch'en, Ts'ai, and Pu-keng, and each is capable of supplying a thousand war chariots. You yourself played a part in these undertakings. Will the other feudal lords fear me now?"

Tzu-ko replied, "Surely they'll fear you, my king! Any one of these three states[7] alone would be sufficient to inspire fear. And how much more so if the might of Ch'u is added to it? How would they dare do otherwise than fear you?"

The overseer of artisans Lu came to the king with a request, saying, "Your Majesty has ordered that a jade baton be broken up and used to ornament the handle of an ax. May I venture to ask for further instructions?" The king entered his inner apartments to see to the matter.

Hsi-fu said to Tzu-ko, "The state of Ch'u looks to you for help. Yet now you do no more than echo the words of the king! If you proceed in this manner, what will become of the state?"

Tzu-ko said, "I'm whetting my blade and lying in wait. When the king makes a move, my weapon will cut him in two!"

The king reappeared and resumed the conversation. At that time I-hsiang, the historian of the left, hurried by. The king said, "He is a good historian. You should observe him well. He knows how to read the Three *Fen,* the Five *Tien,* and Eight *So,* and the Nine *Ch'iu.*"[8]

Tzu-ko replied, "I once questioned him. They say that long ago, King Mu wished to give free rein to his heart by traveling all over the world, leaving his carriage tracks and horses' hoofprints in every region. Mou-fu, the duke of Chai, composed the ode entitled *Ch'i-chao* in order to still the ruler's heart.[9] As a result, King Mu was able to die a natural death at the

7 The text actually says "four states." The older explanation, put forth by Tu Yü, is that Pu-keng was made up of two parts, Eastern Pu-keng and Western Pu-keng. I have followed commentators who opine that "four" here is simply a mistake for "three."

8 No such texts are extant and commentators can only speculate as to their content and provenance. The word *fen* here appears to mean "great." *Tien* or "canon" is a term used for some sections of the *Book of Documents. So* or "inquiry" may refer to some kind of commentary on the Eight Diagrams or eight basic trigrams of the *Book of Changes. Ch'iu* means "hill" but here may refer to some geographical work pertaining to the Nine Provinces of ancient China. The point of the sentence is that the historian I-hsiang is thoroughly versed in the ancient texts.

9 King Mu (r. 1001–947) was an early Chou ruler famous in legend for his fine horses and his rambles about the empire. The ode entitled *Ch'i-chao* is one of the "lost odes," not being included in the *Book of Odes,* and one can only guess at the meaning of its title. Older interpretations take *Ch'i-chao* to be the name of a person; other suggestions are that the title means "Seeking Brightness" (i.e.,

Chih palace.[10] I asked I-hsiang about the ode, but he knew nothing. If I ask him about affairs even older than that, how would he be able to answer?"

The king said, "Can you recite from the ode?"

Tzu-ko replied, "I can. The ode says:

> Serene, serene is *Ch'i-chao;*
> make bright the virtuous tone.
> I think of my king's measures,
> may they be like jade,
> may they be like gold.
> May he gauge his people's strength,
> not be drunken and sated in heart!"

The king bowed and retired to his apartments. He did not eat the food set before him, nor could he sleep soundly at night. But after several days he was still unable to overcome his selfish desires, and so he met with difficulty.[11]

Confucius remarks: An old book tells us, "To overcome oneself and return to propriety is the way of benevolence."[12] Good words indeed! If King Ling of Ch'u had been capable of doing so, how would he have met with disgrace at Kan-ch'i?

The narrative now describes the enmities that King Ling aroused in the past among the officials and powerful families of Ch'u and its neighbors, and the revolt that was precipitated by these discontents.

understanding on the part of King Mu), or "Seeking Return" (return of the king from his imprudent rambles). Or perhaps the word *chao* refers to the Shao music of high antiquity. In the quotation from the ode that appears below, I have left the term untranslated.

10 That is, King Mu was persuaded to give up his plans for a journey and to devote himself to affairs of government. The Chih palace was a detached palace in the state of Cheng.

11 By "difficulty" the *Tso* is referring to the death of the king, as described in the section of the narrative that follows. The king, as indicated by his restless behavior, was fully aware of the remonstrance that Tzu-ko had delivered through the words of the ode. But he was incapable of overcoming his inner nature and reforming his ways.

12 The same statement is found in *Analects* XII, 1: "The Master said: 'To overcome oneself and return to propriety is benevolence.' "

DUKE CHAO 13TH YEAR (529 B.C.)

Earlier, when King Ling of Ch'u became prime minister of the state, he put to death the grand marshal Wei Yen and appropriated his belongings. Later, after he came to the throne, he seized the lands belonging to Wei Chü, and when he moved the state of Hsü, he made a hostage of Wei, a high official of Hsü.[13] Wei of the state of Ts'ai had earlier enjoyed favor with the king, but when the king wiped out Ts'ai, Wei's father died in the fighting.[14] King Ling accordingly left Wei behind and did not allow him to accompany the royal party when he went to Kan-ch'i. Again, at the time of the meeting at Shen (538 B.C.), the official of Yüeh [Ch'ang Shou-kuo] was subjected to insult. The king also seized the city of Chung-ch'ou from Tou Wei-kuei, and likewise seized a city from Tou Wei-kuei's son, Tou Ch'eng-jan, and ordered him to act as overseer of the capital suburbs. Tou Ch'eng-jan had earlier been in the service of the king's brother, the new ruler of Ts'ai.

As a result, the Wei clan, as well as Wei Chü, Wei of the state of Hsü, and Wei and Tou Ch'eng-jan of the state of Ts'ai, all felt they had been treated with impropriety by the king. They accordingly joined with the numerous persons who had been deprived of their offices by the king and, making Ch'ang Shou-kuo, the official from Yüeh, a party to their plans, they initiated a revolt. They laid siege to the city of Ku-ch'eng, seized the city of Hsi-chou, and fortified their position at the latter.

Earlier, when Kuan Ch'i was put to death, his son Kuan Ts'ung went to Ts'ai, where he entered the service of Chao Wu.[15] He said to Chao Wu, "If we do not take this opportunity to restore the state of Ts'ai, it will never be restored! Let me try and see what I can do."

He forged an order from the new ruler of Ts'ai summoning Tzu-kan and Tzu-hsi.[16] When they arrived in the suburbs of the Ts'ai capital, he ex-

13 The murder of Wei Yen is recorded under Duke Hsiang 30th year (543 B.C.). In 533, King Ling forced the small state of Hsü to move to the region of the Yi barbarians.

14 In 531 King Ling murdered the ruler of Ts'ai and later in the year appointed his own younger brother, Prince Ch'i-chi, as the new ruler of Ts'ai.

15 Kuan Ch'i had been in the service of Prince Tzu-nan when the latter was prime minister of Ch'u. In 551 King Kung of Ch'u had both Prince Tzu-nan and Kuan Ch'i put to death because he feared their power. Chao Wu was a former official of Ts'ai who, as we shall see, hoped to see the state, which had been overthrown by Ch'u in 531, restored.

16 The new ruler of Ts'ai was King Ling's younger brother, Prince Ch'i-chi. Tzu-kan and Tzu-hsi were sons of King Kung and younger brothers of King Ling and Prince Ch'i-chi. In 541, when King

plained the situation to them and forced them to conclude an alliance with him. He then made a surprise attack on the Ts'ai capital.

The ruler of Ts'ai was just about to sit down to a meal, but when he saw the invaders, he fled. Kuan Ts'ung instructed Tzu-kan to eat the meal. Digging a hole and offering a sacrifice, he placed the text of the alliance over it, and then hurried the two princes from the scene.[17] He went about Ts'ai in person showing the alliance and saying, "The ruler of Ts'ai has summoned the two princes and is going to restore them to power. He has joined with them in an alliance and has sent them on ahead. He himself will lead his troops and follow after!"

The people of Ts'ai gathered around and were about to seize Kuan Ts'ung, but he said, "The rebels have escaped and are massing their troops. What good will it do to put me to death?" With this they released him.

Chao Wu then addressed the people: "Gentlemen, if you are prepared to lay down your lives for the king, then you had best defy the ruler of Ts'ai and wait to see what transpires. But if you seek peace and security, then you had best side with the ruler of Ts'ai and make events transpire according to your wishes! Moreover, should you defy your superior, where could you go to escape punishment?"

The people replied, "We will side with him!"

They proceeded to acknowledge Prince Ch'i-chi, the ruler of Ts'ai, as their leader and, summoning the other two princes, concluded an alliance with them at the city of Teng. They enlisted the support of the people of the former states of Ch'en and Ts'ai by promising that those states would be reestablished. Thus the three princes of Ch'u, Ch'i-chi, Tzu-kan, and Tzu-hsi, along with Tou Ch'eng-jan and Chao Wu of Ts'ai, led the combined armies of Ch'en, Ts'ai, Pu-keng, Hsü, and She, and along with followers from the four families of Wei Chü, Wei of Hsü, Wei of Ts'ai, and Tou Ch'eng-jan, marched into Ch'u.

When they reached the suburbs of the Ch'u capital, the men of Ch'en and Ts'ai, wishing to commemorate the occasion, asked permission to erect a walled encampment to exemplify the military might of the armies. The ruler of Ts'ai understood their intention but said, "We must hurry! Moreover, our workmen are worn out. I hope you will content yourselves with a palisade." Accordingly they erected a palisade for the armies.

Ling murdered his nephew Chia-ao and seized the throne of Ch'u from him, Tzu-kan fled to Chin and Tzu-hsi fled to Cheng.

17 It was customary when concluding an alliance to dig a hole, place an animal sacrifice in it, smear one's lips with the blood, and place the text of the alliance over the sacrifice. Here Kuan Ts'ung has this procedure carried out so it will appear that the two princes have concluded the alliance with Prince Ch'i-chi, the Ts'ai ruler who fled.

The ruler of Ts'ai dispatched Hsü Wu-mou and Shih P'ai to enter the capital ahead of the others. Enlisting the aid of the chief groom, they put to death Lu, the eldest son of King Ling, and another son, Prince P'i-ti.

Prince Tzu-kan or Pi assumed the title of king, while Prince Tzu-hsi or Hei-kung became prime minister; they encamped at Yü-p'o. Prince Ch'i-chi assumed the office of marshal and went ahead of the others to clear the palace of King Ling's supporters.

He dispatched Kuan Ts'ung to go to Kan-ch'i and contact King Ling's army there, reporting to them on the situation. Kuan Ts'ung said, "Those who return to the capital at once will get their old positions back. Those who are slow about it will have their noses cut off!" By the time the king's army reached Tzu-liang it had melted away.

When King Ling received word of the death of his sons, he threw himself to the ground beside his carriage. "Do other men love their sons the way I loved mine?" he said.

"Even more!" said his attendant. "When petty men get old and have no sons, they know they'll end tumbled in a ditch!"

The king said, "I have killed many sons of other men—how could I help but come to this?"

The overseer of the right Tzu-ko said, "I beg you to wait in the suburbs of the capital till you hear how the people of the state are disposed!"

But the king replied, "The wrath of the populace cannot be opposed."

"Perhaps you could take up a position in one of the larger cities and solicit troops from the other feudal lords."

The king replied, "All the cities have turned against me!"

"Perhaps you could flee to one of the other states and get its ruler to assist you to regain your throne."

The king replied, "Good fortune does not come twice. I would only bring shame on myself!"

Tzu-ko thereupon took leave of the king and returned to the Ch'u capital. King Ling followed the course of the Hsia, intending to enter the city of Yen.[18]

Yü-yin Shen-hai, son of the Ch'u official Yü-yin Wu-yü, said to himself, "My father twice defied the king's command, but the king did not punish him.[19] There could be no greater act of mercy. I cannot bear to see my ruler suffer, nor to ignore the debt I owe for such mercy. I will attend the king!"

18 Hsia is another name for the Han River. Yen was a secondary capital of Ch'u.

19 When King Ling was still prime minister, he had a flag made for his carriage which was like that

He went in search of King Ling and, encountering him at the gate to a village in Chi, took him to his own home.

In summer, the fifth month, the day *kuei-hai,* the king strangled himself at the home of Yü-yin Shen-hai. Yü-yin Shen-hai put to death his own two daughters and buried them with the king.[20]

With King Ling removed from the scene, the narrative now turns to a description of the fate of the leaders of the revolt.

Kuan Ts'ung said to Prince Tzu-kan, "If you do not kill Ch'i-chi, even though you become ruler you will suffer misfortune!"

"I cannot bear to kill him," said Prince Tzu-kan.

"But he can bear to kill you!" said Kuan Ts'ung. "And I cannot bear to linger here any longer!" With this he departed.

Every night the Ch'u capital was startled by reports that King Ling was entering the city.[21] On the night of the day *i-mao,* Prince Ch'i-chi sent men

---

used by the king. Yü-yin Wu-yü, considering this improper, broke the flagstaff in two. Later, after King Ling took the throne, one of Yü-yin Wu-yü's gatekeepers, having committed a crime, ran away and hid among a party of laborers who were building a new palace for the king. Yü-yin Wu-yü, despite the protests of the guards, seized the gatekeeper on the palace grounds and took him home. Both acts were violations of the law but were pardoned by King Ling. They are described under Duke Chao 7th year (535 B.C.).

20 The *Kuo yü,* in a narrative dealing with King Fu-ch'ai of Wu in chapter 19, gives the following account of King Ling's last days:

> The three armies revolted against King Ling at Kan-ch'i. The king, thrown into panic and confusion, wandered all alone through the mountain forest for three days. At last he came upon his porter Ch'ou.
>
> The king called to the porter, saying, "I have not eaten for three days!"
>
> Ch'ou hastened forward to attend the king, who, pillowing his head on Ch'ou's thigh, lay down on the ground. But when the king had fallen asleep, Ch'ou placed the king's head on a clod of earth and abandoned him.
>
> When the king awoke and found himself alone, he crawled on hands and knees till he reached the gate of a village in Chi, but the people at the gate refused to admit him. Finally he entered the home of Yü-yin Shen-hai. There he strangled himself.

Ssu-ma Ch'ien, ever appreciative of a good story, in his own account of the death of King Ling in chapter 40 of the *Shih chi,* combines the *Tso chuan* and *Kuo yü* accounts to achieve the maximum in pathetic effect.

21 The people were unaware of the king's whereabouts and supposed he was still in command of his troops. Prince Ch'i-chi exploited this fact to create panic in the city.

racing throughout the city, crying, "The king is here!" The people of the capital were greatly alarmed.

He also dispatched Tou Ch'eng-jan to run to Prince Tzu-kan and Prince Tzu-hsi and report to them, "The king is here! The people have killed your marshal, Prince Ch'i-chi, and are coming this way! If you act quickly enough you can escape disgrace. The anger of the populace is like flood or fire—you cannot hope to reckon with it!"

When other men came racing by and shouting, "The people are coming!", the two princes both committed suicide.

On the day *ping-ch'en,* Prince Ch'i-chi ascended the throne, taking the personal name Hsiung-chü. He had Prince Tzu-kan buried at Tzu; the latter is hence known as Tzu-ao.[22] He also had a prisoner killed, dressed the body in the robes of King Ling, and dumped it into the Han River. He then fished the body out and gave it appropriate burial in order to pacify the people of the state. He appointed Tou Ch'eng-jan to the post of prime minister.

When the Ch'u armies were on their way back from the attack upon Hsü, they were defeated by the Wu forces at Yü-chang and all five commanders were taken prisoner.[23]

The new ruler, Prince Ch'i-chi, posthumously known as King P'ing, once more enfeoffed the former ruling families of Ch'en and Ts'ai and restored to their original sites the cities that had been moved. He handed out rewards to those who had aided him, dispensed largess and treated the common people with lenience, pardoned offenses and restored offices.

He summoned Kuan Ts'ung and told him, "You have but to name your wish!" Kuan Ts'ung replied, "My ancestors assisted at divinations by the tortoiseshell." The king accordingly appointed him overseer of divination by the tortoiseshell.

The king dispatched Chih-ju Tzu-kung on a courtesy visit to the state of Cheng and instructed him to return the lands of Ch'ou and Li.[24] When Chih-ju Tzu-kung arrived in Cheng and finished announcing his mission, he had still not mentioned the return of the lands. The men of Cheng said, "Reports from along the road indicate that you have some message for our ruler regarding Ch'ou and Li. May we ask you to be good enough to deliver

22 According to Ch'u custom, rulers who were not assigned posthumous names were known by the place where they were buried plus the word *ao.* Chia-ao, the ruler whom King Ling murdered and replaced, is an example.

23 On the attack upon Hsü, see p. 164 above. The five commanders are the marquis of T'ang, the viscount of P'an, the marshal Tu, Wu, the overseer of Hsiao, and Hsi, the overseer of Ling.

24 Territories of Cheng that had earlier been seized by Ch'u.

the message?" But Chih-ju Tzu-kung replied, "I have received no such message."

When he had returned to Ch'u and reported on his mission, King P'ing asked him about the matter of Ch'ou and Li. Chih-ju Tzu-kung doffed his robe and replied, "I mistook my orders and in error failed to deliver the lands."[25]

The king took his hand and said, "Do not fret about it. Go home now. If I need your services, I will send you word."[26]

Some years later, Yü-yin Shen-hai reported to the court concerning the burial place of King Ling, and the king's body was accordingly dug up and reinterred.

The *Tso chuan* brings to a close its narration on the death of King Ling with some scenes pertaining to the king's younger days and the other brothers who preceded and followed him as ruler of Ch'u.

Some years earlier King Ling, before he became king, divined by the tortoiseshell, saying, "May I be given rulership over this realm!" But the response was inauspicious. He threw aside the tortoiseshell and cursed Heaven, saying, "This paltry little realm you will not give me? In that case I'll take it for myself!"

The people of Ch'u were distressed by the king's insatiable desires. Hence they flocked to join the revolt as though they were going to their own homes.

Still earlier, King Ling's father, King Kung, had no heir by his consort, but had five sons by other women whom he favored.[27] Not knowing which one to appoint as heir, he decided to carry out lavish sacrifices to the

25 The doffing of the robe is a gesture indicating that he is deserving of punishment.

26 The narrative does not make clear whether Chih-ju Tzu-kung actually mistook his mission, or merely pretended to do so in the knowledge that the king would secretly approve his action.

27 King Kung reigned 590–560. His sons, in order of age, were King K'ang (r. 559–545), King Ling (r. 540–529), Prince Tzu-kan, Prince Tzu-hsi, and King P'ing (r. 528–516).

mountains and rivers in the kingdom and pray to them, saying, "I beg the gods to choose from among my five sons the one who should become lord of the altars of the soil and grain." He displayed a jade disk at each of the sacrifices, saying, "Whichever son performs his bow at the spot where this jade disk is placed will be the one elevated by the gods. Who will dare to question the choice?"

He and Lady Pa[28] together secretly buried the disk in the courtyard of the ancestral temple of Ch'u. He then ordered his sons to fast and prepare themselves for worship and to enter the courtyard in the order of their age and perform their obseisance.

The future King K'ang's legs straddled the disk when he bowed, the future King Ling's elbow partially covered it, but Tzu-kan and Tzu-hsi were both far away from it. The future King P'ing, being a mere infant, was carried into the courtyard and performed two bows. Both times his hands pressed down right where the cord was attached to the disk.

Tou Wei-kuei instructed his son Tou Ch'eng-jan to support the future King P'ing. But he added, "Whether the king goes against the rules of propriety or disregards the command of the gods, Ch'u will face danger in either case!"[29]

The final scene in the narrative takes place in the state of Chin shortly after Prince Tzu-kan returned to his native state of Ch'u at the summons of Kuan Ts'ung. See p. 168 above. Han Ch'i, son of Han Chüeh, a high official of Chin, and Yang-she Shu-hsiang, a Chin official who had served as envoy to Ch'u and was well versed in its affairs, here discuss the chances for Tzu-kan to succeed in overthrowing King Ling and replacing him as ruler of Ch'u.

28 A favorite concubine of King Kung.

29 That is, King Kung has created a dilemma for himself: if he follows the rules of propriety, which favor the principle of primogeniture, and sets up his eldest son as heir, he will be defying the will expressed by the gods, who favored the youngest son. Hence whatever choice he makes, the state will be imperiled.

When Prince Tzu-kan returned to Ch'u, Han Ch'i said to Yang-she Shu-hsiang, "Will Tzu-kan succeed?"

"It will be difficult!" replied Shu-hsiang.

Han Ch'i said, "Those who share the same hatreds help each other—it's just like the marketplace.[30] Why should it be difficult?"

Shu-hsiang replied, "Since there's no one who shares his likes, who will share his hatreds? In seizing a state there are five difficulties. First, a man may enjoy favorable position but lack the proper associates. Second, he may have associates but lack a host to welcome him. Third, he may have a host but lack a plan. Fourth, he may have a plan but lack a populace to support him. Fifth, he may have the populace but lack a name for virtue.

"Tzu-kan was here in Chin for thirteen years, but among his followers from Ch'u and Chin I have heard of no outstanding men—so he may be said to lack associates. His clan is nearly wiped out and his kin have turned against him—so he may be said to lack a host to welcome him. He has made his move without waiting for a proper opening—so he may be said to lack a plan. He fled abroad and has been away for almost a decade—so he may be said to lack the support of the populace. While he has been abroad, there is no sign he was greatly missed at home—so he may be said to lack a name for virtue. King Ling is tyrannical, but he is not envious of others. In order to become ruler of Ch'u, Tzu-kan will have to overcome these five difficulties and commit regicide against a long-established ruler. Who could succeed in such circumstances?

"The one who will end up in possession of the state of Ch'u is Ch'i-chi. Since he became ruler of Ch'en and Ts'ai, all the area beyond the Fang-ch'eng Mountains is in his grasp. He imposes no harsh or improper demands, and the robbers and bandits in his area have all gone into hiding. He does not permit personal desires to lead him astray, and hence the common people bear him no grudge. The gods gave their command in his favor and the people of the state trust him. Whenever there is disorder among the persons of the Mi surname, it is always one of the younger sons who in the end takes the throne—this is a constant pattern in Ch'u history.[31]

"Ch'i-chi first of all has the protection of the gods. Second, he has the populace with him. Third, he has a name for virtue. Fourth, he enjoys favor

30 That is, there is such widespread hatred of King Ling that many people will join with Tzu-kan, just as merchants in the marketplace all join in striving to make a profit because they hate being poor.

31 Mi is the surname of the Ch'u ruling family. Cf. the words of the Ch'u prime minister Tzu-shang recorded under Duke Wen 1st year (626 B.C.): "The succession in the state of Ch'u customarily comes from among the younger sons."

and eminence. Fifth, he fits the constant pattern. With these five advantages to help him dispel the five difficulties, who could oppose him?

"Tzu-kan's office is only that of overseer of the right. In terms of eminence and favor, he is a mere son of a concubine. When the gods gave their command, he was far away from the jade disk. He lacks eminence, favor has passed him by, the people harbor no affection for him, no one in the state takes his side. How could he ascend the throne?"

"But," said Han Ch'i, "Duke Huan of Ch'i and Duke Wen of Chin—were they not such men?"[32]

Shu-hsiang replied, "Duke Huan of Ch'i was a son of Duke Hsi by his concubine, Lady Wei, and enjoyed favor with Duke Hsi. He had Pao Shu-ya, Pin Hsü-wu, and Shih P'eng to assist him.[33] The states of Chü and Wei acted as hosts when he was abroad, while the Kuo and Kao families were hosts welcoming him in Ch'i.[34] He followed goodness as water flows downward, bowed before goodness and was scrupulous in conduct and circumspect. He hoarded no wealth, gave no rein to his desires; he dispensed largess unwearyingly, sought goodness without ever tiring. Therefore he came to possess the state. And was that not fitting?

"Our former ruler Duke Wen was the son of Duke Hsien by his concubine, Lady Hu, and enjoyed favor with his father. He was single-minded in love of learning, and by the time he was seventeen he had acquired five followers.[35] The senior officials Chao Ts'ui and Hu Yen acted as his belly and heart; Wei Wu-tzu and Chia T'o were his legs and arms. The states of Ch'i, Sung, Ch'in, and Ch'u were his hosts abroad, with the Luan, Hsi, Hu, and Hsien families to host him in his own state. Though he was in exile for nineteen years, he grew more fervent than ever in his determination to return. Dukes Hui and Huai cast the populace aside, but in the case of Duke Wen, the populace actively followed and supported him. In the end there were no other kin of Duke Hsien left who might be ruler, and the people looked nowhere else in hopes of finding one. It was as though Heaven

32 Duke Wen of Chin has been described at length in earlier narratives. Duke Huan of Ch'i (r. 685–643), the other most famous of the Five Hegemons, is mentioned in the *Tso chuan* but his story is not recorded in detail.

33 Worthy men who aided Duke Huan to power. The list does not include Kuan Chung, Duke Huan's famous minister in later years, because Kuan Chung originally favored another contender for power.

34 The state of Chü harbored Duke Huan when he fled abroad in his youth. Wei was his mother's native state. Kuo and Kao were powerful ministerial families in Ch'i who supported Duke Huan.

35 Probably the five men designated on p. 41 above as accompanying the future Duke Wen on his wanderings, i.e., Hu Yen, Chao Ts'ui, Tien Hsieh, Wei Wu-tzu, and the minister of works Chi-tzu, though this list duplicates most of the figures mentioned in the next sentence.

was aiding the state of Chin—who could have taken the place of Duke Wen?

"Thus these two rulers, Duke Huan and Duke Wen, were very different from Tzu-kan of Ch'u. Among King Kung's sons there is one more favored than he, and the state still has its enthroned ruler.[36] Tzu-kan has distributed no largess to the people, nor does he have the support of states abroad. When he left Chin, no one saw him off. When he returned to Ch'u, no one greeted him. How can he hope to win the state?"

36 References to Prince Ch'i-chi and King Ling respectively.

T H I R T Y - T W O

The Death of Duke Chuang of Chu

THE ACCOUNT OF THE DEATH OF KING LING OF CH'U IN THE preceding selection has elements of tragedy and pathos about it that might almost put one in mind of *Richard II* or *King Lear.* By contrast, the following brief death scene is suggestive of pure farce. It centers upon Duke Chuang, the ruler of a small state called Chu in the Shantung Peninsula near the state of Lu. Elsewhere in the *Tso chuan* (Duke Chao 15th year), one of the characters observes that "a man will meet his end doing what he enjoys," and indeed in the *Tso* the particular manner of death is taken as an important key to the individual's personality, and vice versa. Duke Chuang of Chu succeeded his father, Duke Tao, as ruler of Chu in 541, and by the time of his demise was probably well along in years—old enough, that is, to have had better control of his temper.

DUKE TING 3D YEAR (507 B.C.)

Second month, the day *hsin-mao.* The ruler of Chu was on the terrace at the top of the palace gate, looking down into his courtyard. The gatekeeper at the time was dousing the courtyard with water from a pitcher. The ruler, spying him from afar, was greatly annoyed. When he questioned the gatekeeper, the latter said, "Yi Yeh-ku pissed in the court there!"

The ruler ordered Yi Yeh-ku arrested. When Yi Yeh-ku could not be found, the ruler, more furious than ever, flung himself down on his bed with such violence that he fell off into the ashes of the brazier and burned to death.

Before dying, he gave instructions that five chariots be buried with him and five men put to death to accompany his spirit. Duke Chuang was a very excitable and fastidious man, and therefore he came to such an end.

T H I R T Y - T H R E E

The Battle Between Wu and Ch'u at Po-chü

THE NARRATIVE ON THE DEATH OF KING LING OF CH'U ENDED with the accession to the throne of King Ling's youngest brother, Prince Ch'i-chi, who became King P'ing of Ch'u. King P'ing designated his son Chien as crown prince and appointed an official named Wu She to be his chief tutor. But a rival official succeeded in persuading the king that Prince Chien and Wu She were contemplating treason. In 522 King P'ing summoned Wu She to court and subjected him to examination.

Wu She had two sons, Wu Shang and Wu Yün (Wu Tzu-hsü), and the king was advised to summon the sons to court as well so they could not plot against him. The king did so, threatening to kill their father if they did not obey the summons. The elder son, Wu Shang, answered the summons out of a sense of filial duty, though he knew that both he and his father would undoubtedly be put to death. But he urged his younger brother Wu Yün to flee to the nearby state of Wu so that he could live to avenge their father's death. As he put it, "I will do the dying, you can do the avenging." As the sons had expected, Wu She and Wu Shang were put to death in 522. These events are described in the *Tso chuan* under that date, Duke Chao 20th year.

The following narrative is in part the story of how Wu Yün, having fled to Wu, finally succeeded in avenging the death of his father and elder brother. It is also the story of how Wu, a relatively minor state on the seacoast east of Ch'u, gradually built up its military power until, under King Ho-lü, who had seized the throne of

Wu in 515, it was able to inflict a decisive defeat on Ch'u and for a time occupy the Ch'u capital city of Ying.

DUKE TING 4TH YEAR (506 B.C.)

The men of Shen failed to attend the meeting at Shao-ling.[1] The men of Chin instructed Ts'ai to attack Shen. In the summer, Ts'ai attacked and wiped out Shen. In the autumn, Ch'u, because of the action taken against Shen, laid siege to the Ts'ai capital.

Wu Yün at this time was acting as receiver of envoys for the state of Wu and helped to plan campaigns against Ch'u.

After Ch'u put to death Hsi Yüan, the members of the Po family fled from Ch'u.[2] Thus Po Chou-li's grandson Po P'i was acting as prime minister of Wu and also helped to plan campaigns against Ch'u. At this time King Chao had just come to the throne of Ch'u, and no year went by without an attack from the armies of Wu.[3] The ruler of Ts'ai arranged with Wu to send his son Ch'ien and the sons of his high officials to that state as hostages.[4]

In the winter, the rulers of Ts'ai, Wu, and T'ang attacked Ch'u.[5] They tied up their boats at the bend of the Huai River and proceeded by way of Yü-chang, drawing up on one side of the Han River while the Ch'u forces occupied the opposite bank.

The Ch'u marshal of the left Shen-yin Hsü said to Nang Wa, "You patrol up and down along the banks of the Han. I will lead all the forces from beyond the Fang-ch'eng Mountains and destroy the enemy's boats, and then circle back and block the passes at Ta-sui, Chih-yüah, and Ming-ai. Then you can cross the Han and attack the enemy, I'll strike them from the rear, and we're bound to inflict a crushing defeat."[6]

After this plan had been decided upon and was being put into effect,

1 In the third month of this year the rulers of the northern states met at Shao-ling to lay plans for an attack on Ch'u. The meeting was ostensibly called by a minister of the Chou court but in fact was instigated by Duke Ting of Chin, who hoped thereby to gain control over the other states; his efforts in this direction failed. Shen, a small state neighboring and allied with Ch'u, declined to attend the meeting.

2 The Ch'u official Hsi Yüan was slandered by a rival and put to death along with the members of his family in 515 B.C. At that time the members of the Po family, who had been allies of the Hsi family, fled to the state of Wu. Po Chou-li of the Po family, as we have seen on p. 131*n*12, was originally from Chin.

3 515 marked the first year of King Chao's reign. He was the son of King P'ing.

4 The ruler of Ts'ai at this time was Marquis Chao (r. 518–490).

5 The ruler of Wu at this time was King Ho-lü, who had arranged the assassination of his predecessor and seized the throne in 515. T'ang was a small state between Ts'ai and Ch'u.

6 Nang Wa was prime minister of Ch'u at this time. Greedy and suspicious by nature, he had put to death many officials of Ch'u and aroused hatred among the smaller states such as Ts'ai and T'ang.

Hei, an official of the city of Wu-ch'eng, said to Nang Wa, "The Wu war chariots are made of wood, while ours use leather trappings and will not last for long.[7] You had best engage in battle as quickly as possible!"

And another Ch'u official, Shih Huang, said to him, "The people of Ch'u hate you and favor the marshal. If the marshal destroys the Wu army's boats on the Huai, blocks the Fang-ch'eng passes, and then carries out an attack, he alone will get all the credit for defeating Wu! You had better engage in combat as quickly as possible, or you will never escape censure."

Nang Wa accordingly crossed the Han River and drew up his lines on the other side. In the region from Little Pieh to Big Pieh mountains, he fought three engagements with the enemy, but realized that victory was impossible. He was about to flee when Shih Huang said, "You were happy enough to manage affairs while they were going well, but now there's trouble, you want to run away! Where do you think you can run to? You must stay here and die! If so, you'll be pardoned for your earlier error."[8]

Eleventh month, the day *keng-wu:* the two armies drew up their lines at Po-chü in Ch'u. When King Ho-lü's younger brother, King Fu-kai,[9] came to pay his early morning respects, he said to King Ho-lü, "Nang Wa of Ch'u is a heartless man and none of his officials have any intention of dying in his cause. If I lead off with an attack on him, his men are certain to flee. Then the bulk of the army can follow me up and we are bound to win victory!"

King Ho-lü refused permission for such a move. But King Fu-kai said, "This is a case where a subordinate, seeing his duty, must carry it out without waiting for orders! If I die on the field today, Ch'u can surely be invaded!" He then led the five thousand men under his command and initiated hostilities by making an attack on Nang Wa's men.

Nang Wa's men fled, the Ch'u army was thrown into panic, and the Wu forces inflicted a major defeat. Nang Wa fled to the state of Cheng. Shih Huang mounted Nang Wa's chariot, pretending to be Nang Wa, and died in battle.

The Wu troops pursued the Ch'u army as far as the Ch'ing-fa River, where they prepared to attack once more. But King Fu-kai said, "Even an animal, if pressed too hard, will turn and fight, to say nothing of a man. If they know there's no escape and they must fight to the death, they are bound to overpower us. But if we make those who have already crossed the

7 Because rain and dampness will cause the leather to deteriorate.

8 That is, for crossing the Han and attacking too soon.

9 The title "King" here is an anachronism. Fu-kai did not take this title until the following year, 505 B.C., when he made an unsuccessful attempt to replace his older brother as ruler of Wu, as we shall see in the pages that follow.

river believe they have escaped, then those still on this side will scramble to get across as well and will have no will to fight. When they're halfway across the river, that will be the time to attack!"

They adopted this plan and once more inflicted a defeat. The Ch'u soldiers who had already crossed the river had begun preparing a meal, but when the Wu men arrived on the scene, they fled. The Wu troops ate the meal and then set off in pursuit once more, defeating the Ch'u troops at Yung-shih. They fought a total of five engagements, until they reached the Ch'u capital at Ying.

On the day *chi-mao* the Ch'u ruler, accompanied by his youngest sister, Mi Pi-wo, left the city. When he crossed the Chü River, the Ch'u official Chen Yin-ku went in the same boat with the king. The king arranged to have elephants with lighted torches tied to their tails stampeded in the direction of the Wu forces.

On the day *keng-ch'en* the Wu forces entered Ying. The commanders occupied the Ch'u palaces in accordance with their respective ranks. Prince Tzu-shan occupied the palace of the prime minister.[10] King Fu-kai, wishing the palace for himself, was about to attack the prince when the latter, frightened, abandoned it, leaving it for King Fu-kai to occupy.[11]

The Ch'u marshal of the left Shen-yin Hsü, after withdrawing as far as Hsi, returned and inflicted a defeat on the Wu forces at Yung-shih, but was wounded in the action.

Earlier in his career he had been in the service of King Ho-lü of Wu, and he was therefore ashamed at the thought of being taken prisoner by the Wu forces. He said to his officers, "Who will see to it that my head does not fall into enemy hands?"

One of his men, Wu Kou-pi, said, "I'm a man of no rank, but will I do?"

"In the past I've misjudged your true worth!" the marshal said. "You will do fine." He fought three engagements with the enemy and was wounded each time. "I'm of no more use now!" he said.

10 Prince Tzu-shan was a son of King Ho-lü of Wu.

11 The *Tso chuan* at this point says nothing about acts of destruction carried out by the Wu forces or by Wu Yün (Wu Tzu-hsü) against the Ch'u royal house. The *Ku-liang* Commentary, under Duke Ting 4, however, states: "The Wu forces . . . destroyed the ancestral temples, moved their racks of musical instruments, and whipped the grave of King P'ing." The whipping of the grave of King P'ing, who died ten years previously, in 516, is also mentioned in *Lü-shih ch'un-ch'iu* ch. 14, *Shou-shih,* and in *Huai-nan Tzu* ch. 20. In the *Shih chi* it is depicted as a personal act of vengeance carried out by Wu Tzu-hsü against the ruler who put to death his father and elder brother. Thus, in the biography of Wu Tzu-hsü in *Shih chi* 66, we read: "Later, when the Wu forces entered Ying, Wu Tzu-hsü searched for King Chao. Failing to find him, he proceeded to dig up the grave of King P'ing of Ch'u, expose the corpse, and inflict three hundred lashes upon it." (See my translation of the biography in *Records of the Historian* [New York: Columbia University Press, 1969], p. 22.) Apparently when the *Tso chuan* account was compiled, this part of the Wu Tzu-hsü legend had not yet taken shape.

Wu Kou-pi then spread out his lower garment, cut off the marshal's head, and wrapped it in the garment. He concealed the bundle on his person and made off with the head.

The king of Ch'u, after crossing the Chü River and the Yangtze, entered the marsh of Yün-meng. As he was sleeping, bandits attacked him and struck at him with a halberd. The royal grandson Yu-yü shielded the king, taking the blow on his own back, and was pierced in the shoulder.

The king fled to Yün.[12] The Ch'u official Chung Chien carried the king's younger sister on his back and followed after. Later, when Yu-yü gradually regained consciousness from the blow he had suffered, he too followed the king.

Huai, the younger brother of Tou Hsin, lord of Yün, wanted to assassinate the king.[13] "King P'ing killed our father!" he said, "It's only right that I kill his son!"

But Tou Hsin said, "If a ruler punishes one of his ministers, who would dare resent the action? The ruler's command is like that of Heaven. When one dies because of Heaven's command, who would think of resenting it? The *Odes* says:

> The soft he does not gobble up,
> the hard he does not spit out;
> he does not abuse the lonely, the widowed,
> does not fear the strong, the mighty.[14]

Only the benevolent man can behave in this manner. Shunning the strong but persecuting the weak is not bravery. Profiting from a man's distress is not benevolence. Destroying one's clan and cutting off its sacrifices is not wisdom. If you insist upon committing such offenses, I will have to kill you!"

Tou Hsin and his younger brother Tou Ch'ao thereupon fled with the king to the state of Sui.

The Wu forces went in pursuit of the king of Ch'u, saying to the men of Sui, "Ch'u has wiped out all the descendants of the Chou house who were established along the Han River.[15] Now Heaven, making clear its will, is

12 A small state that had earlier been swallowed up by Ch'u.

13 Tou Hsin was the son of Tou Ch'eng-jan, an official we have seen on pp. 168–172 helping King P'ing to power. Later, in 528, King P'ing had Tou Ch'eng-jan put to death because of his avarice but assigned his son Tou Hsin to a post in Yün.

14 "Greater Odes," *Cheng min,* Mao no. 260.

15 Sui, a small state on the northern border of Ch'u, was ruled by a branch of the Chi family, the Chou royal family, as was the state of Wu. The men of Wu here are pointing out that in earlier times

inflicting punishment upon Ch'u, and yet you take steps to conceal the Ch'u ruler. What fault do you find with the Chou royal house, that you behave in this manner?

"If you will consider the debt of gratitude you owe the Chou royal house, and will extend your kindness to our ruler by encouraging Heaven to work its will, we will be much beholden to you. In that case, the lands north of the Han River will be yours for the taking."

The king of Ch'u occupied a position north of the palace of the ruler of Sui, while the Wu forces were south of the palace. The king's elder brother, Prince Tzu-ch'i, who resembled the king, proposed that he impersonate the king and in this way enable the king to flee. "If I am handed over to the enemy," he said, "Your Majesty will surely be able to escape."

The people of Sui divined by the tortoiseshell to see if they should hand over Prince Tzu-ch'i, but the response was unfavorable. They therefore addressed the Wu forces in these words: "Because Sui is a small, out-of-the-way state situated close to Ch'u, it has had to depend upon Ch'u for its existence. For generations we have sworn to ally ourselves with Ch'u, and to this day have never departed from that custom. If we were to turn our backs on Ch'u now that it is in difficulty, how could we serve your ruler in a spirit of good faith? It is not the king of Ch'u alone who poses a threat to your authorities.[16] If you can somehow restore peace and order within the borders of Ch'u, then we will of course heed your commands."

The Wu forces thereupon withdrew from Sui.

Lü Chin had earlier been a servant in the household of Prince Tzu-ch'i, and it was he who talked the men of Sui into promising to conceal King Chao and Prince Tzu-ch'i. Later King Chao wished to thank him openly, but he declined, saying, "I would not want it to seem as though I tried to profit by the king's distress."

The king made an incision in the flesh over Prince Tzu-ch'i's heart and with the blood concluded an alliance with the men of Sui.[17]

there had been a number of small states north of the Han River that were ruled by members of the Chi family, but that these had all been wiped out by Ch'u. Wu thus appeals to its fellow clansmen of Sui to honor their Chou ancestors and join in opposing the "barbarian" state of Ch'u.

16 That is, though you may seize the person of King Chao, you will still have to face the threat of reprisal from the officials and people of Ch'u.

17 He uses Prince Tzu-ch'i's blood to consecrate the alliance because the prince had earlier offered to sacrifice his life by impersonating the king.

While King Chao of Ch'u was being pursued by the Wu invaders and their allies, an official of Ch'u journeyed north to the powerful state of Ch'in to seek military assistance. Ch'in at this time was under the rule of Duke Ai (r. 536–501).

Earlier, Wu Yün became friends with a Ch'u official named Shen Pao-hsü. When Wu Yün fled from the country, he said to Shen Pao-hsü, "I am determined to overthrow the state of Ch'u!"

"Do your best!" said Shen Pao-hsü. "You are capable of overthrowing it. And I surely am capable of raising it up again!"

Later, when King Chao had fled to Sui, Shen Pao-hsü journeyed to Ch'in to plead for military assistance. "The state of Wu," he said, "is a huge swine, a long snake little by little eating away at the states of China proper, and it has begun by committing outrage against Ch'u. Our ruler has lost custody of his altars of the soil and grain and has been driven into the wilderness. He has dispatched his humble servant to report his distress, saying, 'These barbarians are never surfeited. If they should become your neighbors, your border lands will be troubled. Before Wu has had time to settle things, you should come and take your share of territory, for if Ch'u is to be destroyed in the end, its lands had best become yours. But if you should be gracious enough to preserve our state from destruction, we will serve you for generation after generation!"

The Ch'in ruler had this message relayed to Shen Pao-hsü: "I have heard what it is you would command. You may retire for the time being to the quarters assigned you and I will consider the matter and report to you later."

But Shen Pao-hsü replied, "My ruler has been driven into the wilderness and I do not even know where he is hiding! How could your humble servant dare to take his ease at such a time?"

Then he leaned against the wall of the court where he was standing and began to wail, his voice never ceasing day or night. He refused to allow so much as a spoonful of water to pass his lips.

After seven days, Duke Ai of Ch'in recited the ode *Wu yi.*[18] Shen Pao-

18 "Airs of Ch'in," Mao no. 133, a poem describing soldiers about to set off on a campaign. The Ch'in ruler quotes it particularly for the lines, "The king calls out his army, / we put in order our halberds and lances," etc., which indicate to Shen Pao-hsü that Ch'in will go to the aid of Ch'u.

hsü bowed his head nine times in gratitude and at last consented to take a seat. The Ch'in army was thereupon dispatched.

DUKE TING 5TH YEAR (505 B.C.)

Shen Pao-hsü returned with the Ch'in army, the Ch'in commanders Tzu-p'u and Tzu-hu leading a force of five hundred war chariots to go to the rescue of Ch'u.[19] Tzu-p'u said, "I am not familiar with the Wu manner of fighting." He therefore had the men of Ch'u engage the Wu forces in combat first, and then he joined in at Chi in Ch'u. He inflicted a major defeat on King Fu-kai of Wu at Yi.

The men of Wu captured the Ch'u official Wei Yeh at Po-chü, but his son led the Ch'u forces that had fled in rout and went to join Prince Tzu-hsi.[20] Together they defeated the Wu armies at Chün-hsiang.

In autumn, the seventh month, Prince Tzu-ch'i of Ch'u and the Ch'in commander Tzu-p'u wiped out the state of T'ang.[21]

In the ninth month, King Fu-kai returned to Wu and set himself up as king. Then, having fought with the real king, Ho-lü, and been defeated, he fled to Ch'u, where he and his descendants became known as the T'ang-ch'i family.

Though the Wu forces had earlier defeated the Ch'u forces at Yung-shih, the Ch'in forces in turn defeated the Wu forces. The Wu forces withdrew to a position at Chün in Ch'u. Prince Tzu-ch'i of Ch'u wanted to burn them out, but Prince Tzu-hsi said, "The fathers and elder brothers of our state died fighting there and their bones lie exposed in the fields. If you cannot gather up the bones, but instead set fire to the area, it will never do!"

But Prince Tzu-ch'i replied, "The country is in peril! If the dead have consciousness, surely they can continue to enjoy their old sacrifices. What harm can it do if the area is burned?"[22]

He set fire to the region and then attacked, defeating the Wu forces. He also attacked at Kung-hsü Valley, where the Wu forces suffered a major defeat. With this the Wu ruler finally returned to his own state.

19 This represented a fighting force of 37,500 men.

20 A son by a concubine of the former Ch'u ruler, King P'ing.

21 T'ang, it will be recalled, was a small state that had joined Wu in the attack on Ch'u.

22 The important thing is that the state should not perish so that its citizens can continue to offer sacrifices to the spirits of their dead. The fate of the bones of the dead is of secondary importance.

Earlier, the Ch'u official Yin Yü-p'i had been taken prisoner by the Wu forces. He asked to be allowed to be sent to Wu ahead of the Wu ruler, and in this way eventually managed to escape and make his way back to Ch'u.

Shen Hou-tsang, younger brother of Shen Chu-liang, lord of She, had accompanied his mother when she was taken prisoner and carried off to Wu.[23] But he returned to Ch'u alone without waiting for her, which so angered Chu-liang that for the rest of his life he would never look directly at his younger brother.

King Chao of Ch'u reentered the capital city, Ying.

Earlier, when Tou Hsin heard that the Wu invaders were quarreling over who should occupy which of the Ch'u palaces,[24] he said, "I've heard that where there's no yielding, there's no harmony, and where there's no harmony, it is impossible to carry out a long-range campaign. If the men of Wu fall to quarreling over Ch'u, disorder is sure to result, and if there's disorder, they will surely go home. How could they ever gain firm control over Ch'u?"

When King Chao fled to Sui and was about to cross the Ch'eng-chiu River, Wei, the overseer of Lan, helped his wife and family across the river but refused to let the king use the boat. After peace had been restored, King Chao wanted to put him to death for this. But Prince Tzu-hsi said, "Nang Wa brought on his downfall because he thought only about settling old scores. Why imitate his example?"

"You're right," said the king, and he restored Wei to his old post. "This way I can remind myself of my former errors," he said.

King Chao handed out rewards to Tou Hsin, the royal grandsons Yu-yü and Yü, Chung Chien, Tou Ch'ao, Shen Pao-hsü, the royal grandson Chia, Sung Mu, and Tou Huai. Prince Tzu-hsi said, "Please drop Tou Huai from the list!" But the king said, "Great virtue cancels out a small grudge—such is the Way."[25]

Shen Pao-hsü said, "I acted for the ruler, not for myself. If my ruler is safe, what more could I wish? Moreover, I criticized Tou Ch'eng-jan for being greedy—should I be the same myself?"[26] In the end he refused to accept any reward.

King Chao wanted to arrange a marriage for his younger sister Mi Pi-wo,

23 Shen Chu-liang and Shen Hou-tsang were sons of the Ch'u marshal of the left Shen-yin Hsü.

24 See p. 183 above.

25 The fact that Tou Huai and his brother Tou Hsin helped King Chao to escape to Sui canceled out the fact that Tou Huai had earlier proposed to kill the king. See p. 184 above.

26 In 528 B.C., when Tou Ch'eng-jan was put to death; see note 13 above.

but she refused, saying, "Any proper young woman shuns all contact with men, yet I allowed Chung Chien to carry me on his back." It was arranged that she should become the wife of Chung Chien, and he was assigned the post of overseer of music.

When King Chao was in Sui, Prince Tzu-hsi used the king's carriages and vestments in order to prevent panic on the roads and set up a temporary capital at P'i-hsieh.[27] Later, when he learned where the king was, he went and joined him.

King Chao ordered the royal grandson Yu-yü to build a wall around the city of Chün. When he came to the king to report on the completion of the work, Prince Tzu-hsi asked how high and how thick the wall was, but Yu-yü replied that he did not know.

Prince Tzu-hsi said, "If you couldn't do the job properly, you should have refused it! You don't even know how high or how thick the wall is—what *do* you know?"

Yu-yü replied, "I tried to refuse by saying I could not do it, but you insisted! Every man has things he can do and things he cannot do. When the king encountered bandits in the marsh of Yün-meng, I took the blow of their halberd, and the mark of it is still here!" He slipped off the upper part of his robe and showed them his back. "This was something I *could* do! But what you did at P'i-hsieh—that I couldn't do!"[28]

As a postcript to the above account of the battle of Po-chü and the invasion of Ch'u by King Ho-lü of Wu, I append here a moralizing speech by Prince Tzu-hsi, delivered in 494 when he was prime minister of Ch'u, in which he discusses the qualities that allowed King Ho-lü to carry out this operation successfully, and the reasons why no similar success is to be feared from King Ho-lü's successor, King Fu-ch'ai. King Ho-lü died in 496 of wounds received in a battle with the neighbor-

27 At this point Prince Tzu-hsi did not know the whereabouts of the king, but he disguised this fact by using the king's carriages and vestments and pretending to set up a new capital so as to avoid causing panic among the people of the state.

28 Yu-yü is implying that when Prince Tzu-hsi impersonated the king and set up a temporary capital at P'i-hsieh, he actually had it in mind to usurp the throne for himself.

ing state of Yüeh. He was succeeded by his son Fu-ch'ai, who ruled Wu from 495 until 473, when the state was finally wiped out by its rival, Yüeh.

DUKE AI 1ST YEAR (494 B.C.)

When the Wu armies took up a position in the state of Ch'en, the officials of Ch'u were all terrified, saying, "Because Ho-lü knew how to use his people, he was able to inflict defeat on us at Po-chü. Now we hear that his successor is even more competent. What shall we do?"

Prince Tzu-hsi said, "You gentlemen should worry only about disharmony among yourselves. You need not fret over Wu.

"In past years, Ho-lü's meals had no variety of flavors, his living quarters no double-layered mats, his rooms no raised foundations. His vessels were without color or carving, his palaces had no pleasure terraces, his boats and carriages no trimmings. In his clothes and other articles of use he took care to select what was not costly. When he was in his capital, if Heaven sent down calamity or pestilence, he went about in person to visit the orphaned and widowed and distribute supplies to the poor and suffering. When he was with his troops, he waited till hot meals had been handed out before venturing to eat, and if he had any tasty dishes, he shared them with his foot soldiers and carriage men. He treated his people with pity and compassion and joined in their cares and delights. Therefore his people never wearied of his service, and died for him without counting it a loss. Our own former prime minister, Nang Wa, behaved in an entirely different manner from this, however, and thus brought defeat upon us.

"Now I hear that when Fu-ch'ai stays in one place for more than a few nights, he must have terraces and pavilions, embankments and ponds, and for a one-night sojourn concubines and maids are needed to wait on him. Even on a day's outing his every wish must be satisfied, games and amusements must attend him. He surrounds himself with the rare and unusual, thinks only of spectacles and diversions. He looks on his people as though they were foes and each day thinks up new tasks for them. Before anyone else can do so, he is certain to inflict defeat upon himself. How could he possibly defeat us?"

THIRTY-FOUR

The Battle Between Ch'i and Lu at Ch'ing

THE FOLLOWING NARRATIVE CONCERNS A MINOR CLASH between the forces of the powerful northeastern state of Ch'i and its smaller neighbor Lu that began at a place called Ch'ing in Ch'i. The account is of interest because it involves several persons who are mentioned in the Confucian *Analects,* notably Confucius' disciples Jan Ch'iu and Fan Ch'ih, and because it includes comments by Confucius on the action.

It is also noteworthy because it reveals the situation in Lu at this time with regard to the ruling ducal house and the powerful Chi family, whose three branches, Meng-sun, Shu-sun, and Chi-sun, were known as the Three Houses of Huan because they were descended from three sons of Duke Huan (r. 711–694) of Lu. The three branches of the Chi family had for generations served as high ministers to the dukes of Lu, and gradually came to overshadow the ducal house in power and influence. Finally, when Duke Chao openly challenged their authority by launching an attack upon them in 517, they forced him to flee to Ch'i. Attempts to effect a reconciliation between the duke and the Chi family ended in failure, and Duke Chao died in exile in 510.

The *Tso chuan,* after describing Duke Chao's death under that year (Chao 32), records a discussion between two officials of Lu on the causes for the duke's failure, which runs in part as follows:

> The rulers of Lu have for generations pursued a course of error, while the Chi family have for generations practiced diligence. Thus the people of Lu have forgotten who their ruler is. Though he has died abroad, who is there to pity him? The altars of the soil and grain are not always tended by the same

family, ruler and subject do not remain in their respective positions forever. From ancient times this has been so. Thus the *Odes* says:

> The high banks become valleys,
> the deep valleys become hills.[1]

The descendants of the rulers of the three dynasties of antiquity are mere commoners today—as you well know!

At the time dealt with here, the most junior of the three branches of the Chi family, the Chi-sun, headed by Chi K'ang-tzu, exercised the greatest degree of authority.

DUKE AI 11TH YEAR (484 B.C.)

Eleventh year, spring. Because of what happened at Hsi, Kuo Shu and Kao Wu-p'i led the Ch'i army in an attack on us, advancing as far as Ch'ing.[2]

Chi K'ang-tzu, the head of the Chi-sun family, said to his steward Jan Ch'iu, "The Ch'i army at Ch'ing must intend some action against Lu. What shall we do?"

Jan Ch'iu said, "Let one family stay behind to guard the capital and the other two go with the duke to defend the border."[3]

"I have no power to arrange that," said Chi K'ang-tzu.

"Then have the other two lie in wait on this side of the border," said Jan Ch'iu.

Chi K'ang-tzu made this proposal to the leaders of the other two families, but they refused to agree. Jan Ch'iu said, "If they won't agree, then the ruler should not venture out of the capital. Let one of you lead his forces and fight with his back to the walls of the capital. Whoever fails to side with you will be no citizen of Lu. The families of Lu officials in the capital are more numerous than the war chariots of Ch'i. If one family concentrates on attacking one chariot, they can surely prevail. What have you to worry about? It is hardly surprising that the heads of the two other families have

1 "Lesser Odes," *Shih-yüeh-chih-chiao,* Mao no. 193.

2 In the preceding year Duke Ai of Lu and the ruler of Wu had attacked Ch'i, taking up a position in Hsi in Ch'i. The present attack, led by two officials of Ch'i, is in retaliation for that action. The *Spring and Autumn Annals,* being a chronicle of Lu, speaks of an attack on Lu as an attack on "us," and the wording of the *Tso chuan* has been made to conform to that style here.

3 Jan Ch'iu probably means that the Chi-sun family should defend the capital while the other two families accompany the duke, though he is careful not to be that explicit in his statement.

no desire to fight. The government these days rests with the Chi-sun family. Now, when the responsibility lies with you, if the men of Ch'i attack Lu and you are not able to fight them off, it will be your disgrace! How can Lu hope to maintain its rank among the feudal leaders!"

Chi K'ang-tzu ordered Jan Ch'iu to accompany him to court and wait for him beside the Chang family moat. Shu-sun Wu-shu, head of the Shu-sun family, summoned Jan Ch'iu and questioned him about the plans for battle.

Jan Ch'iu replied, "Gentlemen may have far-reaching plans, but how would a petty man like myself know of such things?" When Meng I-tzu, head of the Meng-sun family, pressed him for an answer, he replied, "Petty men gauge their talents before speaking, and weigh their strength before taking on a task."

Shu-sun Wu-shu said, "Obviously you do not consider us the kind of men worth talking to!" He withdrew and began inspecting his war chariots.

Meng Wu-po, son of Meng I-tzu, commanded the army of the right, with Yen Yü as his carriage driver and Ping Hsieh as his right-hand attendant. Jan Ch'iu commanded the army of the left, with Kuan Chou-fu as his carriage driver and Fan Ch'ih as his attendant on the right.[4] Chi K'ang-tzu said, "Fan Ch'ih is too young!" But Jan Ch'iu replied, "He knows how to carry out orders."

The Chi-sun family forces consisted of seven thousand armed men, and Jan Ch'iu had a force of three hundred men from the city of Wu-ch'eng to act as his foot soldiers. The old and young men guarded the palace, while Jan Ch'iu's forces took up a position outside the Yü Gate of the capital. Five days passed before the army of the right joined them.[5]

Kung-shu Wu-jen,[6] when he saw the defenders of the city, wept and said, "Military assignments are irksome, taxes are heavy, our superiors don't know how to plan, our officers don't know how to die in the line of duty—how can the people be well governed? And if I speak of others in this way, dare I shirk my own duties?"

The Lu armies fought with the Ch'i army in the suburbs of the Lu capital, the Ch'i army advancing from Chi-ch'ü. At first the Lu forces were unwilling to go beyond the moat around the capital. Fan Ch'ih said to Jan Ch'iu,

4 Both Jan Ch'iu and Fan Ch'ih were disciples of Confucius and are depicted in numerous places in the *Analects* in conversation with the Master, though there is no direct reference to the military action described here.

5 The implication is that Meng Wu-po and his troops had no real heart for the battle.

6 A son of Duke Chao of Lu. Here he functions like a Greek chorus, commenting dolefully upon the prospects for the battle.

"It is not that the men are unable to advance, but they don't trust you. Please repeat to them three times the promises regarding rewards and punishments and then order them to cross over."

When this had been done, the troops followed their orders and the Lu forces closed with the Ch'i army.

The Lu army of the right fled back to the city. The Ch'i men pursued it, the Ch'i officials Ch'en Kuan and Ch'en Chuang crossing the Ssu River. Meng Chih-ts'e of Lu was the last to enter the city, having guarded the rear. But he drew an arrow and began whipping his horses with it, saying, "It's just that the horses won't go forward!"[7]

The men under Lin Pu-niu, a Lu company commander who was in the rear, said, "Should we make a dash for it?"

"Who is there to run from?" said Lin Pu-niu.

"Then should we take a stand here?"

"What would be so admirable about that?" said Lin Pu-niu. He then proceeded on his way in a leisurely fashion and was killed in the fighting.

Jan Ch'iu's forces killed eighty armed warriors, and the men of Ch'i were unable to reform their army. Spies sent out at night reported that the men of Ch'i were preparing to retire from the field. Jan Ch'iu three times sent to Chi K'ang-tzu asking permission to pursue them, but Chi K'ang-tzu refused.

Meng Wu-po remarked to someone, "I was no match for Yen Yü, but I made a better showing than Ping Hsieh! Yen Yü fought very nimbly. I had no heart for fighting, but at least I knew how to keep silent, unlike Ping Hsieh, who shouted, 'Spur the horses and let's be gone!' "

Kung-shu Wu-jen and his favorite page Wang Ch'i rode together in the same carriage and both were killed in action. Both were interred in coffins. Confucius said, "The boy knew how to handle a shield and halberd and defend the altars of the soil and grain. It was right not to bury him with the rites of a minor."

Jan Ch'iu used his spear against the Ch'i army and so was able to penetrate their ranks.[8] Confucius said, "How righteous of him."

7 He did not want it to seem that he was making a show of bringing up the rear.

8 Ordinarily the right-hand attendant in the carriage should wield the spear or halberd, not the commander. But because Fan Ch'ih was young and inexperienced, Jan Ch'iu wielded the spear in his place.

T H I R T Y - F I V E

The Revolt in Wei

AFTER THE DEATH OF DUKE LING OF WEI, WHO HEADED THAT state from 534 to 493, a long and complex power struggle ensued which is recorded in the *Tso chuan* in considerable detail and stretches over a period of many years. Confucius had visited Wei in the time of Duke Ling, and did so again at a somewhat later period, and several of his disciples, as we shall see, were involved in the succession struggles there. Hence the account of the revolt in Wei is of particular importance to students of the life of Confucius and his followers. I will not attempt to present here all the numerous entries that deal with Wei's protracted period of troubles, but will concentrate on the three most famous scenes in the saga.

The first occurs in 496, three years before the death of Duke Ling, and concerns Duke Ling, his consort Nan Tzu, and K'uai K'uei, a son whom he had designated as heir. Nan Tzu, who was apparently not the mother of K'uai K'uei, had an unsavory reputation, for reasons suggested in the narrative. According to *Analects* VI, 28, Confucius had an interview with her when he was visiting Wei, and this so scandalized his disciple Tzu-lu that the Master was obliged to swear by Heaven that nothing improper had taken place during the meeting.

DUKE LING 14TH YEAR (496 B.C.)

Duke Ling, the ruler of Wei, in order to please his wife Nan Tzu, summoned Sung Chao to Wei.[1]

1 Nan Tzu was a daughter of the ruling family of Sung and was rumored to have had an affair with Sung Chao or the ducal son Chao, also a member of the Sung ruling family and possibly her brother. He was noted for his good looks; see *Analects* VI, 16.

When a diplomatic meeting took place at T'ao, the Wei heir apparent K'uai K'uei went in order to present the city of Yü to the ruler of Ch'i, who was attending the meeting. As K'uai K'uei was passing through the countryside of Sung, he heard one of the peasants singing this song:

> Now that you've taken care of your randy sow,
> why not send home our handsome swine?[2]

The heir apparent, chagrined at what he heard, said to his retainer Hsi-yang Su, "When I go to pay my respects to the mistress, you must go with me. She will grant me an interview, and when I glance around in your direction, then kill her!" Hsi-yang Su agreed to do so.

They went to pay their respects to the duke's wife, Nan Tzu, who granted the heir apparent an interview. Three times he glanced around, but Su failed to step forward. When the duke's wife saw the expression on the heir apparent's face, she screamed and ran away, crying, "K'uai K'uei is trying to kill me!" Duke Ling took her hand and helped her climb up to the terrace.

The heir apparent fled to Sung.

The second scene takes place just before and at the time of Duke Ling's death in 493.

DUKE AI 2D YEAR (493 B.C.)

Sometime earlier, Duke Ling of Wei went on an outing to the suburbs of the capital and his son Ying acted as his carriage driver. The duke said, "Now that I have no son, I'll make you my heir."[3] Ying made no reply.

2 The "sow" of course is Nan Tzu and the "swine" Sung Chao.

3 Ying was a younger son of Duke Ling. In saying that he has no son, the duke is referring to the fact that his designated heir, K'uai K'uei, had fled the state.

Another day, when the duke repeated the statement, Ying replied, "I am not worthy to guard the altars of the soil and grain. I hope my lord will reconsider the matter. There is my lord's consort in the upper hall to be considered, and in the lower hall, the various dignitaries of the state. If my lord were to issue a command without consulting them, it would only cause disgrace."

In the summer, Duke Ling of Wei died. His consort, Nan Tzu, said, "It is commanded that the ducal son Ying be made heir apparent. That was the duke's command!"

Ying replied, "I am different from the other sons.[4] Moreover, the duke expired in my arms. If there had been any such command, surely I would have heard it. Furthermore, there is Ch'e, the son of the prince who fled, who is here."[5]

In the end Ch'e was made ruler of Wei.

Though K'uai K'uei had the backing of powerful forces in the state of Chin, to which he had eventually fled, he was not able to assert his claim to the rulership of Wei at this time. He did, however, manage to gain control of the city of Ch'i in an outlying region of Wei, from whence he eyed the reign of his son Ch'e, watchful for an opportunity to overthrow him.

DUKE AI 15TH YEAR (480 B.C.)

K'ung Yü of the state of Wei married Lady Po, the elder sister of K'uai K'uei, and she bore him a son named K'uei. K'ung Yü had a servant named Hun Liang-fu who was tall and handsome, and after K'ung Yü died, the man had clandestine relations with Lady Po.

When Lady Po's brother, the heir apparent K'uai K'uei, was residing in the city of Ch'i in Wei, Lady Po sent Hun Liang-fu as her messenger to him

4 Probably he was a son by a concubine.
5 The son of the heir apparent K'uai K'uei.

there. The heir apparent said to him, "If you help me to enter the capital and take control of the state, I will see that you wear the cap and robes of a high official, ride in a high official's carriage, and are pardoned three offenses that would ordinarily incur the death penalty." The two men entered into an alliance, and then Hun Liang-fu went to request Lady Po's cooperation.

In the intercalary month of this year, Hun Liang-fu and the heir apparent entered the capital and took shelter at a garden estate of the K'ung family. At dusk the two of them muffled themselves in women's robes, mounted a carriage, and with the page Lo as their driver, proceeded to the K'ung family mansion. When Luan Ning, the senior retainer of the K'ung family, asked the driver who they were, the driver reported that they were women relatives of the family. Eventually they were able to make their way to Lady Po.

Lady Po, having finished her dinner, took a halberd and led the way for the group, with the heir apparent and five men, all armed, following after and carrying a pig.[6] They cornered Lady Po's son K'ung K'uei in the privy and forced him to swear an alliance with them. Then they threatened him until he agreed to ascend the terrace.[7]

Meanwhile, the K'ung family's senior retainer Luan Ning was preparing to drink wine, but before the meat he was to eat with it had finished roasting, he received word of the revolt. He sent someone to report to Tzu-lu,[8] ordered Shao Hu to prepare a carriage and horses, and then, after passing around the wine beaker and eating the roast meat, he attended Ch'e, the ruler of Wei, and fled with him to Lu.

Tzu-lu was about to enter the city when he encountered Tzu-kao just emerging.[9] "The gates are already shut!" he said.

"I'll have a look anyway," said Tzu-lu.

"It's too late. Don't get mixed up in the trouble!" said Tzu-kao.

"I earn my living from them—I can't hope to escape their trouble!" said Tzu-lu. Tzu-kao eventually fled from the city.

When Tzu-lu entered the city and reached the gate of the K'ung family mansion, he found the ducal grandson Kan guarding the gate. "It's no use going in now!" said Kan.[10]

6 The blood of the pig was to be used in sealing an oath of alliance.

7 From which he could address persons in the courtyard below and inform them of Prince K'uai K'uei's intention to seize power.

8 Also called Chung Yu; one of the best known of Confucius' disciples. At this time he was in the service of the K'ung family.

9 Also called Kao Ch'ai, another disciple of Confucius. He was an official of Wei.

10 Because the ruler, Ch'e, had already fled the city. Ch'e is known by the unusual posthumous title

Tzu-lu said, "It's the ducal grandson—the one who pursues profit but runs away from trouble! I'm a little different—if I profit from their stipend, I feel bound to help them with their worries!"

Just then a messenger emerged from the gate and Tzu-lu slipped inside.

Tzu-lu said, "What can the heir apparent do with K'ung K'uei? Even though he kills him, there are others who are certain to carry on the struggle!"

Later, Tzu-lu said, "The heir apparent is a coward. If we set fire to one side of the terrace where he is, he will surely release K'ung K'uei!"

When the heir apparent heard this, he was frightened and ordered his men Shih Ch'i and Yü Yen to descend from the terrace and block Tzu-lu's approach. Carrying halberds, they attacked Tzu-lu and in the process severed the cords that held on his hat.

Tzu-lu said, "When a gentleman dies, his hat does not fall off!" He retied the cords of his hat before he died.

When Confucius heard of the revolt in Wei, he said, "Tzu-kao will probably come to Lu, but Tzu-lu will die there."[11]

K'ung K'uei set up Prince K'uai K'uei, posthumously titled Duke Chuang, as ruler. Duke Chuang disapproved of the men who had managed the government in the past and wanted to do away with them all. Before taking such steps, he said to the minister of instruction Man Ch'eng, "For many long years I suffered hardship abroad. Now I want you to have a taste of what it's like!"

After Man Ch'eng returned home, he reported this to Ch'u-shih Pi and together they plotted to attack the duke, but their plans came to nothing.

This did not end the long period of troubles in Wei. Prince K'uai K'uei proved unable to consolidate his position and in 478 was driven from power and murdered. A period of great confusion ensued, until in 476 Prince K'uai K'uei's son Ch'e, the

of Ch'u Kung or "The Ousted Duke" because, as we see here, he was driven out of the capital and deprived of the rulership of Wei—by his own father, Prince K'uai K'uei, as it happened.

11 In *Analects* XI, 13, Confucius is recorded as saying: "Yu (Tzu-lu), now—he will not die a natural death." There is no indication when he said this, but it may well have been on this occasion.

Ousted Duke, was finally restored to rule. He continued in power until his death in 470.

THIRTY-SIX

The Revolt of the Lord of Po in Ch'u

PO KUNG OR THE LORD OF PO WAS A TITLE BESTOWED ON Prince Sheng, a grandson of King P'ing of Ch'u. In 479 B.C., Prince Sheng led a revolt that resulted in the death of several high officials of Ch'u and briefly disrupted the reign of King Hui (r. 488–432). To clarify the background of the revolt, the *Tso chuan* begins its narrative by briefly summarizing the career of Prince Sheng's father, Prince Chien.

Prince Chien was the heir apparent of King P'ing, who reigned from 528 to 516. One of Prince Chien's tutors was an official named Fei Wu-chi, who was sent to the state of Ch'in to fetch a bride for the prince. The bride proved to be of such unusual beauty that Fei Wu-chi urged King P'ing to take her into his own harem, a suggestion which the king was happy to follow. Having thus ingratiated himself with the king, Fei Wu-chi began to fear retaliation from the prince and accordingly slandered the prince to his father, asserting that he was plotting revolt in the city of Ch'eng-fu, to which he had been assigned. King P'ing issued an order for the prince to be put to death, but the latter was warned in time and fled for refuge to the state of Sung. This took place in 522. These events have already been touched upon on p. 180 above. The same year, internal trouble in Sung obliged the prince to leave that state and go to Cheng. From Cheng he went to Chin and there, as we see in the paragraphs that follow, he plotted treacherously against the people of Cheng. When his duplicity came to light, he was put to death. This information is recapitulated here as a preface to the account of the activities of Prince Chien's son Sheng, which occupies the main part of the narrative.

DUKE AI 16TH YEAR (479 B.C.)

When Chien, the heir apparent of Ch'u, encountered slander, he fled from Ch'eng-fu to Sung. Then, to avoid the disturbance caused by the Hua family, he left Sung and went to Cheng. The people of Cheng accorded him very favorable treatment.

He then went to Chin, where he joined the men of Chin in a plot to launch a surprise attack on Cheng. To implement the plot, he asked Cheng to readmit him, and the men of Cheng accordingly took him back and treated him as before.

The men of Chin sent a spy to meet with Prince Chien and fix a date for the surprise attack on Cheng. But Prince Chien had behaved in a violent and tyrannical manner toward the people of the town assigned to him as his private domain, and the townspeople brought charges against him. When the men of Cheng investigated, they discovered that the prince had been in collusion with a spy from Chin. They accordingly put him to death.

The narrative now turns to the subject of Prince Chien's son Sheng, depicting two officials of Ch'u in a discussion over whether or not to summon Sheng home to Ch'u. Tzu-hsi, a prince of the Ch'u royal family and prime minister of Ch'u, has figured prominently in the account of the clash between Wu and Ch'u on pp. 187–190 above. The lord of She is Shen Chu-liang, a Ch'u official who has appeared on p. 188 above. (The title "She kung" or "lord of She" is sometimes translated as "governor of She.") He appears several times in the *Analects* in conversation with Confucius or his disciples.

Prince Chien's son Sheng was living in Wu. Tzu-hsi wanted to call him home, but the lord of She said, "I have heard that Sheng is deceitful and disorderly. Would that not bring injury to the state?"

Tzu-hsi said, "I have heard that Sheng is trustworthy and brave. Summoning him will do no harm. We'll station him in the borderlands and let him serve as a bastion to guard the state."

The lord of She said, "Adhering to benevolence is what I call being trustworthy, and practicing righteousness is what I call being brave. I have heard that Sheng cares only about doing what he has sworn to do, and seeks out men who are ready to die. Surely he has some private aim in mind.[1] Just doing what one has sworn to do is not trustworthiness, and dying when the time comes is not bravery. You are bound to regret this!"

Tzu-hsi, ignoring the advice, summoned Sheng and assigned him to a place on the border between Ch'u and Wu, making him lord of Po.

Sheng requested that Ch'u launch an attack on Cheng, but Tzu-hsi said, "Ch'u is not ready for that yet. If it were, I would not forget your grievance."

Later, Sheng repeated his request and Tzu-hsi agreed to carry it out. But before the army had been mobilized, the men of Chin attacked Cheng, and Ch'u came to Cheng's aid, concluding an alliance with it.

Sheng, enraged at this, said, "There is a man of Cheng here in our midst![2] My enemy is not far off!" He set about whetting his sword.

P'ing, the son of Prince Tzu-ch'i, went to see him and said, "Young prince, why are you whetting your sword?"

Sheng replied, "I am known for my frankness, and I would not be frank if I failed to tell you the reason, would I? I'm going to kill your father."[3]

P'ing reported this to Tzu-hsi. Tzu-hsi said, "Sheng is like an egg that I spread my wings over and hatched. As things stand in Ch'u now, if I should die, who but Sheng could serve as prime minister or marshal?"

When Sheng heard this, he said, "The prime minister has gone mad! If he succeeds in dying a natural death, it will be no fault of mine!"

Despite this, Tzu-hsi did not change his attitude.

Sheng said to his retainer Shih Ch'i, "The king and the two high ministers —if we have five hundred men in all, we can dispose of them!"[4]

Shih Ch'i said, "We cannot get that many." Then he said, "South of the marketplace there is a man named Hsiung I-liao. If we can enlist him, he will be worth five hundred men."

1 That is, he is planning to attack the men of Cheng in revenge for his father's death.

2 He is referring to Tzu-hsi who, by aiding the state of Cheng, has become Sheng's enemy.

3 Tzu-hsi is actually P'ing's uncle, but the term "father" is often used rather loosely.

4 The king is King Hui; the two high ministers are Prince Tzu-hsi, the prime minister, and Prince Tzu-ch'i, the marshal.

Shih Ch'i accompanied Sheng and they went to meet with Hsiung I-liao. Sheng, after talking with the man, was pleased and proceeded to tell him why he had come. Hsiung declined to join the undertaking. Sheng instantly threatened him with a sword, but he remained unmoved.

"He does not fawn at the prospect of gain, or flinch before a threat," said Sheng. "He will not betray another man's words merely in order to seek favor."

He let the man go.

The men of the state of Wu attacked the region of Shen in Ch'u. Sheng, the lord of Po, defeated them and requested permission to remain armed and to present his spoils to the ruler. When permission was granted, he used the opportunity to initiate a revolt.

In autumn, the seventh month, he killed Tzu-hsi and Tzu-ch'i at court and threatened the king. Tzu-hsi covered his face with his sleeve before he died.[5]

Tzu-ch'i said, "In the past I served my ruler with my brute strength. I must end my life in the same manner." He tore a camphor tree up by the roots and used it to slay his attackers until he himself was killed.

Shih Ch'i said, "Burn the storehouses and put the king to death—otherwise you will never succeed!"

The lord of Po said, "That is impossible! Putting the king to death would be ill-omened, and burning the storehouses would leave us without supplies. How would we get along?"

Shih Ch'i said, "Take possession of Ch'u, govern its people well, and serve the spirits with reverence—then you can elicit plenty of favorable omens and collect more supplies as well. What is there to worry about?"

But Sheng rejected the advice.

The lord of She was in Ts'ai at this time, and everyone in the area beyond the Fang-ch'eng Mountains said, "Now is the time to enter the capital!" But the lord of She said, "I have heard that those who embark on dangerous ventures in hopes of a lucky outcome are never satisfied in their ambitions, but keep on till they topple of their own weight." When he heard that Kuan Hsiu of Ch'i had been put to death, then he moved against the capital.[6]

5 Indicating his shame at having failed to heed the warnings against the lord of Po.

6 Kuan Hsiu, an official of Ch'u, was noted for his worth. He was said to have descended from Kuan Chung, the famous high minister of the state of Ch'i in the time of Duke Huan of Ch'i; hence he is referred to as Kuan Hsiu of Ch'i.

The lord of Po wanted to make Tzu-lü the new king, but Tzu-lü refused.[7] The lord of Po attempted to threaten him with arms, but Tzu-lü replied, "Young prince, if you will first bring peace and tranquility to the state of Ch'u, put the royal house in order, and then extend your patronage to me, that would accord with my wishes exactly. In that case, how would I venture to object? But if you overturn the royal house in your obsession with gain, and take no thought for the state of Ch'u, I can never go along with you even though I am threatened with death!"

In the end the lord of Po put Prince Tzu-lü to death and forced King Hui to go with him to the government storehouses at Kao-fu. Shih Ch'i acted as overseer of the gates there, but an official of Ch'u named Yü Kung-yang dug a hole in the wall of the king's quarters and, bearing the king on his back, made off with him to the palace of Lady Chao.[8]

The lord of She also arrived at the palace. When he reached the north gate, he met someone who said, "My lord, why are you not wearing a helmet? The people of the state look to you with expectation as they would to a loving parent. And if you should be wounded by an arrow from one of the rebel band the expectations of the people would be shattered! Why, then, do you fail to wear a helmet?"

The lord of She accordingly donned a helmet before proceeding on his way. Then he met another person who said, "My lord, why do you wear a helmet? The people of the state look to you with expectation as they look forward to a good harvest. Day after day they await you. If they can see your face, they will be comforted. For as long as they know you are not dead, their spirits will be lifted up and they will parade your cause like a flag to rally the nation. But if you hide your face in a helmet, you shatter the expectations of the people. Is that not a grave error?"

The lord of She then removed the helmet before proceeding on his way. He also encountered Chen Yin-ku, who was leading the forces under his command to go to the assistance of the lord of Po.[9] The lord of She said, "If it were not for those two gentlemen, Ch'u would never have become the state it is![10] If you turn your back on such virtue and follow a rebel, how can you hope to survive?"

Chen Yin-ku thereupon joined the forces under the lord of She. The lord of She sent him, along with other men of the state, to attack the lord of Po.

7 He was a son of King P'ing by a concubine.

8 The consort of King Chao and mother of King Hui.

9 The Ch'u official Chen Yin-ku has already appeared on p. 183 above, assisting King Chao to flee the invaders from Wu.

10 The prime minister Tzu-hsi and the marshal Tzu-ch'i, both of whom played key roles in saving the state at the time of the invasion from Wu.

The lord of Po fled to the mountains and hanged himself. His followers kept his whereabouts a secret. His retainer Shih Ch'i was captured alive and questioned about the death of the lord of Po. Shih Ch'i replied, "I know where he died, but that worthy gentlemen charged me not to reveal it."

"If you don't speak, we'll boil you alive!"

Shih Ch'i said, "In this sort of undertaking, if you win, you become a high official; if you don't you are boiled alive. That's the way it is—why should I object?"

They proceeded to boil Shih Ch'i alive.

Prince Yen fled to the region of K'uei-huang in Wu.[11]

Shen Chu-liang, the lord of She, for a time filled the two offices of prime minister and marshal. Then, after peace had been restored to the state, he appointed Ning as prime minister and K'uan as marshal.[12] He himself retired to live out his old age in She.

11 Prince Yen was a younger brother of Sheng, the lord of Po.

12 Ning was the son of the late prime minister Tzu-hsi; K'uan was the son of the late marshal Tzu-ch'i.

THIRTY-SEVEN

Attitudes Toward the Supernatural

THE FOLLOWING COLLECTION OF BRIEF EPISODES, CULLED from different sections of the *Tso chuan* and arranged in chronological order, will give some idea of the typical attitude displayed in the *Tso* toward questions relating to portents, the service of the spirits, and other supernatural concerns. In reading these passages, it is well to keep in mind the pronouncement of Confucius recorded in *Analects* VI, 22: "To treat the spirits and gods with reverence but keep one's distance from them may be called wise."

The first excerpt deals with a strange battle of snakes in the capital of the state of Cheng. At the time of the incident, Duke Li (r. 700–697; 680–673), the ruler of Cheng, had been forced to flee the state and was residing abroad. In 680 his efforts to regain control of the state and return to his capital were finally successful. The battle of the snakes that had taken place six years previously was interpreted as an omen of this event.

DUKE CHUANG 14TH YEAR (680 B.C.)

Earlier, the snakes living within the city and those from outside had engaged in battle in the middle of the southern gate to the capital of Cheng. The snakes living within the city died. Six years later, Duke Li of Cheng returned to the capital.

When Duke Chuang of Lu heard of this, he questioned his minister Shen Hsü about it, saying, "Are there really such things as portents?"

Shen Hsü replied, "When people have something they are deeply distressed about, their vital energy flames up and takes such shapes. Portents arise because of people. If people have no dissensions, they will not arise of themselves. When men abandon their constant ways, then portents arise. That is why these particular portents came about."

The next two items concern the practice of human sacrifice. Archeological excavation at Shang dynasty sites has revealed that human sacrifices were carried out by the Shang people on the occasion of royal burials or the consecration of buildings or city walls, and presumably on other occasions as well. In most cases the victims were probably slaves or prisoners of war. References in literary sources dealing with the succeeding Chou period indicate that the practice was continued in Chou times, at least sporadically, though it is vehemently condemned by thinkers of the period.

DUKE HSI 19TH YEAR (641 B.C.)

In the summer the duke of Sung ordered Duke Wen of Chu to use the ruler of Tseng as a sacrifice at the shrine of Tz'u-sui. He hoped in this way to win over the Yi barbarians of the east.[1]

The marshal Tzu-yü of Sung said, "In ancient times the six domestic animals were not used interchangeably.[2] For a minor affair one does not use a large sacrifice. And how would one ever dare use a human being? Sacrifices and prayers are carried out for the sake of human beings. The people act as hosts to the gods. If one uses a human being as a sacrifice, what god will ever accept it?

"Duke Huan of Ch'i insured the preservation of three states that would

1 The Sung ruler is Duke Hsiang (r. 650–637). On the ruler of Tseng, see note 3 below. The shrine was on the Sui River in present day Honan; the deity worshipped there was apparently revered by the Yi people of the east.

2 The six domestic animals, which were used for sacrifices, are the horse, ox, sheep, pig, dog, and fowl. Tu Yü's commentary interprets the sentence to mean that horses were not used in sacrifices to the horse deity (a constellation worshipped as the ancestor of horses), and so forth, but I have taken it in what seems to be its more natural meaning.

otherwise have perished and in that way won over the other feudal lords, but even then men who were concerned about righteousness claimed that he was lacking in virtue. Now the ruler of Sung holds one meeting of the feudal lords and treats the rulers of two feudal states with brutality.[3] And in addition he wants to use one of them in sacrifices to some unknown and disreputable spirit being![4] He hopes in this way to become a hegemon among the feudal rulers, but that will be hard, will it not? He will be lucky if he dies a natural death!"

DUKE HSI 21ST YEAR (639 B.C.)

In the summer there was a great drought. Duke Hsi of Lu wanted to burn the shaman Wang alive.[5]

Tsang Wen-chung said, "That won't remedy the drought! Repair your inner and outer city walls [in order to give employment to the people]. Eat simply, reduce expenses, pay heed to agricultural matters, encourage people to share. These are what you should tend to. What can shaman Wang do? If Heaven wants him killed, it shouldn't have brought him into existence in the first place. And if he can really cause a drought, then burning him alive will only make it worse!"

3 The ruler of Sung held a meeting of the feudal lords in the third month of this year, at which time he seized the ruler of T'eng. In the sixth month he seized the ruler of Tseng. T'eng and Tseng were tiny states in the area east of Sung.

4 The word translated here as "disreputable," *yin*, also means "excessive" or "obscene," and is often employed in early texts to stigmatize sacrifices or other religious activities of which the Chinese disapproved. It is not clear whether they used the term because of some element in the worship or lore of the deity that they regarded as immoral, or simply because the deity did not belong to the pantheon approved by the traditions of Chou culture.

It may be noted that, although the *Tso chuan* narrative strongly implies that the ruler of Tseng was actually sacrificed at the shrine, the *Kung-yang* and *Ku-liang* commentaries offer a less horrifying interpretation. Commenting on the *Spring and Autumn Annals* entry under Duke Hsi 19th year that says the ruler of Tseng was "used," both state that this means that the ruler was struck on the nose and the resulting blood used to smear the sacrifical vessels with. I leave the reader to judge the plausibility of such an interpretation.

The *Tso chuan* mentions two other instances of human sacrifice. One is recorded under Duke Chao 10th year (532 B.C.), when reference is made to a prisoner or prisoners of war being sacrificed in the state of Lu. The other occurs the following year, when King Ling of Ch'u wiped out the state of Ts'ai and used its heir, Prince Yin, the son of Duke Ling of Ts'ai, as a sacrifice to Mt. Kang in Ch'u. In both cases, the *Tso* follows the notice of the sacrifice with a speech expressing vigorous condemnation of the act.

5 Presumably because the shaman's prayers had failed to produce rain or because he was thought to be in some way responsible for the drought. Some commentators believe that the shaman indicated here was a woman.

The duke followed this advice. The year was one of dearth, but the people suffered no harm.

The following brief narrative concerns the ruler of Chu, a small state in Shantung adjoining Lu, and the concept of *ming,* fate or destiny, which may refer either to one's mission in life or one's allotted life span. The discussion plays on these two meanings of the word.

DUKE WEN 13TH YEAR (614 B.C.)

Duke Wen of Chu divined by the tortoiseshell to determine if he should move his capital to the city of Yi. The historian who conducted the divination replied, "The move will benefit the people but not their ruler."

The ruler of Chu said, "If it benefits the people, it benefits me. Heaven gave birth to the people and set up a ruler in order to benefit them. If the people enjoy benefit, I am bound to share in it."

Those around the ruler said, "If by taking warning from the divination you can prolong your destiny, why not do so?"

The ruler replied, "My destiny lies in nourishing the people. Whether death comes to me early or late is merely a matter of time. If the people will benefit thereby, then nothing could be more auspicious than to move the capital."

In the end he moved the capital to Yi. In the fifth month, Duke Wen of Chu died.

The gentleman remarks: he understood the meaning of destiny.

In the episode that follows, an event of seemingly prodigious nature is reported to Duke P'ing of Chin. When the duke questions his wise adviser Shih K'uang or Music Master K'uang, the latter adroitly uses the opportunity to deliver a reprimand. The narrative concludes with remarks by another sage of Chin, Yang-she Shu-hsiang.

DUKE CHAO 8TH YEAR (534 B.C.)

Eighth year, spring. A stone spoke in Wei-yü in Chin. Duke P'ing of Chin questioned Shih K'uang, saying, "How can a stone speak?"

Shih K'uang replied, "A stone cannot speak. But perhaps something took possession of it. If not, then the people who reported it must have made a mistake. Nevertheless, I have heard it said that if enterprises are not undertaken at the proper time, resentment and grumbling will arise among the people. And then even things that do not speak will do so.

"Now our halls and palaces are lofty and lavish, and the people's strength is impaired and exhausted. Resentment and grumbling continually arise, for the people cannot go on living as human beings. It is hardly surprising that a stone should speak!"

At this time the ruler of Chin was engaged in building the palace at Ssu-ch'i.

Yang-she Shu-hsiang of Chin remarked, "Shih K'uang's words are those of a gentleman. The words of a gentleman are trustworthy and capable of proof. Therefore resentment never comes near him. The words of a petty man are irresponsible and lacking in proof. Therefore resentment and blame fall on him. This is what the *Odes* means when it says:

> Pitiful is he who cannot speak!
> His words have barely left his tongue
> when his body encounters distress.
> Lucky is he who can speak!
> His skillful words are like a current
> bearing his body to a place of rest.[6]

6 "Lesser Odes," *Yü wu cheng,* Mao no. 194. I have translated the lines in a way that seems to fit the context here. Interpretations put forward by commentators of Han and later times give the lines a quite different interpretation, taking the term *ch'iao yen,* translated here as "skillful words," to be pejorative, i.e., "clever words" or "artful words."

"When the Ssu-ch'i palace is completed, the other feudal lords will surely turn against Chin, and our ruler will suffer blame. This gentleman, Shih K'uang, understands this."

Tzu-ch'an, the wise statesman of the state of Cheng, has been described in detail in chapter 30 above.

DUKE CHAO 19TH YEAR (523 B.C.)

There was a great flood in Cheng. Dragons fought with one another in the deeps of the Wei River outside the Shih Gate of the Cheng capital.

The people of the state asked permission to perform sacrifices to them. But Tzu-ch'an refused, saying, "When we fight, the dragons do not watch us. When the dragons fight, why should we watch them? We might pray for their removal, but the river is after all their home. If we ask nothing of the dragons, the dragons will ask nothing of us."

This ended the matter.

Chapter 33, on the battle between Wu and Ch'u at Po-chü, described how King Chao of Ch'u was temporarily driven from his capital by the Wu invaders in 506–505 B.C. As we have seen there, King Chao was eventually able to return to his state and resume rule. Some years later, in 489, the Wu forces invaded the small state of Ch'en on Ch'u's northern border. Ch'en had for generations been an ally of Ch'u and King Chao was bound by oath to defend it. Though by this time he was in poor health, he chose to be faithful to his oath and died, presumably of illness, as he was launching an attack on the Wu invaders. Immediately after describing his death, the *Tso chuan* records the following two incidents concerning omens that were thought to pertain to the king's destiny.

DUKE AI 6TH YEAR (489 B.C.)

This year there was a cloud like a flock of red birds that pressed in on either side of the sun and flew in the sky for three days. King Chao of Ch'u sent an envoy to consult the grand historian of the Chou court concerning its meaning. The grand historian replied, "It concerns the king's own person. But if he will perform a propitiatory sacrifice, the ill effects can be shifted to the prime minister or the marshals of the state."

King Chao said, "If an illness that threatens the heart and bowels of the nation should be shifted to the legs and arms, what good would that do?[7] If I have not committed any grave error, would Heaven cut short my life prematurely? And if I have committed a fault, I must accept punishment. How can I shift it off on others?" So in the end he refused to perform a propitiatory sacrifice.

Some years earlier, when King Chao was ill, divination was made by the tortoiseshell and the answer given: "The Yellow River is exercising a malign influence."

The king, however, declined to perform sacrifices to the Yellow River. When his officials begged him to carry out such sacrifices in the suburbs of the capital, he replied, "Under all three dynasties of antiquity, with regard to sacrifices it has been ordained that one shall not sacrifice to mountains or rivers beyond the borders of one's own domain. The rivers that Ch'u sacrifices to are the Yangtze, the Han, the Chü, and the Chang. Whatever good or ill fortune comes to us comes from these alone. Though I may be a person of no virtue, I have done nothing to offend the Yellow River!" In the end he declined to perform the sacrifice.

Confucius said: King Chao of Ch'u understood the Great Way. No wonder he did not lose his kingdom.

7 In Chinese rhetoric the ruler represents the heart or mind of the state and the chief ministers are the legs and arms.

I N D E X

OTHER WORKS IN THE COLUMBIA ASIAN STUDIES SERIES

TRANSLATIONS FROM THE ORIENTAL CLASSICS

Major Plays of Chikamatsu, tr. Donald Keene 1961
Four Major Plays of Chikamatsu, tr. Donald Keene. Paperback text edition 1961
Records of the Grand Historian of China, translated from the Shih chi of Ssu-ma Ch'ien, tr. Burton Watson, 2 vols. 1961
Instructions for Practical Living and Other Neo-Confucian Writings by Wang Yang-ming, tr. Wing-tsit Chan 1963
Chuang Tzu: Basic Writings, tr. Burton Watson, paperback ed. only 1964
The Mahābhārata, tr. Chakravarthi V. Narasimhan. Also in paperback ed. 1965
The Manyōshū, Nippon Gakujutsu Shinkōkai edition 1965
Su Tung-p'o: Selections from a Sung Dynasty Poet, tr. Burton Watson. Also in paperback ed. 1965
Bhartrihari: Poems, tr. Barbara Stoler Miller. Also in paperback ed. 1967
Basic Writings of Mo Tzu, Hsün Tzu, and Han Fei Tzu, tr. Burton Watson. Also in separate paperback eds. 1967
The Awakening of Faith, Attributed to Aśvaghosha, tr. Yoshito S. Hakeda. Also in paperback ed. 1967
Reflections on Things at Hand: The Neo-Confucian Anthology, comp. Chu Hsi and Lü Tsu-ch'ien, tr. Wing-tsit Chan 1967
The Platform Sutra of the Sixth Patriarch, tr. Philip B. Yampolsky. Also in paperback ed. 1967
Essays in Idleness: The Tsurezuregusa of Kenkō, tr. Donald Keene. Also in paperback ed. 1967
The Pillow Book of Sei Shōnagon, tr. Ivan Morris, 2 vols. 1967

Two Plays of Ancient India: The Little Clay Cart and the Minister's Seal, tr. J. A. B. van Buitenen 1968
The Complete Works of Chuang Tzu, tr. Burton Watson 1968
The Romance of the Western Chamber (Hsi Hsiang chi), tr. S. I. Hsiung. Also in paperback ed. 1968
The Manyōshū, Nippon Gakujutsu Shinkōkai edition. Paperback text edition. 1969
Records of the Historian: Chapters from the Shih chi of Ssu-ma Ch'ien. Paperback text edition, tr. Burton Watson. 1969
Cold Mountain: 100 Poems by the T'ang Poet Han-shan, tr. Burton Watson. Also in paperback ed. 1970
Twenty Plays of the Nō Theatre, ed. Donald Keene. Also in paperback ed. 1970
Chūshingura: The Treasury of Loyal Retainers, tr. Donald Keene. Also in paperback ed. 1971
The Zen Master Hakuin: Selected Writings, tr. Philip B. Yampolsky 1971
Chinese Rhyme-Prose: Poems in the Fu Form from the Han and Six Dynasties Periods, tr. Burton Watson. Also in paperback ed. 1971
Kūkai: Major Works, tr. Yoshito S. Hakeda. Also in paperback ed. 1972
The Old Man Who Does as He Pleases: Selections from the Poetry and Prose of Lu Yu, tr. Burton Watson 1973
The Lion's Roar of Queen Śrīmālā, tr. Alex and Hideko Wayman 1974
Courtier and Commoner in Ancient China: Selections from the History of the Former Han by Pan Ku, tr. Burton Watson. Also in paperback ed. 1974
Japanese Literature in Chinese, vol. 1: *Poetry and Prose in Chinese by Japanese Writers of the Early Period,* tr. Burton Watson 1975
Japanese Literature in Chinese, vol. 2: *Poetry and Prose in Chinese by Japanese Writers of the Later Period,* tr. Burton Watson 1976
Scripture of the Lotus Blossom of the Fine Dharma, tr. Leon Hurvitz. Also in paperback ed. 1976
Love Song of the Dark Lord: Jayadeva's Gītagovinda, tr. Barbara Stoler Miller. Also in paperback ed. Cloth ed. includes critical text of the Sanskrit. 1977
Ryōkan: Zen Monk-Poet of Japan, tr. Burton Watson 1977
Calming the Mind and Discerning the Real: From the Lam rim chen mo of Tsoṅ-kha-pa, tr. Alex Wayman 1978
The Hermit and the Love-Thief: Sanskirt Poems of Bhartrihari and Bilhaṇa, tr. Barbara Stoler Miller 1978
The Lute: Kao Ming's P'i-p'a chi, tr. Jean Mulligan. Also in paperback ed. 1980
A Chronicle of Gods and Sovereigns: Jinnō Shōtōki of Kitabatake Chikafusa, tr. H. Paul Varley 1980
Among the Flowers: The Hua-chien chi, tr. Lois Fusek 1982
Grass Hill: Poems and Prose by the Japanese Monk Gensei, tr. Burton Watson 1983
Doctors, Diviners, and Magicians of Ancient China: Biographies of Fang-shih, tr. Kenneth J. DeWoskin. Also in paperback ed. 1983

STUDIES IN ORIENTAL CULTURE

18. *The Lotus Boat: The Origins of Chinese Tz'u Poetry in T'ang Popular Culture,* by Marsha L. Wagner 1984
19. *Expressions of Self in Chinese Literature,* ed. Robert E. Hegel and Richard C. Hessney 1985
20. *Songs for the Bride: Women's Voices and Wedding Rites of Rural India,* by W. G. Archer, ed. Barbara Stoler Miller and Mildred Archer 1986
21. *A Heritage of Kings: One Man's Monarchy in the Confucian World,* by JaHyun Kim Haboush 1988

COMPANIONS TO ASIAN STUDIES

Approaches to the Oriental Classics, ed. Wm. Theodore de Bary 1959
Early Chinese Literature, by Burton Watson. Also in paperback ed. 1962
Approaches to Asian Civilizations, ed. Wm. Theodore de Bary and Ainslie T. Embree 1964
The Classic Chinese Novel: A Critical Introduction, by C. T. Hsia. Also in paperback ed. 1968
Chinese Lyricism: Shih Poetry from the Second to the Twelfth Century, tr. Burton Watson. Also in paperback ed. 1971
A Syllabus of Indian Civilization, by Leonard A. Gordon and Barbara Stoler Miller 1971
Twentieth-Century Chinese Stories, ed. C. T. Hsia and Joseph S. M. Lau. Also in paperback ed. 1971
A Syllabus of Chinese Civilization, by J. Mason Gentzler, 2d ed. 1972
A Syllabus of Japanese Civilization, by H. Paul Varley, 2d ed. 1972
An Introduction to Chinese Civilization, ed. John Meskill, with the assistance of J. Mason Gentzler 1973
An Introduction to Japanese Civilization, ed. Arthur E. Tiedemann 1974
Ukifune: Love in the Tale of Genji, ed. Andrew Pekarik 1982
The Pleasures of Japanese Literature, by Donald Keene 1988
A Guide to Oriental Classics, ed. Wm. Theodore de Bary and Ainslie T. Embree; third edition ed. Amy Vladek Heinrich, 2 vols. 1989

INTRODUCTION TO ORIENTAL CIVILIZATIONS

Wm. Theodore de Bary, Editor

Sources of Japanese Tradition, 1958; paperback ed., 2 vols., 1964
Sources of Indian Tradition, 1958; paperback ed., 2 vols., 1964; 2d ed., 1988
Sources of Chinese Tradition, 1960; paperback ed., 2 vols., 1964

NEO-CONFUCIAN STUDIES

Instructions for Practical Living and Other Neo-Confucian Writings by Wang Yang-ming, tr. Wing-tsit Chan 1963
Reflections on Things at Hand: The Neo-Confucian Anthology, comp. Chu Hsi and Lü Tsu-ch'ien, tr. Wing-tsit Chan 1967
Self and Society in Ming Thought, by Wm. Theodore de Bary and the Conference on Ming Thought. Also in paperback ed. 1970
The Unfolding of Neo-Confucianism, by Wm. Theodore de Bary and the Conference on Seventeenth-Century Chinese Thought. Also in paperback ed. 1975
Principle and Practicality: Essays in Neo-Confucianism and Practical Learning, ed. Wm. Theodore de Bary and Irene Bloom. Also in paperback ed. 1979
The Syncretic Religion of Lin Chao-en, by Judith A. Berling 1980
The Renewal of Buddhism in China: Chu-hung and the Late Ming Synthesis, by Chün-fang Yü 1981
Neo-Confucian Orthodoxy and the Learning of the Mind-and-Heart, by Wm. Theodore de Bary 1981
Yüan Thought: Chinese Thought and Religion Under the Mongols, ed. Hok-lam Chan and Wm. Theodore de Bary 1982
The Liberal Tradition in China, by Wm. Theodore de Bary 1983
The Development and Decline of Chinese Cosmology, by John B. Henderson 1984
The Rise of Neo-Confucianism in Korea, by Wm. Theodore de Bary and JaHyun Kim Haboush 1985
Chiao Hung and the Restructuring of Neo-Confucianism in the Late Ming, by Edward T. Ch'ien 1985
Neo-Confucian Terms Explained: Pei-hsi tzu-i, by Ch'en Ch'un, ed. and trans. Wing-tsit Chan 1986
Knowledge Painfully Acquired: K'un-chih chi, by Lo Ch'in-shun, ed. and trans. Irene Bloom 1987
To Become a Sage: The Ten Diagrams on Sage Learning, by Yi T'oegye, ed. and trans. Michael C. Kalton 1988
The Message of the Mind in Neo-Confucian Thought, by Wm. Theodore de Bary 1989

MODERN ASIAN LITERATURE SERIES

Modern Japanese Drama: An Anthology, ed. and tr. Ted Takaya. Also in paperback ed. 1979
Mask and Sword: Two Plays for the Contemporary Japanese Theater, Yamazaki Masakazu, tr. J. Thomas Rimer 1980
Yokomitsu Riichi, Modernist, Dennis Keene 1980

Nepali Visions, Nepali Dreams: The Poetry of Laxmiprasad Devkota, tr. David Rubin	1980
Literature of the Hundred Flowers, vol. 1: *Criticism and Polemics,* ed. Hualing Nieh	1981
Literature of the Hundred Flowers, vol. 2: *Poetry and Fiction,* ed. Hualing Nieh	1981
Modern Chinese Stories and Novellas, 1919–1949, ed. Joseph S. M. Lau, C. T. Hsia, and Leo Ou-fan Lee. Also in paperback ed.	1984
A View by the Sea, by Yasuoka Shōtarō, tr. Kären Wigen Lewis	1984
Other Worlds; Arishima Takeo and the Bounds of Modern Japanese Fiction, by Paul Anderer	1984
Selected Poems of Sō Chōngju, tr. with intro. by David R. McCann	1989
The Sting of Life: Four Contemporary Japanese Novelists, by Van C. Gessel	1989